Unfinished

JOHN W. GALLER

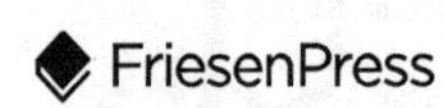

One Printers Way
Altona, MB R0G 0B0
Canada

www.friesenpress.com

First Edition — 2024

ISBN
978-1-03-919748-0 (Hardcover)
978-1-03-919747-3 (Paperback)
978-1-03-919749-7 (eBook)

1. PHILOSOPHY, METAPHYSICS
2. SELF-HELP, MEDITATIONS

Distributed to the trade by The Ingram Book Company

This is for the young and fresh minds. But even if they never read this, it has at least helped me to cope with our missing mental capacities. Being a man is not enough anymore. Become an overman. But, ladies first . . .

> "Talent hits a target no one else can hit; Genius hits a target no one else can see. "
>
> —Arthur Schopenhauer

Table of Contents

Preface	VII
Introduction	IX
Unfinished	XI
Chapter 1: The Big Picture	1
Chapter 2: Metaphysics	15
Chapter 3: Capitalism	21
Chapter 4: Democracy	72
Chapter 5: Religion	81
Chapter 6: Psychology	97
Chapter 7: Philosophy	113
Chapter 8: Capacity	124
Chapter 9: Mental Capacity Chess	157
Chapter 10: Quantum Physics	173
Chapter 11: Meditation	181
Chapter 12: New Rules	205
Chapter 13: Closing	214
Gratitude	223

Preface

Welcome!

Because of my dismay with human depression, which I identify as suppressed anxiety of idiot compliance, the absurd was nagging. So, I started *Unfinished*, a book about mental depth. As I progressed, I sometimes got torn away from continuing because I thought there was no use in explaining to others, and realizing that many people had already expressed what we need to raise the mental bar did not help. So, I remained torn, piecing mental capacity together for myself. Mental capacity is a present mystery, like seeing the pyramids of Giza. They simply sit there, enormous, silent monuments, inviting questions. How did they get there? What are they?

Still torn from the confidence that I was on to something of consequence with *Unfinished*, I continued to look for a genuine message. My research led me to discover books I had missed before, such as *The Rebel* by Albert Camus and *Mind into Matter* by Fred Alan Wolf. This research was a journey, and I appreciate having arrived here, now. Regardless, it still mildly disappoints to be late. Where to go next now seems more urgent than before.

It is a gift to find the right literature early in life, even when one is not aware at the time that they've found treasure and only later discover that it was so. It is difficult to know what one should read first. Influence and education can assist and direct, but life, with its demands, will shape what one could have read, and insights often appear late because experience is fertile. These insights are capacities, and they change us. I therefore recommend reading *The Rebel* if you want to understand more about human incapacity. Looking at Camus's other works will also help one understand why his Nobel Prize in literature was so well-deserved.

Eventually, I found what the message had to be in *Unfinished*. It had to be about mental capacity tools and where to find them. Like a manual to put everything into perspective from a pure consciousness point of view and to instruct on how one can be a nihilist with purpose: a nihilist that won't tolerate capitalism. A manual for how we can eliminate capitalism altogether. Since our lives won't have to be a byproduct of capitalism anymore, I will suggest practical alternatives that are attainable right now. This is a book about actions, because only what we do will be of consequence.

I have packed my enthusiasm into these pages. Machiavelli wrote *The Prince* as a manual for capitalist princes. My target is the middle class. I wrote a manual for the herd in despair. Slightly like Goethe wrote *Faust*, so we might care.

Introduction

Beginning is the first step of becoming, just like the first pages in a book will get a reader interested. What interests a reader, and what is worthwhile to write about? We are numb from information excess and nearly everything has already been done. Even so, a lot of information is repetition, and not much is original or important. And if we consider what is practical, the first thing that may come to mind are cookbooks. They are hands-on and fun, and everybody likes to eat. I pondered what other information would be as practical and could be implemented into action ourselves. When we watch TV, we rarely put what we have learned into action. The same applies to a lot of the books we read. Most books tell stories or report and can be divided into fiction, facts, and opinions. Let's review how to organize opinions since I spend little time analyzing fiction.

1. There are objective opinions, based on generally accepted facts and supported by science.
2. There are subjective opinions, which are personal perspectives.

What I reveal in *Unfinished* is my subjective perspective. It includes some philosophy, history, political views, metaphysics, and quantum physics. I include these topics because they are all necessary to connect to the absurd that I want to expose. Hopefully, some of you can then draw actionable, practical applications from these connections.

What always inspired me was reading philosophy because it is subjective idealism. Reading about ideas is the bridge between what we claim to know and what we eventually choose to believe. Still, just because we have learned to believe something does not mean that we will deliberately act on our new belief. Choosing comes first, and it is always subjective, as are most situations at first sight.

The core of my story is to expose how absurd our behaviour is as a species. Some of it may be seen as accurate or inaccurate—this will largely depend on your point of view. Eventually, one will have to admit that I present substance. I cannot prove if parts of my theory are fact. However, one could ponder them as fiction. Like a story to read in between the lines and tell children by a campfire.

In essence, *Unfinished* is about how we spend most of our time as spectators for the participating rich. It is irrelevant whether we tolerate this or not. It is a problem, and I have chosen to address it.

I present my story from two opposing sides to dissect the same problem, although both sides happen simultaneously. On the one side, I explain that managing the conditions of capitalism is what we do. Yet, what we truly need is to end capitalism. Agreed, this seems impossible to accomplish. Still, I am convinced that we can develop the mental capacity to actually get this done. On the other side, I elaborate about the capacity of our own consciousness, which all beings and matter have in common. I break this consciousness down, with logical deconstruction, into an abstract theory, and invite even the most skeptical to consider it. I can already predict that some will profess that they know better. But what are they doing with their information? Can they feel what they teach and make an impact towards improving what we are capable of? Mental capacity is unfinished and surprisingly not a thought—it is a feeling. And this feeling reveals that the single thought of capitalism is just an absurd little misfit.

Capitalism is nothing, and consciousness is something. Be prepared for content that is structured with factual and imaginary scenarios, and how we can connect these very present opposites of nothing and something. Some concepts may seem repetitive, but that is intentional to make them sink more deeply into the domain of consideration. It is obvious that we seem to drown in disasters of our own creation. Nevertheless, most of these disasters are just caused by thoughts. So, what can we choose?

Implement this: What we choose directly impacts us all. Beginning starts with a choice. Remember that we tend to begin with our first impression. But think again, wait, then choose a next step. Do not comply.

Or don't. Don't even think about it and enjoy yourself.

(As above, throughout this book I will give you practical options to implement into your life when I present the big questions. I will also give you the alternative if you prefer to continue as part of the herd.)

Unfinished

What is unfinished in our lives are our constantly occurring thoughts and what we project from these thoughts. Where do these thoughts come from and what do we become? Just as we become what we eat, we will become what we think. What we become are unfinished opportunities, and I want to describe some of these opportunities, even if only to entertain. For example, what does quantum physics have to do with how we can improve societies and remedy misery? I will leave that up to you to decide later. We have come a long way and are now even beginning to understand the quantum universe. But from that perspective, why do we still behave like Neanderthals in business suits?

Unfinished is about having better thoughts in order to take better actions against the capitalist disaster. Our true life source is consciousness, not thoughts. So, preserving this planet as a species with mental potential requires that we remember pure consciousness more often. Consciousness is always present and is a constant prior to any thought arising. Isolation is the best way to experience it.

Capacity thought also requires isolation, and I have to confess that I write alone and stay away from people. Writing for me is the second-best alternative to isolation in silence (let's not call it meditation). It provides time to meet myself. Liberated from the herd, the media, and the never-ending chore of fitting into our materialist expectations. Once I deconstruct that external noise and chatter into something private and neutral, then a sense of calm capacity emerges. In that silence, the journey of internal contemplation begins, and where I go is often unpredictable. It allows me to let life emerge moment by moment.

In that environment, one discovers that there are never choices that emerge in a moment. Something will appear without having to be chosen. Choosing comes later. Therefore, where does what appears in our awareness come from? This is phenomenology.

We perceive life as happening to us. But what if we project every moment into the present ourselves? That would be a new perspective on existence. Further, why do we think about the things we think about? What makes us what we are? These are existentialist questions that also ask what one is among everybody else.

Society is like a bunch of individual herds that are conditioned to conduct themselves as they're told to, and every herd holds distinct social beliefs. Eventually, we assess ourselves as individuals within these herds and compare.

But at birth, we are alone, innocent, and simply breathing. We helplessly wait to be nurtured and stimulated, and then we grow into children. That fundamental, initial waiting while simply breathing will always be there until our last breath expires and death meets us alone again.

Therefore, capacity conduct is waiting and breathing in the unfinished now. It is not default compliance because of herd adaptation and fear. Yet something as simple as waiting seems impossible because we're always busy with what's next. We're on cruise control as we engage with our ongoing lives. Most of the time, we don't even realize that we are, in fact, still breathing. It may sound boring to do, yet waiting in the silence of now helps us understand and accept any situation better. Many situations are already out of our control, so we have to welcome them, regardless if we tolerate them or not. Still, patiently accepting does not mean love. The word *love* is too broad and imprecise to convey my intended meaning. Love may be a compromise for both approval and disapproval based on judgment, whereas unconditional acceptance is not. Unconditional means neutral, with no correlation to anything, not even love. One could say that I am talking in circles here, and that I am not isolating how to accept anything. Right! Unfinished is exactly that.

Chapter 1:

The Big Picture

Suppose we can accept that the entire cosmos, including infinite universes, consists of various energies. We could then conclude that perception is only a part of these energies in our isolated and observable universe. We could also conclude that what we observe and experience in sequences of moments appears as (but is not) a continuum of linear time.

Now (literally), when did linear time begin and when does it end? And is the experience of time only restricted to visible locations in infinite universes? I am about to challenge the concept of the human standard model of linear time by asking the following questions: What if our present perception, at this very unfolding moment, could be the residue of something that has already happened in a medium without time? What if our perception in the constant present was also projected previously by this timeless source and differs from what our concept of perceivable physical linear time actually represents?

Initially, this seems impossible. In our standard model of perception, we assume that we can't perceive something that was previously projected by ourselves. But what if both projecting and perceiving happen simultaneously?

This is a bit of a leap from what we are used to because in theory we never look at a source that can project our unfolding reality in time as a separate entity. We don't consider that it can actually exist independently from the medium we call perceivable time. We think that we experience perception as happening to us. But what if we create it?

Assuming we can actually create reality as we perceive it, then is capitalism the best we can come up with? Absurd, right?

This what-if scenario intends to show that our perception is experienced from the future because it was already created in the past simultaneously by ourselves and then reveals itself in the very present simultaneous moment as the now. And that now just keeps coming.

So, where does this now come from if it was not projected by us?

It could be described in a formula as:

The future projected from the past by consciousness,
simultaneously happening in the present = infinity experienced

Because this format of instantaneous perception is simultaneous, it would have to be infinite. The arrow of time does not travel from the future to the past. There is no arrow of time. All we can ever experience is only instant perception. Seems obvious because we are always in the present.

Therefore, simultaneity is actually perceived with our perception as linear, and it only seems to progress linearly to give consciousness meaning at a pace, which we call time, in a self-observing universe. Otherwise, there would be no event horizon for perception to occur. Therefore, we think of time as a fourth dimension. But I propose that time, as an enduring concept and as a fourth dimension, does not exist. There is no room for time in simultaneous! What we experience is a perception dimension of time that consciousness produces because it observes itself.

If I asked you what infinity looked like, what would you say? You might say deep space. And I agree, but that is only from a visible perspective of our perception.

In the standard model of linear time, all three positions—the future, the now, and the past—seem like separate entities. But they actually flow into each other. No one situation remains; there is constant flow. There is only now, and it is always present. If time is a dimension in itself (in the now), then we are time as well. And if we are time, then time must be conscious, because we are conscious. So are time and consciousness one and the same or are they dual, as in observing each other? As explained, I think they are one and the same, not dual. Since awareness springs out of consciousness and is the process of observing itself, then that makes us self-aware as time.

Regardless of if I'm right or wrong, why is this important?

Well, all this takes place before we even begin to think or recollect. We can't seem to predict the future, but some say they can. Predicting the future could make sense because when everything happens simultaneously, there is no future. And when we recall the past, we do so in the present. We recollect the past as memory because it already happened, which seems linear. Memory is like experiencing the past instantaneously in the now. If time flows as an arrow in itself (as a fourth dimension), then we should not be able to recall what has already gone. But we still have a record or memory that we can recall, which confirms that time must be conscious if we are time. In essence, we should be able to recall every second of our lives because we have already experienced them, but our memory is incomplete and our surface awareness forgets most of it.

My view is that our memory recall is incomplete because infinity has to project forwards (to the future) for perception to occur. If it didn't, it would create a paradox and contradict itself. If infinity projected backwards (to the past), then we would exist from death towards birth and get younger and unlearn every day. That would be bizarre, and evolution would be unable to unfold. It would be devolution and outfinity (a new word).

Even the word *infinity* is obscure. It describes *in* and *finite*, meaning within limit. However, infinite is endless, always, and simultaneous. Why is the suffix -finite even in this word?

At first glance, infinity experienced seems a difficult concept to imagine, but quantum physics can help us explain further. Measurements in quantum physics have proven that event sequences of particle measurements are affected by the actual processes of measuring them. It's like the measurements affect what is about to happen. This means that the particle quantum environment is impossible to analyze with certainty in terms of what particles actually and precisely reveal in terms of their position, when they were in that position, and their momentum. Consequently, there are no constants among particles anywhere, and they will also never be in the same particular position ever again.

Everything is always moving simultaneously as energy in space. So is consciousness as infinite transcendence. Therefore, Immanuel Kant's transcendence is consciousness: the thing-in-itself.

We widely accept the theory that particles are influenced by conditional variables according to Heisenberg's uncertainty principle. These variables also include the actual process of measuring. But how does the process of measuring something influence the end result? It appears that the end result is aware that it is being measured. Or more precisely, we can witness how our measurements seem to observe themselves, as if they were already present before they happened. This would only be possible if that self-awareness was already projected previously. Somewhat clear and concise, but we still miss it.

According to Schrödinger's theory, an event can exist or not, and a photon can be both a wave and a particle (this is from his cat in a box theory). We know that a wave function only seems to become a particle when it collides with something. Yet, if there is nothing to collide with, then the wave never collapses! What makes the wave collapse? Therefore, our standard physics view only applies when we look at perception from the dual (consciousness + time) and linear perspective.

If we look at this from an infinite, non-dual, and simultaneous (consciousness and time as one) perspective, then this non-dual simultaneous entity must be our own consciousness. And this non-dual entity projects our dual linear perception. I repeat, we can recognize that consciousness is that non-dual infinity from which we become aware. And as we become aware, we observe the process. But the observation is also the awareness. So, the loop closes and is not linear. In other words, consciousness observing itself is what makes the photon wave function collapse. The David Bohm interpretation of the photon wave collapse in quantum science also suggests that this may be the case.

Further and beyond, the definition of an infinite simultaneous moment would obviously be much faster than the speed of light because instantaneous is beyond speed. And infinities of simultaneity would be eternal, which also means that there could be no death of consciousness because it is eternal. So, maybe don't wish for a better next life. Instead, wish for a better physical death in this one.

Such an eternal perspective also helps support the simultaneous multi-verse theories that science already predicts. Further, it invites that the quantum physics term of entanglement is the residue of what our non-dual eternal consciousness projects and instantly perceives in a dual sense as existence, at a linear pace we call time. And we can feel this without having any thoughts! So, pay attention: consciousness, awareness, and observation all exist before a single thought can even develop.

Psychology recognizes a subconscious, meaning a hidden conscious state beyond consciousness. What I suggest is that the subconscious is consciousness and that the consciousness of psychology is awareness.

There can't be a subconscious of consciousness because that would be a sub-infinity. Yet, hidden layers of awareness exist, like in dreams, hypnosis, and trance.

Further, once we start to consider that consciousness is not a physical phenomenon produced by the brain, then we can expand towards accepting that consciousness can exist without a brain, without a body, and without time as an eternal entity in itself. The brain is only a bridge or filter to provide organic and physical coherence in linear observable time. We can then progress to accept that our physical format and how we perceive physical experience is a revelation of the eternal in an organic human body.

No wonder there is an imagined need to believe in a god. But that so-called god is the self-awareness process in itself. Again, like Kant wrote, the thing-in-itself. This concludes that this eternal source exists independently and is an absolute priori.

Now, how do I prove this?

I can't.

But what if? There is evidence, and I present valid questions. Can others prove that I am mistaken? Can science prove that what I propose is not the case? We have to admit that science struggles to explain how the reality of perceivable existence actually unfolds.

We perceive it, but what is it?

We have to accept that only existing consciousness can, by necessity, cause thoughts. We mistake that awareness and thinking are existence produced by the physical brain (which is dual), but that is simply an assumption to explain away the fundamental consciousness mystery.

Religion explains it away with gods. But neither brain nor god produces consciousness because without consciousness, neither exists. If we are simple bio-matter that creates consciousness with a brain, then where and when would a god move in? And if we are simple bio-matter that expires at death, then where would going to hell or heaven appear? Is it not obvious that there is much more going on here?

Thoughts are also not consciousness in itself. A thought is only an eventual single point of reference within awareness that depends on a previous event. Each thought that springs from an existing sensory event then creates further sequences of events that we imagine and can then progress into situational causation.

As mentioned, the in-itself consciousness does not seem to require any thoughts at all, and you can test this by recognizing that you are aware and that you can perceive your awareness without thinking. Try this right now by closing your eyes. . . It just is, and it keeps coming. . . It's like we see a forest (awareness), but we don't see the trees (thoughts). You can experience plain consciousness by feeling that you are aware. You don't think up awareness. You feel presence. Consciousness has to recognize itself as awareness before it develops thoughts. Therefore, your consciousness is always present before you can even think that you are aware.

If we think that consciousness has to imagine (projecting) experiencing awareness, then this would also mean that the universe would have to think of itself to exist. Yes, this would mean a self-aware universe, making brains and gods obsolete as sources of consciousness. Follow this with the question, what other source could make the universe think of itself?

Because nobody then or now was able to explain this, religions have chosen to call this source God (or gods). Religions state that God created the universe as a secondary creator. If there was such a second-party god, then what created it? God must be the thing-in-itself. No. Male prophets created religion and used the concept of God as an explanation for their inability to explain what caused conscious existence in a self observing universe. And that divine excuse was exploited to enforce control.

Instead, what if we replace a second-party dual god with a non-dual consciousness to project the physical universe? Therefore, consciousness would be the universe and it would be aware of itself in the present. Once we consider this perspective, suddenly things make more sense. The universe not only appears to exist in itself, but it unfolds into various dimensions such as dark matter, dark energy, the visible universe, and other dimensions that we can't even imagine.

Consciousness is the thing-in-itself that Kant wrote about 250 years ago. He recognized it, but the controlling males were not ready for that then, and still aren't (with a few exceptions). More on that later.

Without consciousness, the visible universe could not be perceived as awareness. It is therefore absurd to recognize a concept of a dual God as the creator of the universe and consciousness.

Non-dualism means that the label *God* is consciousness, and this also means that all of us are God because we are conscious. This would explain why some claim that God speaks to them—they are actually speaking to themselves. It may also explain other mental disorders.

Further, the fact that conscious existence as a whole seems to be necessary, because we experience it by default, confirms that conscious existence must be an eternal necessity. Otherwise, how else could we define a necessity that exists in itself? An eternal necessity that appears but never had a beginning.

Nietzsche could have been interpreted incorrectly when he said that God was dead, because his dual God never existed. God is just another word for eternal consciousness, which is non-dual. If consciousness was dead, we would not be aware. What Nietzsche really meant when he said God is dead is that man killed the concept of God by finally recognizing God as a dual delusion.

God still remains a mystery to most, and so does capitalism. Therefore, I declare that capitalism is dead because we should be able to recognize that it is a delusion as well. Capitalism is not the big picture. Consciousness is!

Briefly, once man became aware of observing the self, males took over and invented ruling with fear. Then they discovered that religion can be a companion to ruling and that it could be used to induce even more fear from a threat that does not even exist (God). Men ruled in the names of kings and the divine. Then ruling became imperialist theft and the power of religion became capitalism that replaced faith with greed. Consequently, we can now enjoy our miserable global living conditions.

That's all it is, summed up in a single paragraph. Does capitalism not sound like an absurd amount of wasted time? But, it is not what we are. It is only how we learned to behave because of males.

Another perspective

My daughter studies astrophysics, and I wrote her a note to consider:

- Existence is necessary while math is not, and math proves this with logic. If existence was not necessary, we could not experience it. It simply exists in itself and from itself, and it would be absurd to ask for an external dual cause of it (such as God) because we can only perceive it internally as a feeling (even without thoughts).

– Math is not necessary, and it is not necessary to experience it. If it was, we could not exist without it. But we do, and we don't feel math. Therefore, the same applies to thoughts, just like math is also a thought. Thoughts are not necessary to existence. They are independent from perception (awareness springing from consciousness).

  This isolates the concept of occurring necessity, regardless of thoughts.

  Remember when René Descartes said, "I think, therefore I am". But what is the actual "I"? Is "I" a thought or a thing-in-itself? In other words, did he say, "I think, therefore I am a thought of I"? That still does not explain what he, the "I," actually is. He sure made an impact with his original quote, but he was not accurate! His quote is actually reversed. To be more precise: "He is, and therefore he thinks".

  Now, allow me to label existence quantum dynamics. It is different than quantum mechanics because mechanics is math, as in reference points in science, and perceived in linear time. Quantum dynamics is the medium to explain how existence (the universe and being) can observe itself without thought and without linear time. (This is what confused Descartes, but then again he also had to be careful to satisfy religion.)

Conclusions:

- Existence observes itself because it is non-dual infinity experienced, and it projects awareness.
- Our perception, in our awareness, is what we experience but that has already happened.
- We only perceive the dualism of our self-projection and self-observation as the residue of simultaneity.
- Consciousness would have to be the cause of itself because it perceives what it projects.

- Consciousness projects the awareness process that we call senses and thought, which identifies with a self—an "I," as in a causal being. But we are not a being; we are consciousness, becoming aware as a being.

Down to zero:

> This consciousness as an infinite presence and thing-in-itself is faster than the speed of light. It would not require linear time, it would be broader than the uncertainty principle, and it would not include gravity as a relative condition of space-time.
>
> In other words, this is eternal being. Would this eternal consciousness be a thing or a cause? If it were either, it would be dual. But "in itself" means that something is the cause of itself, which is non-dual. This is why Leibniz asked, "Why is something nothing, and nothing something?" It is kind of like asking, what is zero? Zero has no value, but it is still zero. An existing empty value, in between negative and positive values, representing nothing or neutral as something.
>
> Therefore, within the limited capacity of thought, quantum mechanics is the widely accepted medium for how consciousness reveals itself within the event horizon of linear thought. But quantum dynamics is the essential priori to experience an event horizon at all.
>
> Love you,
>
> Dad

My daughter's broad initial answer was that everything is a matter of perspective. Correct—that it is. However, a perspective is still a thought. Consciousness is not.

Further proof leading towards existentialism

Test this. Close your eyes and feel that "forever now" I described earlier. How exactly do you feel about it? It simply keeps coming, fantastic, out of nowhere, regardless of thoughts. You're not only alive—there is more. And this forever now occurs at the same pace for all of us. It is what consciousness is in itself.

It is the same source that makes the grass and flowers sprout in spring, all by itself.

This is the thing-in-itself before reasoning even begins that Kant recognized! The same thing-in-itself that the wise Nietzsche should have paid more attention to. He called Kant's thing-in-itself and its transcendence a "backdoor philosophy." A rather grave mistake for a mind of his capacity. His genius was occupied with becoming an overman (beyond man). The mistake is that he missed that becoming an overman is still only a dual thought, because becoming depends first on being (which is non-dual). Somewhat a lack of perspective and words on his part. Curiosity demands that we should also be interested in being, which is prior to thinking. Even so, Nietzsche expressed his fruit of thought with very refined language and represents the psychological value of how to separate oneself from mass views and compliance. His healing writing is art indeed. But he does not answer, what is being?

As mentioned, one of the magic terms in quantum physics is quantum entanglement. It means that particles on the smallest scale seem to be aware of what other particles are doing, even when they are far apart. Einstein called this "spooky action at a distance," and he was not a fan of quantum theory because he did not know what he did not know at the time (sorry, Albert).

Since science has now grown into particle accelerator quantum experiments, Albert today would most likely consider changing his view. The silhouette of his shadow still dims the light at the end of the quantum tunnel. Today, he would have to concede that eternal is actually beyond light speed.

Contemporary scientists remain determined to find theories that unify current physics models. They measure repeatable consistencies in research and box things up until there seems no point of return or expansion. Unless one can prove otherwise with mountains of data escaping the box, plenty of experts bicker about who is right or wrong about the substance of reality. But what does the substance of reality actually mean? Even language finds it challenging to explain what real is. Science simply can't fully explain what happens in the present moment, despite rigorous research.

A theory cannot be an experience because a theory is a thought, whereas an experience is a feeling. This is why I ask, do we feel the present moment that just passed as the residue of the previously projected future, or did it just fall away to the past after we experienced it as a thought?

What we know is that everything that we observe in the moment appears to be an energy. We call this energy reality, yet this observable reality only represents about 4% of the big cosmic energy picture. What is going on with the other 96% of energy that we now believe exists but is invisible during linear observable time?

From an abstract necessity point of view, it seems irrelevant whether we can explain existence or not. If it wasn't necessary, it wouldn't be happening! Therefore, existence always remains unfinished. And in that unfinished existence in itself, from the non-dual point of view of self-aware consciousness, is where mental potential begins and genius sprouts!

We recognize that there is more to experiencing reality than science can explain. Where we can expand is with pure feeling practices such as deep meditation. There, beyond data and science, we can seek mental range within consciousness itself.

For example, can science explain a feeling like love? Can science clarify the entanglement of particles with the mind and explain whether consciousness exists beyond the brain or body? These are the questions that bring us to our widely accepted limits where not knowing begins.

We have established that consciousness (prior to awareness) is infinity projected and experienced simultaneously by ourselves. It appears as a dual experience when we perceive it, because duality depends on separated conditions. However, when all conditions are experienced simultaneously, then they actually are non-dual. We only perceive dualism as a fragmentation of the same. This non-dual experience of being differs compared to the dual awareness of becoming.

Try sensing *being* again and notice how it arrives, remains, sustains itself, and flows on, all while you can't grasp any of it. It all happens in that instant of sequential nows we experience as perception. This ever-renewing now is the purest experience we have of being. Without it, nothing further can occur. When we retract into every single moment of being ourselves and investigate more about our internal space, we find a space where we rarely spend much time in. But we should!

What happens next is *becoming*, and this is where the capacity for solutions to our problems can begin. We become reasoning causalities of these sequential nows in perception (time), regardless of remembering what we actually are. Before we become anything, we have to elevate ourselves to thoughts. Then we can become the causalities of our invented and entangled thoughts.

We always expand towards the awareness of becoming like we're rushing through traffic to get to the next red light. We process causes and effects and relate them to our imagined selves that are seeded with ideas from the past and imagined expectations. This is reasoning that provides coherence in awareness.

However, consciousness in itself is something far more advanced and vast, and it does very well without reasoning thought. It does not require cause and effect at all. It just is, and it provides presence and an awareness of itself. It is independent, silent, and unfinished potential. There is genius in its silence.

We have to pay more attention to this pure potential, instead of mostly being distracted by following causal thoughts. This potential is the same source that grows a plant. You cannot tell what the plant will grow and look like. And for that restless *becoming* mind, engaging in seeking potential in the silence of a simply *being* presence is too slow and boring. This restless and reduced *becoming* mind is only a tiny fraction of what infinite *being* (genius) is.

Let us compare the difference between consciousness and thought with a metaphorical game of chess, where consciousness is the chessboard and the pieces, and the mind is the game that unfolds when we play with the pieces on the board according to the rules. We look at the game as a whole entity, and begin to make strategy plans. The duality in this case is to visually experience chess with the hardware, and playing the game with our minds. The material and the thought strategy combined are the non-dual process called chess. In other words, without the board and pieces, we could not play the game with our minds. Both hardware and game depend on each other as a whole. The same applies to consciousness and awareness.

In this case, consciousness would simply be (as in *being*) the material board and the pieces. And once the thoughts get involved, we begin to form (as in *becoming*) our game in awareness. We never think about the actual board and pieces. They are just material that exists. Instead, we mostly think about how to play the game.

Experts know that the game follows predictable strategies in the opening, middle, and endgames, and that players (not computers) can make mistakes and still win with well-planned combinations. The game is a somewhat logical process puzzle. It does not matter if one is an experienced or a new player. The point is playing, and that is *becoming*.

We know that without the board and the pieces, playing would not be possible. Without knowledge of the game, the board and pieces are useless and cannot be utilized for any playing strategy. They simply exist. The hardware's purpose is to serve as the tool for the game. One might assume that the game rules are more important than the hardware. However, one cannot apply the rules without it.

In comparison, our consciousness is the hardware. This is our true nature. We are present and represent nothing except presence in terms of existence. We cannot define the purpose of consciousness until we learn some rules. So, what is more important, the existing hardware or knowing how to play the game? We become completely absorbed in the experience of playing the game that we completely forget about the hardware. Thoughts apply the rules, start moving the pieces, and the game evolves into something.

Life is the same! Through our self-awareness, we also become something through a process, and we mistake this process for our actual self. But priori consciousness is independent of a self and has no need for an actual self. It is in itself, without a self. The self we think we are is only a fabricated identification within our perceivable environment.

If distinguishing awareness from consciousness bores you, then contemplate what dullness is. Boring is another word for contemplating stillness, and it is far more interesting than what the restless circular mind can ever offer. You will find that Buddhism, Taoism, and Zen will also confirm that identifying with a self is not our true nature and that this self is an illusion of thought. In fact, these doctrines reach even further by saying that all activities are dualistic processes. Only when we observe them together as a whole (non-dual) do they depend on each other. Again, this is like how we observed the duality between the physical chess board and the thoughts combined to be understood as a (non-dual) game.

This is how consciousness allows awareness to fabricate a self with thought while simultaneously allowing to forget itself. Therefore, we project our reality out of consciousness, just like we project a game with our thoughts. But then, here comes the mystery again: How can we project what we observe simultaneously?

I'll give you another example. We can observe that our awareness becomes fragmented when we pay attention during a chess game. We think about the game so intensely that we even forget that we exist. The sages say that "seeing exists, but we can't see the seer," or in other words that the eye cannot see itself. It follows then that to the eye, the seer is invisible but still exists. Like the seer is emerging out of nothing. How can we project the act of seeing from nothingness?

Science says that seeing is one of our senses generated by the brain reading the light reflecting on the retina and so on. But this process is immediate, and our whole body responds instantaneously to what we see. And out of nothing means consciousness. See what I mean? This is not just happening to us.

Hence, this nothing, which I call a mathematical zero, best describes what non-dual is. In addition, nothing cannot be one because one is an entity, and it is one more than zero. Zero still represents a value because it is something as a non-value. Therefore, *non-dual simultaneous* is not as in one, but as in zero.

Anyway, we cannot remain in the state of zero. We have to progress to pay more attention to the source for all this. We constantly experience something out of nothing, then get lost in thought, and then forget about the source that caused the thought in the first place.

Yes, we need thoughts. They are important for us to function, and they can be profound. I will entertain later with some chosen philosophy and use the game of chess again as a metaphorical mental development structure. Chess strategies are similar to the structure of a paragraph: there is an initial opening point, then a supporting point, then another supporting point to support the support. However, all components and sequences are leading to an endgame, which has a concluding point. Mental ability also begins with an initial point and moves through a coherent process to arrive at a concluding point. This sounds logical, but this is not how we operate. We lose coherence in our processes and then explain them away with something else.

My point is a fundamental existentialist one: Can we behave like a mental capacity species? I will mention later that disasters seem to generate the capacity for urgency in us. Urgency comes from necessity, as seen in military conflicts, disasters, and health lockdowns. Why can we only create urgency because of necessity? And at what point exactly does necessity become necessary as it relates to lingering misery?

These are existentialist questions, but what does existentialism have to do with disaster relief? What I want to show is that once we are past necessity, we seem to lose coherence. When we watch a disaster on TV, extreme polarities unfold right in front of us. On one hand, we witness disaster, and on the other, we just move on because we can and proceed with our day. It's not that we are unsympathetic; it's that we lose coherence!

Chapter 2:

Metaphysics

One can fall away from it all

When you miss a step and experience a moment where you almost fall, your state of mind alters to high alert for a few seconds until you can regroup. This is like another awakening while awake. A feeling, not a thought. A moment in between thoughts.

During such moments, compliance with anything disappears. Nothing is left but the very moment. In such moments, we find undisturbed, eternal consciousness. Believe me, once we spend more time there, everything becomes ridiculously unimportant. I made up this poem in German;

Der neue Tag ist noch nicht wahr,
der vorhergehende ist vergangen,
dass unendliche Jetzt hat immer begonnen,
wo man nur ist, und nichts ist weit,
weil hier gibt es keine Zeit.
—Das ist Unendlichkeit erlebt.

[The new day is not yet true,
the previous one has passed,
the eternal now has always begun,
where one only is, and nothing is far,
because here exists no time.
—This is infinity experienced.]

P.S. I wrote this in German because the words rhyme and seem balanced, while the English version does not rhyme and is choppy.

Under that tree, the Buddha must have felt that he was falling away from it all and into the very moment. Assuming his existence, he understood that the very moment was more profound than any thought would ever be. It must be the actual effortless falling in itself (the process of arriving in between thoughts) that is the enlightenment process. An immense sense of lifting off into the freedom from any attachment. I encourage you to explore that true freedom which comes from disconnecting from your thoughts entirely.

Zen spoils this non-effort falling with discipline, rigidity, and riddles such as koans. What for? Falling and being can happen without complications. Simply sitting and being in Heidegger's Da-sein. There is no need for koans like "the sound of one hand clapping" or "you are one with the sound of the bell." Koans are thoughts as well.

Nothing

Without thought, there is a void that is even more empty than nihilism, yet this emptiness still holds a presence. Nihilism denies former beliefs, but still asks for purpose, even when it is meaningless. Purpose is also a thought. Again, what for? Why explain what we cannot explain? That is what nothing is, and it will always remain as such. The Tibetans call this *suchness* or *evenness*, an effortless abiding that still is something. Where bliss appears out of nowhere, as a well-being feeling emerging from nothing. And that is enough.

Therefore, enlightenment is a feeling and not a thought or a destination, and it is already present when one falls into it. We all have the ability to feel enlightenment already, but we still seek it.

Then there was a guy called Jesus (not Brian, his neighbour in *Monty Python*) that had nothing and died for nothing to cleanse nothing of sin. What sin is there when there is only nothing? All these saints fall away from everything to be content with nothing. By abandoning their own selves, they discovered what remained: eternal nothing.

To deny one's own self is a concept. However, this just means to deny the thought of one's self. There always is a presence of a self without thought inside of us, and that is priori being (consciousness). How can we deny that? It's always there.

When Eastern religions declare that one should deny the self, it can be confusing when not explained with clarity. They do not isolate consciousness in particular. They teach to calm the mind and to distract from thought with

Soma (body posture), breathing exercises, and concentrating on images and concepts. They isolate how to recognize the back-and-forth wobble between thoughts and feelings, and the gap (experiencing no thought). And eventually one should merge with the eternal nothing.

So why bother to calm any thoughts? They only exist because we cause them to exist. It's borderline absurd to calm what we cause. They also emphasize that thoughts are empty, but they focus on the thoughts themselves rather than the gaps between our thoughts. In these gaps we experience self observing consciousness, and this is the medium that is crucial to refine our being. To think about calming thoughts and their emptiness are still thoughts. However, calming thoughts helps to ground people, and it is better than not being aware of the option to do so.

Even compassion is a thought, and it is only necessary when accepting others' thoughts and actions that cause suffering. Without suffering, compassion becomes unnecessary. Humans not only cause suffering, but they also choose to suffer by wanting, regardless of whether they deny it or not.

Anyway, how we behave is just thought—especially incompetent thought—but there is so much more than just thought.

Imagine nothing out in space where there is an immediate nothing, and the entire cosmos floats in this nothing. There we can expand into infinity, as infinity, where infinity can only end in nothing as well. So why bother with anything in our minuscule minds of thought when that space of nothing sustains everything? But we forget about it. Yes, it is incomprehensible that we mostly miss it and that we need to remind ourselves of it.

Others have to have more thoughts and more of something. And if it was not for the benefit or profit of something, then most would actually do nothing. So, here we are again. Nothing, nothing, nothing. . . Absurd, right? So, what can we do? We always crave something in this nothingness, which is why we find nothing boring. Instead, we choose to be busy. This busy, a thought, is an epidemic that stretches into systems and delusions and on and on. Even so, all emerges out of nothing. Just like bliss does.

Urgency and Complacency

It is 4 a.m. There are earthquakes in southern Turkey and northern Syria. A few minutes later, there is massive destruction and thousands are buried because of lousy building codes. The news spreads, rescue operations develop, and millions in relief funds are being released to help in the short-term. Further north, millions are released as well to support the Ukraine war against renegade Russia. This is a long-term help campaign. In both of these cases, there is immediate action and sustained urgency with global unity. Suddenly, capitalist imperialism and religions disappear into the background. We tend to unite and move beyond after immediate disasters.

Simultaneously, millions are displaced, thousands starve, and pollution is rampant, yet there is neither short-term, nor long-term urgency. Capitalist imperialism and religions clearly take centre stage here, where billions in delayed relief fund complacency are an accepted condition of greed.

There is a severe polarity between immediate support for a specific cause and ongoing relief complacency for another cause. We don't send construction equipment, food, and medical supplies with the same disaster sense of urgency to countries plagued with famines and civil wars. In other words, we are incapable of behaving appropriately when it comes to lingering man-made disasters.

Regardless, these aforementioned scenarios cost billions because everything is a profit-seeking business. Everybody has to get paid. And without profit-seeking, the earthquake scenario would not be nearly as severe. While we can't control earthquakes, we can control how well buildings remain standing with better building codes, which would result in fewer deaths.

While that unfolds, there is BRICS (Brazil, Russia, India, China, South Africa) whose main objective is to undermine the US dollar in world finance. Their view is that American and European plundering has lasted long enough and that they no longer have to comply with their demands. BRICS nations understand that a military or territorial conflict would be too costly and devastating, so they attack silently, by hedging natural resources and currencies. A severely devalued dollar would have global consequences and is an actual threat to the US. However, the better news is that a severe dollar devaluation would create much more equality for everybody else.

A previous approach similar to BRICS was when Europe tried to financially unite behind the euro in 1999. In that case, not all of the nations that wanted to join were welcome. A nation had to produce and contribute enough GDP to qualify. Again, discrimination that only favours the best. The UK left the EU in 2020, and they also never adopted the euro. They kept their pound sterling. In other words, it was all a prime capitalist failure for the UK.

When the intent is to unite, then why not accept the same currency and stick to the plan? Well, it's a typical royal British trademark to want to be special. Like driving on the other side of the road, building ramp aircraft carriers, and being so very proud. So, the USA is now their best financial option to tag along with. But both nations are under heavy debt loads, and they both conceal negative financial threats against their systems. To make their currencies stronger, they control inflation and interest rates, and the US has been reprimanding smaller private banks for insolvency. They claim that their federal and larger banks are secure enough to protect global financial stability, but if we could test their liquidity to cover their cash deposits, they would come up short. They are also overextended on high-risk and commercial real estate loans. To make a long story short, their banks can't balance their assets with their liabilities. So in a way there is urgency to balance global finance, but there is complacency to reveal the truth.

Accurate balance sheets are a default requirement for every business. The feds enforce the same default requirement for banks, but they allow them to take higher risks even if their affairs do not balance. Meanwhile, the rich conceal their wealth somewhere else. It may be hidden offshore or in investment firms like BlackRock and Vanguard that invest in the largest companies such as Apple, Pfizer, and so on. They do some direct lending to companies that are screened with a fine-tooth comb and don't carry nearly as much risk as the banks. They rake in profits to invest more into the select and privately pampered businesses of the rich. On top of that, they compound dividends and interest on interest. They do nothing else but move funds. The rich don't report record profits; they hide them and pay lawyers to find loopholes in the tax systems. Money is the ultimate power and they disguise whatever they want with savvy balance sheets. However, their influence only works in a capitalist system, and the single reason why the rich get richer is because we, the middle class, comply with complacency. There is no urgency to isolate the rich.

At the same time, most governments report deficits to sustain their societies, which are financed with taxes. The polarity is severe: the rich hide their riches while governments constantly and publicly expand their debt. And again, it is all because we let them—because we're such obedient slaves.

What is incomprehensible is that all of this industriousness and financial power cannot come up with a remedy to ease global poverty and misery. This is capitalism at its best!

We, the middle class, truly struggle to comprehend what this actually does to us as a species. And what is seriously underestimated is that the middle class is by far the strongest force that can change the whole planet. When the middle class unites with decisive action, then there is no need to wait for governments and the rich to solve our suffering.

Capitalism is a disease, not a living standard, and we miss the big picture that there are plenty of other options.

Chapter 3:

Capitalism

"Imagine"

You are on the coast of North Africa in the early nineteen hundreds. It is a pleasant afternoon and you are sitting on the veranda at a low-priced beach-side hotel. You are among intellectuals that have escaped the political and philosophical grind of Europe. Scattered groups are enjoying the scene and participating in relaxed conversation. You are sinking into the depth of your own intentions and exchange free thought with others. Liquid and mental spirits flow, and you feel comfortable with the minds that share and dare to dream.

You discuss Marx, Dostoevsky, Mill, Kierkegaard, and Nietzsche. This is where existentialism got a stronger foothold to grow into Camus, Sartre, Heidegger, and Arendt, and Europe was ready to receive them first. They were celebrated because the western herd needed something new to emerge from the colonial and religious leftovers. The renaissance of existentialism drilled deeper into the psychology of what *being* meant for an individual and how to cope with default imperial capitalism. Imagine that day and what was at issue. . .

The problem

To be spectators of the rich is a fundamental existentialist problem for the rest of the global population. We comply with the illusion that humanity can't evolve away from a materialist profit-seeking system. Even religions are subject to it in their own sheepish ways. And, it is not enough to just criticize it all.

We rooted the word imperialism in the Latin word *imperium*, which means supreme power. Ancient history mostly pursued and reported about empires, and to this very day, we still do the same. But to me, supreme power means evolving as a capacity species rather than achieving supreme domination over others.

Today, the scope of empires is far more complex than when the Romans ruled with swords and shields over land. Our current empires are not only about territorial ambitions. The new empires are marketing, business, finance, cyber, and many others, and the participation in these empires is all happening simultaneously. Now, everything is about hoarding and everything hinges on profit. This is how imperialism morphed into capitalism.

All empires are self-interested and strive for control over competition, but that is still a tribal drive at best. Modern empires are perhaps a small step up from the Neanderthals, yet they still compete and don't get along. From a mental capacity perspective, empires of any kind belong in museums.

As mentioned, the principal issue for an empire is the pursuit of control and to limit others in the name of profit. And we did this first in our heads! It was only our thoughts that created capitalism and other political ideologies. Nothing else did. We regurgitated imperialist thoughts, we enforced control, we took military action, and secret services had their own plans. There are ghost agencies and agents that wipe people out while covering up the erasure as if it never happened. And the cover-ups lean on pathetic laws such as "not guilty beyond reasonable doubt": if nobody saw it, then it never happened. Like it was nothing.

However, it is actually a fake nothing that really is something, but it is lied away with other thoughts. The liars get away with calling deliberate eliminations imaginary conspiracies. It is irrelevant whether we tolerate the slaughter of people or the disappearance of species. There is always some guy with a bigger gun or threat that has to have it all. Comply or die! Does this sound like high IQ to you?

We can remain in apathy and denial that capitalism is vile. Like rats on a sinking ship, we hold on with tooth and nail to whatever we have accumulated, all while calling ourselves civilized. It is no wonder that to the average citizen, who has been conditioned to the intellectual capacity of a bag of donuts, this grotesque existence seems to be the ultimate. But of course, since we can reduce ourselves to phenomena that will never happen, such as delusions and hope, there is no intellectual capacity required. Consequently, we become prey to oppression.

But that does not apply to you, of course. It only applies to everybody else.

Are you entertained by now, or are you enraged by the fact that someone has the audacity to poke at such sensitive nerves? It is rude indeed, but this is how we behave, and again, it is irrelevant whether we tolerate it or not.

Can we transcend capitalism into mental capacity, or should we eliminate it?

The existential question of the past was, can we transcend capitalism into mental capacity? Well, it sounded like an option. But when greed is the priority and nothing slows it down, then we have a runaway train. And since the lure of credit keeps the social herd interested in consuming to no end, that train keeps picking up speed. The perfect exploitation tool for consumption is credit. Consequently, credit provokes the herd to spend, and spending before earning is the crucial deception of the capitalist model.

Corporations depend on credit as well, and they even pay their workers with credit. Jobs are created for production, and the products are expected to generate future revenue. They call this investing in opportunities with credit. This all sounds good, and corporate balance sheets can even look balanced with future revenues that are based on speculation. But what if the products don't sell? It does not seem to matter. We simply sell overproduction at a discount or loss and keep going. In other words, we build more with more resources on debt.

Some companies may have backlogs because they can't keep up. And what do they do? They borrow more to catch up. As a result, we operate on inflated debt economies and everything is based on future speculations. And the more we speculate, the higher the risk of failure. However, we have learned to live with risk and tend to think that we can get away with it. But eventually, we reach a point of no return where we can't stop that runaway train. So how can we transform a heavily loaded, high-speed runaway train into a nice little afternoon joyride? We can't, because physics won't allow it. But we still think we can find a way.

The same principles apply to capitalism. We insist that capitalism can turn into something good despite the fact that it has progressed too far into the uncontrollable.

The cream of the capitalist crop is the financial environment. Speculating on markets and securities is the absolute, and since nobody speculates on losing, they all speculate on greed. The low-IQ intent that someone can gain or lose based on market conditions is theft within legal capitalist parameters, and the securities that they trade are only partially backed by cash money. It would be impossible to cash in all securities at once. Securities only represent predicted future promises and values. They have no other function whatsoever besides a future trade for something else. The entire global surface population revolves around this single concept.

Marx explained in 1867 in his *Capital* that overproduction would lead to exploitation and societal corruption. But he did not expand further to say that over-lending and over-speculating would cause even more severe problems. We don't seem to register that everything in a capitalist environment is simply an invitation to gamble. The rich earn interest on their investments and securities, which leads to even more interest, and so on. The microbe, middle class, corporate slaves deliver the fuel with their payroll deposits flowing through the banks. It's just simple math that the gap between the wealthy and middle class will continue to widen indefinitely.

The rich have no debt, and they don't work—this is exactly what we all need as well! And we can actually accomplish this in a society that does not revolve around profit. Capitalist insanity is not a destination. It is a mental problem! We need a herd awakening to not only improve, but reverse engineer our capitalist asylum. But again, it is too late for that. All kinds of simultaneous domestic wars are draining the planet of resources. It's economic recycling—wars and conflicts are necessary to sustain capitalism. For example, the United States made money off Desert Storm. They spent billions on warfare, only to earn more billions on arms production and rebuilding contracts. They engage in liabilities to earn future assets. Is that brilliant or insane or both?

If we review the constitution of the United States, we find that the great American dream is founded on their view of freedom. A wonderful concept if it would include the rest of the world. Is the self-declared American world police actually promoting global freedom, or is it serving American hoarding? I guess it is a matter of perspective. Most of the American population are decent people, but what their government represents is a global problem. I doubt that the average individual citizen approves that their administration is involved in everything.

Everything is only about transactions. No wonder the Russians and the Chinese are always pissed off. They want a piece of the transactions as well. The US has become the poster nation of capitalism. Since I live in Canada, which almost completely depends on US relations and trade, I must come off as a hypocrite, criticizing my own lifestyle. However, I don't exactly fit the hypocrite profile. My family and I would give up everything for a chance at a new capacity start somewhere. But in the meantime, I remain hiding here in my fortunate bubble, writing in my basement in order to convince the young capacity minds to be fearless and to challenge the compliance herd with their courage.

Capitalism puts us all to sleep. P. D. Ouspensky, George Gurdjieff, and Helena Blavatsky observed that society is asleep, but they were ahead of their time and isolated themselves with that view. They ran seminars and retreats, and Blavatsky developed Theosophy, which is a combination of religion and philosophy. That was a hundred years ago, and society was not ready to receive them. However, the herd is never ready at first sight, but when they do finally get on board, they insist they all knew a long time ago. This is where greed surfaces again. Society is unfair, and many try to take credit for other people's work.

The mob is always so competitive. And it is bizarre that the animal kingdom's concept of survival of the strongest should somehow justify why they compete. We're not animals, and nature is capable of growing in harmony and balance. If survival was solely based on strength, only lions would survive on the grassland plains, which is clearly not the case.

In a capitalist animal kingdom, most aspire to be lions, and when they become lions, they eat each other. But real lions don't actually eat each other. The "survival of the fittest" mentality is clearly a detrimental concept for humans. Capitalism shows that strength without moderation and balance is an evolutionary disability. It causes the prolonged suffering of not knowing our neighbours and even killing them. And once a nation has killed its neighbours, it does not attend their funerals. Where are former nations buried? Their tombstones could read:

Here we rest because the imperialists invaded the weak,
the clever deceived the less fortunate,
those with knowledge did not teach,
and those who accumulated did not share.

The Dalai Lama says that we have to have more compassion. However, compassion only addresses the symptoms of already-present despair. Compassion makes both sufferers and the compassionate feel better. But the problems that cause suffering remain. For the capitalists, compassion is only a word—and an inconvenience.

Trading with compassion and without profit is a viable option for an intelligent species. But it is absurd and boring to capitalists. Governments spend trillions on weapons and armies. Could these fortunes instead be invested in construction equipment to restore neglected nations and environments? There would be just as many jobs, and a good reason to join such an environmental army.

We already have many anti-capitalist movements going on, and they all have good intentions. But establishing non-profits, shared business, and moderate capitalism takes too much time to implement. And these well-intentioned conversions are still subject to exploitation by the sinister rich. What the anti-capitalist movement needs is another target, but it's one that no one mentions. That target is to eliminate capitalism.

Implement this: Define what we should progress towards. Is it profit or retrofit?

Or don't. Embrace capitalism as progress and consume yourself to extinction.

What does consciousness have to do with capitalism?

Ultimately, we are not only conscious (aware), but we are consciousness in itself, and in our awareness we experience capitalist materialism. Therefore, capitalism is only a single thought of ours. That narrows things down significantly! We don't have to follow all of our thoughts, and we can learn how to ignore thoughts through meditation. So why can't we ignore this one thought? We don't need to limit ourselves to this single concept of running petty little capitalist empires. Let's look at this more closely with the help of the Oxford Dictionary:

> Capitalism: An economic and system in which a country's businesses and industry are controlled and run by private owners for profit, rather than by the government.

What stands out the most in this definition is "controlled by private owners for profit." Looking even more closely, here are the definitions for controlling, private, and profit:

> Controlling: 1. Not showing emotion; having one's feelings under control. 2. Under the control of someone or something.
>
> Private: Belonging to or for the use of one particular person or group of people only.
>
> Profit: A financial gain, especially the difference between the amount earned, and the amount spent in buying, operating, or producing something.

And we just revolve around this? The pursuit of profit for the private sector or for the state? Apparently, that is the best we can be! And what is even more disturbing is that our lives are just by-products of the cause. Capitalism is how we do what we do, but *how* does not necessarily satisfy *why*.

The consequences of a single thought

Does our global surface activity seem like a happy environment? I think you know the answer. Why is misery so widespread? Even in such conditions, we are asked to be positive. To just lock it all up and chill. To pretend, be an example, and lead. For what, exactly?

At issue is the single capitalist thought, along with the fact that we still believe that *all* humans are to blame for the misery we experience. In a way they are because they invented capitalism, but we can't blame all of humanity when it was males in particular that misled us. Capitalism sprouted specifically out of male imperialist thought, and such thought is as concerning as cancer is for a body. Both can grow out of control, contaminating the host.

Higher living standards and submitting to global capitalist compliance are not remedies for human suffering. They are the cause of suffering! Like a hidden pandemic that causes involuntary complications. Forced compliance with capitalism is an inconvenience that most recognize as suffering. Even so, an even stronger driver that causes societies to suffer is fear.

There is fear everywhere, and it is caused by ideologies, religions, and finances. Our standard upbringing instills fear in us, which is why we are afraid for the rest of our lives. But fear is only a tool for the control of weak minds.

We think we are stuck in the predicaments of fear and compliance because we are told we can't escape them. We are told that a utopian society without profit is a delusion. Why do we follow what we're told?

Capitalists call any opposing ideology a conspiracy. But they never mention that capitalism is a conspiracy as well. Their theory is based on a single ignorant thought: taking! And they are afraid of any other social system. Granted, the inventions that capitalist concepts produced are remarkable, but they all revolve around profit. If we removed all that profit seeking, we could still function well. So, we clearly have to change how we think about taking.

We over-analyze thoughts (awareness). What we need to focus on more is their source (consciousness). Descartes's "*Cogito ergo sum*" ("I think, therefore I am") should have been, "I am, therefore I think." This changes everything from a mental depth perspective. It means that this always-present "I" is there first, and as you become aware of it, it becomes the thought of an "I." Then you forget your source consciousness and follow your thoughts, which follow others.

We can even reach beyond Hegel, Husserl, Heidegger (the three *H*s), Sartre, and Arendt when we clearly divide consciousness from awareness in phenomenology. As mentioned, consciousness is the eternal source, and awareness is only an experience that springs from that source. Both combined become infinity (eternal) experienced, and this is what we miss. We also miss that our capacities can reach far beyond capitalist thought. For example, those with near-death experiences consistently describe out-of-body experiences involving instant communication without language (telepathy). How is that even possible when the brain remains in a clinically dead body and all sense awareness, including thoughts, are mute?

Information and urgency

It may appear that information is everything, but it is actually a little less than everything. Urgency is everything!

People's habits and choices determine how they interpret information. Wittgenstein even said, "If we spoke a different language, we would somewhat perceive a different world," and "Whereof one cannot speak, thereof one must be silent." If this really was the case, it would be much quieter out there, but in reality, it sure is loud. Some organizations choose to slyly transcend loud information and delve into silent manipulation instead. We may not even be aware that what we experience is being deliberately done to us, but even when we do, we crave it and can't seem to imagine how to expand beyond.

Allow me to help.

In our materialist bubble, we go through our day consuming relentless industrious information in various formats. Unconvincing information that orbits around capitalist myths and its shrunken democracies. When everything, including opinions, can be bought, it should be noted that idealistic democratic values will shrink, and that behind that purchased democratic veil is our capitalist fiction.

Capitalism is primarily responsible for global resource depletion. It is destruction and exploitation that we don't want, but that relentlessly continues to occur. Ironically, capitalists even promote environmental cleanup initiatives for problems that they cause in the first place. They are always the good guys. All these global environmental organizations continue to spin their wheels in the financial mud of global cleanup. However, this can't be done with money—there will never be enough! We need construction armies and volunteer work instead of paid contracting. The ruthless truth remains: unless the mindset of the stale materialist empires is erased, there is no possibility of restoring our resources quickly or efficiently. We are beyond the point now to analyze this any further. This certainty stares right at us.

In addition, our massive appetite to consume forces all the less-developed nations to compete in the demand caused by capitalism as well. We all know this, right? I only mention it to humour our incapacity, because all this chaos is just based on information, and justifying the capitalist fiction will only temporarily destroy the surface of this planet. This is fun.

Rest assured that Earth will get past us humans, regardless of authorities that continue to ramble on about conserving the planet. Our materialist perspective treats Earth like it's an imaginary future entity somewhere else, even though we're living on it now. For example, there was a recent agreement to preserve a third of the planet in national parks by 2030. Thumbs up, well done, getting it together finally. But, from the time of writing in 2022, why will this take eight years? When COVID hit, we had immediate lockdowns—emphasis on immediate!

Obviously, this partial, eight-year protection project lacks urgency, and we should have implemented it fifty years ago. Haven't we learned by now that taking sincere action is more important than organized delays, and that information cannot replace results? Immediate action produces results tomorrow.

The capitalist machine grinds away our resources every day and organizes deliberate delays to accumulate profit. Again, it is irrelevant if we tolerate it or not! We hear excuses like, "Unfortunately. . ." "It's complicated. . ." "There are legal issues. . ." or, "We cannot simply stop." Many already scream that we have to implement urgency, and I also plea that we have to move beyond delays to get things done.

Our so-called civilized and value-defending politicians, courts, governments, municipalities, and on, and on, and on, and on, and on take years to potentially, somewhere, somehow, someday, finally turn a project into a maybe, which is evidently too slow. (This was not a run-on sentence). This is the runaround that we are being served. They always talk the talk, but they only deliver constant delay instead of results.

There is nothing to talk about. We just need to turn the capitalist sewer off. The environment needs more than conservation; it needs intervention. In order to shut off the capitalist sewer, materialist capitalism must be surgically removed.

Obviously, we should still react when conditions go from bad to worse. But despite our increased, instant awareness via our devices, we still allow ourselves to ignore clear and concise facts. We assume that we have more time for more delays, and that more drastic action is not required until much later. The imperialist delusion to take whatever we want remains. And then, periodically, some celebrity will chime in to remind us that only half the world is still starving to death and education levels have improved. Well, those advancements took fifty years and are not really accomplishments. They are just excuses to decorate the capitalist promise and to sell a celebrity brand. At the same time, we also exterminated another 25% of wildlife. These celebrities expect us to listen to them, even while they represent everything that is wrong.

The public demands the rich pay more taxes. Realistically, what would that do? Nothing, in principle, because just throwing more money into that same burning pit of misery does not get us out of it. The extra revenue generated by rich people's taxes will not impact the middle class. It will be another slush fund for something else. The rich will still get richer, and more of the same will continue to occur. And the delay acrobats, also known as lawyers, will be paid to defend them and to protect our global incompetence, all with twisted language. Getting paid is what matters in the lawyer microcosm. They represent nothing, period.

Capitalism creates information about delusional ambitions, tolerates slaughter, and neglects entire continents. Capitalist media reminds the middle class to keep donating to global delay charities. Sure, let's beat up the broke slaves for charity, while the rich trade trillions. Bizarre is an understatement. There is always an urgency to spend and produce, but moderation and reducing are just information. Welcome to the incapacity circus!

Agreed, it may seem absurd that a nobody like me is daring to challenge our highly praised living standards, because, after all, they are what living the capitalist dream apparently craves. But if this is living the dream, then we must either have a nightmare or not be dreaming at all.

Apologies, but I can't clarify it any further. We simply overestimate capitalist information. Math clearly shows that overproduction and over-lending make capitalism unsustainable. There is simply too much demand for everything. Many have and continue to criticize it, explain what could be done, and bore with facts, just as I am doing right now.

So, let's say in a few sentences what others explain in essays: Capitalism is just a single thought concept. It is a licence to pollute for temporary financial dictatorship and information and credit are the tools to enforce it. I call it temporary because diluted democratic voting only creates delusional longevity. And I call it a dictatorship because there is no freedom when we self-inflict financial slavery to satisfy our own temptations.

Where does money come from?

The trap is that our own pervasive temptations make it easy for us middle class to overextend ourselves. Everything comes at a cost and is overpriced, and an individual can only borrow a limited amount. That borrowing limit is about 45% of one's net worth. However, this amounts to nothing when one has no net worth.

Mental capacity can resist temptation, and moderation should be measured through the availability of common foods, shelter, and basic social care rather than net worth.

In comparison, if we applied the individual 45% net worth parameter to the banking system, then banks and federal reserves would not exist. But they do because they can just print money (securities), call them bonds, sell them for cash, then lend out that cash as credit. When was the last time you printed money? Unlike them, you have to earn it or else become addicted to credit and comply to paying interest. Again, it is irrelevant if we tolerate it or not. We still crave it, since they make it so accessible and possible. They astutely tease and build their business on personal weakness. The temptation to buy things beyond our means with credit is overwhelming. These bankers ramble on about it with dazzling language, and we selectively hear and willingly accept their premeditated deception.

But my ears only hear about investing in delusions. So forgive me, but we are a compliance joke of our own making. We are the joker on the cover of this book.

As previously mentioned, the ideas I'm about to suggest not only *can* have, but *will* have an immediate impact on everything if people act on them! To be blunt, we, the middle class, have to implement much-needed urgency ourselves and force a complete reset of our global monetary systems. Yes, call me a dreamer. But what if? I repeat, *what if?*

Obviously, all this talk from the rich authorities does not produce adequate results to benefit the middle class and less developed nations. Having an attainable dream offers far more actionable capacity than just reducing oneself to compliance. Waiting in compliance is not an option, hoping is delusion, and talking louder is just noise that doesn't work. There comes a point where we all have to acknowledge that things well-done are far superior to things well-said.

Turmoil, pollution, and poverty have brought us where?

If we preserved things in the first place, then there would be much less of a mess. Let's be crystal clear that the government does not have the delayed obligation to clean up and manage disasters. Their job is to prevent them!

If they want to run empires, then they must run them with the capacity to reduce, reuse, and renew. We cannot accomplish global materialist preservation without decent social preservation as a foundation.

Safeguarding the environment is now widespread social rhetoric, but it only exists to soften the harsh facts that are already present. The predicament is, how can anyone protect what they can't control? Once pollution is present, it is already too late. Pollution is the worst kind of evidence that our pretentious imperialism is leaving behind. Cleaning up that evidence is necessary, but not a remedy. Prevention is!

Let's circle back. Societies don't get along and they can't protect what they can't control while they talk about preserving the globe. Can we be more contradicting? The epic problem is that we are out of control on so many fronts that it is quite a task to even focus on where to begin. Here are a few well-known front-line issues:

- The ocean's fish stocks are about to collapse, and we're still fishing.
- The world is on fire, and we're still burning fuel to produce energy. Energy demands are at an all-time high to extract and deplete even more resources.
- We ship goods globally instead of producing them locally, and then we fill our landfills with overproduction.
- We produce for profit so we can hide profit, and waste so we can bury waste.

No matter the political structure each individual empire has, they are all only chasing consumption to satisfy the banks, the investment groups, and the state. They replace mental capacity with economic capacity, just like religious faith can replace facts.

What kind of creature falls for this kind of masochism and cannot find a remedy for it?

Implement this: Why do we still comply? Incubate this information and recognize that compliance is self-destructive.

Or don't. We are incapable, and you are fine with that. After all, you are more afraid of mental engagement than compliance.

Why is everything important?

When everything is important, then nothing is important. Following is not important, unless you have decided on what to follow personally. Everything becomes trivial when we get lost in details. We are all taught to prioritize, but when everything is important, then how do we prioritize?

The media is a means of communication, and people desire freedom of speech. Nonetheless, what is the point? What does uncensored freedom of speech actually produce? Media, as it is presented, does not offer productive coherence, and is not a collaboration tool. It is a tool for mayhem! The media is in the business of selling things, whatever they may be. Its mantra is profit, not fact or coherence. Anyone with a glimmer of moderation would never need commercials to buy products. Media divides and criticizes and is the ideal manipulation tool for capitalism.

So, what is actually important?

Here is the unimportant:

- Money and the laws that are written to protect it, plus the additional laws written to obstruct those same laws.
- Religion.
- Capitalist consumption.
- Wars.
- Celebrities.
- Following the herd.

Here is what's important:

- Living in the moment.
- Being aware, but without thoughts.
- Having compassionate awareness for each creature, as without it we lose coherence that we are all one.
- Retreating rather than reacting and following.
- Conducting oneself with mental capacity, which does not comply with anything unless it is chosen.

Now that we know what is actually important, what's next? What I suggest may sound less than exciting, but know that at least none of it is conditioned compliance.

Mental capacity recognizes that imperialist capitalism divides our species on so many levels. The United States of the un-united is the best example to substantiate this. For example, consider citizens being armed at home. The US currently has more guns than people, and their American dream unfolds more like a mental disorder. Think about it: if we had the tiniest spark of mental capacity, then what would we need guns for? But imperialism steels itself with guns, which demonstrates that there is even less than a spark of enlightenment present.

Every management book today preaches teamwork, and guns are absent there. So how is war coherent with basic management principles?

Implement this: Capacity conduct is to follow what is important to you personally, and it cannot be manipulated.

Or don't. Continue to not understand what is important and make compliance to everything default. It's so much easier. If it wasn't, we would not even watch commercials.

Three worlds

The "third world" is an expression from the Middle Ages. There was the blue-blooded royalty, the church, and the third world—the ones that were the most, the common folk. Today we recognize the G20 developed imperialist system with corporations (instead of royals), governments (instead of the church), and the wealthy, middle, and poor classes in these societies (as the third world).

This imperialist system does not include the rest of the underdeveloped nations across the globe. They are the G175 (about 195 nations). There they are divided into the rich, poor, and famine classes. A much shorter and less convoluted list.

On a global general scale there are three worlds as well. The developed world, the less developed world, and the secret world. The secret society is not recognized at all, otherwise it would not be secret, but they run everything.

The global financial economy also has three divisions based on credit rating. Less developed countries are commonly known as lower standard entities (the G175). Higher standard perimeters are set by the developed countries (the G20) because they invented them. Last, there are the ones that have no money and no credit, and will never have or qualify for either.

Ratings like AAA credit were designed to discriminate even further, and the mission of AAA-rated countries is to manipulate the less developed into becoming just like them one day. This is despite the fact that doing so is actually impossible! The less developed would never be able to repay the debt that they would incur to accomplish this. Some countries are even so indebted already that they can't even service the debt interest. It is a fact that the gap between developed and less developed nations grows irreversibly larger as time progresses. There will never be any equality, ever!

Our personal situations of being in perpetual debt are now a default. In a capitalist system, if one has no money, then one will never have any money. Credit is not money; it is an obligation with benefits. Consequently, the middle class actually also becomes a third world even in developed nations.

One can save a little here and there and stay inspired by the American dream, but get real people. One will only ever be a slave to that delusion. The sobering truth remains that the well-being of minority capitalism is financed by the misery of the majority population, and capitalists sleep well at night because they are conditioned to view these conditions as a privilege. Depleting resources and outsourcing to cheap labour is normal in the name of profit. They justify selfish living standards with ease.

If we had decent global living conditions for all, then economies and lifted living standards would not be necessary. It is oppression that causes indecent living conditions, and this is also visible in the "living the dream" US, where there is a lot of poverty as well. Additionally, their second amendment, the right to bear arms, makes people paranoid about personal possession and security. Consequently, anybody over eighteen can buy a gun, and the arms trade is a massive industry. They sell guns on the premise of freedom and self-defence, but what are they defending? Is it their financial oppression that limits the freedom they crave? As I mentioned, there are more weapons than people in the States. Consequently, they have daily shootings and frequent mass shootings. So, is it more effective to control the guns or remove them? The Republicans politicize religion and guns simultaneously with their opinion platforms. The other party, the Democrats, asks when stricter gun controls can be implemented to reduce gun violence. But that is the wrong question. Regulating guns is not the answer. Eliminate the second amendment!

The mental range question is: When can we end the imperialism that causes guns in general? The American dream is a leftover myth of ambition from the seventeenth century, and the global mental defect that capitalism represents progress for mankind is only attractive for calculating fools. Let's not forget that imperialism led to capitalist materialism, and socialism/communism formed in opposition.

Previously, welcoming the US and NATO as the world police may have been a temporary option to restore balance after WWII. But now it is an insult to BRICS (Brazil, Russia, India, China, South Africa), who can now be considered another third world. It used to be West versus East, but now we have to include BRICS standing between them.

Implement this: Imperialist materialism creates third worlds. Tell your boss that you will take some days off and withdraw all your financial resources from the bank (provided you actually have any).

Or don't. Admire the capitalist clowns in their mansions and let them entertain you. Show up for work on time, suck up to your boss, and vote for liars that ramble on about the nothing that they've labelled democracy. Just keep going with what's laughing at you every day.

Capital

Marx wrote the massive volume *Capital* which explains how commodities affect labour and advises us to be more aware of how and where we establish values. He published the first volume in 1867 after laborious research. He was not only an idealist but also an economist. Since he was always poor, like most of the industrialized middle class, he wanted to make the new global economies aware of what capitalism would do to humanity.

The capitalists understood that his message attacked their ideals, and then they labelled him a communist because he wrote *The Communist Manifesto* with Engels. Most people don't even know that the *Manifesto* was written nineteen years before he published *Capital*. The *Manifesto* was a labour union manual for unifying against exploitation by the wealthy, whereas *Capital* was an economy manual for isolating the warning signs of overproduction and the detrimental effects of profit seeking.

Capitalists propagate that communism opposes capitalism, and that propaganda is still present today. When *Capital* was published, it clearly exposed how capitalism would eventually become unsustainable and even destroy itself. It described how greed and overproduction would consume resources until nothing was left. Still, Marx is known as the father of the left-wing revolution rather than the Nostradamus of economy. The capitalists always painted Marx as the evil tamer of free enterprise.

A few years later, Nietzsche took note, said that God was dead, and wrote a book called *The Antichrist*. But he did not completely identify who the Antichrist actually was. As far as I understood him he meant Saint Paul, but he also meant that man undermined faith and therefore killed God. Then, for me, Marx clearly identified who the Antichrist was; his name is Capitalism.

When Marx and Engels wrote *The Communist Manifesto*, they tried to build a union party to represent the common folk (proletariat) that were already helplessly oppressed by the wealthy middle class (bourgeoisie) back then. The *Manifesto* attempted to unite and level society as a whole, but it was too extreme in execution because it basically asked for a revolution. So, it did not have much success in restraining or even moderating the already well-established capitalist machine that was rooted in imperialism. In fact, it had the opposite effect: it was to become the evil doctrine that opposed organized capitalist greed.

It was already too late, because organized colonial theft was already too widespread, and greed was the new faith. Communism became the perfect scapegoat to confirm and glorify capitalism. It seems obvious to me that Marx wrote *Capital* to explain in capitalist terms that society inevitably cannot control the rising levels of class and national inequality. The consequences of overproduction for profit that he wrote about were not just built on ideas. They contained straightforward mental capacity principles built on accurate math. He anticipated that capitalism would suffer from the abuse of overproduction. But he could not have anticipated that capitalism would also command the overproduction of credit, and that the consequences of this could only end up in financial collapse. The capitalists know this, but they lie about it with hyper-inflated balance sheets to protect wealth at all costs. Legal idiots at large.

The Communist Manifesto made us aware of class and overproduction principles. However, the global remnants of imperialism were not ready to receive class reform or reduced economies, which is what the *Manifesto* was asking for—a revolution. And back then, with a Napoleonic mind set, that could only translate into civil or even military conflict. Marx simply reacted to the oppression that he was used to. He understood the rich and declared war in theory because the rich are indecent.

What he should have declared was a psychiatric evaluation for a societal model that embraced capitalism, and instigated reform with construction troops to develop all nations instead of leaving it to the capitalists to crucify each other. Imagine where we would be today if the men back then had had enough wit to see the mental capacity side of our species. Yet, dumb and dumber got away with ignoring Marx, and now we are waiting until they eventually go extinct.

I have a better idea, and it does not require a revolution with bloodshed and military action. I propose that we just fine-tune what is already in place with a little financial reset. For example, all currencies would be eliminated and all debt forgiven. Moving forward, trade (not profit) would be made with one new global trading medium. The IMF (International Monetary Fund) which lends money, would be changed to IGFM (International Global Fund Management), which would distribute that global medium. They would distribute trading funds equally to all nations, and the countries that need the most support would be first in line.

This sounds impossible, but think about it. If we eliminate finance and profit from the capitalist equation, we would have a capacity system. Who would care about the ones losing all their wealth?

Once all global debt and individual debt was forgiven, then all individuals would receive a pension. Trade would be encouraged first before using the pension, and everything would have the same value on a global scale. There would be no more hoarding allowed. Consequently, getting along would be much easier. Yes, it sounds like a lot of adjusting, but this is actually possible. Only the wealthy would insist that this is crazy and impossible.

So, how can we make the assumed impossible possible, and even probable, with our inbred capitalist mindset? The G20 countries would declare that this is lunacy and never even attempt to accept it because they would lose their advantage. They would all have to take a few steps back in order to establish equal values everywhere. Meaning, all their surpluses would be shipped to underdeveloped countries, and overproduction would have to stop. A fundamental reset like this is the one and only way that all nations could ever become equal! Rich people would have to downsize and they would not profit anymore. There would be no such thing as offshore tax evasion anymore. Instead of profit seeking, the new desired capacity would be non-profit trade and sharing.

Still sounds impossible, right? But it isn't at all when we, the middle class, simply stop complying with what we are currently doing. We can initiate this all by withdrawing our bank deposits and stopping going to work at the same time, globally.

Let's try it. We already have elements of global foreign aid principles in place to expand on. Sound insane? Maybe so! But it isn't as insane as global capitalist conflict.

As mentioned, it is interesting that only disasters can stimulate substantial global foreign aid. If man truly has the ability to develop global thinking, then disaster aid should be available all the time. And since capitalism is also a disaster, then it should just be normal.

Further, when one collective currency medium re-establishes value, then the rich can keep whatever they have. They just can't use their wealth to invest and grow more. They already have plenty. Their wealth cannot be converted into the new global medium, and they would be encouraged to donate their assets.

Above all, it would be of no use to hoard a common value currency anymore, because nothing would be for sale for profit. There would be no benefit of having anything in excess. Everything would be on a trading basis, and supply and demand would be significantly reduced. Our new value established society could then move beyond our organized trash and clean it up.

If we want to evolve as a species, we have to have the capacity to trust in an entirely new system based on personal capacity and integrity. And once greedy accumulation is extinguished, then why would there be a need for corruption? When equality becomes default, would we have as many drug problems?

Yes, the most reluctant people to this kind of reset will be the wealthy, because they have much to lose and will have to adapt to less. And the ones that will benefit greatly are the ones that have nothing or little. They will become equals, and this will be most of our population!

If we all have equal opportunities, then there is no need for identity theft, fraud, cyber fraud, black markets, and so on. In other words, intelligent beings understand that it would suffice to have equal trading values and that everybody should have enough because we actually have enough!

Only then can we truly focus on preserving the planet and moving into space. Once a global value fund (let's call it that) is managed by IGFM (International Global Fund Management), then they can use all the global banks as distribution centres. Every single community would get what they needed.

With the reset, having more would not get you more. Instead, having less would get you more. Imagine that!

How do we calculate values?

Understanding the capitalist fundamentals of supply and demand can help us to some degree.

The demand to alleviate misery is strong in many countries, and the supply of commodity products to do so is actually available in many of them. But the authorities of the nations in need can't afford enough of these products because they are too expensive, and the ability of charities to provide these products is either not sufficient, or in some countries, not available at all.

Simultaneously, capitalist stock market prices for commodities increase due to wars and famines. Again, misery is good for business. Other good examples are drugs and medical treatment. I had a minor foot surgery to remove a parasite in Nazca, Peru in the mid-eighties. The surgery was $17 and the prescribed antibiotics were $12. I asked the doctor what his salary was, and he replied that it was $280 per month. Now imagine what this treatment would have cost in any of the G7 countries. Probably a hundred times more for the surgery alone. How are such vast differences even possible? The capitalists will say it is because costs are much lower in underdeveloped countries. Maybe so, but the process and treatment are the same.

Supply and demand are reasonable product performance indicators. However, when they become a capitalist excuse to drive price inflation, then performance turns into abuse. It's bizarre: the more we earn, the more we pay for the exact same thing we could get cheaper somewhere else.

Theoretically, if we were to desire nothing in excess, then materialistic values would become obsolete and as a result, demand would not exist. So, what drives demand? Is it actual lack of supply, or is it the capitalist myth?

It's simple: if we need more of something, then we should produce more and not raise the price. If products are scarce, then we should wait until there is more. I mean, when there are no fish left in the ocean, we will have to stop fishing. We won't be able to just raise the price of fish when there are none.

Capitalists always blame demand on immediate desire or volume and not on necessity. And they charge more right away to reduce demand. Therefore, values can be inflated even when it isn't necessary at all. If everything costs the same, was traded with a unified currency, and global distribution was equalized, then there would be no need for price inflation. And if we run out of a product, then we would find alternatives.

But right now, we don't do this. We just charge more, and only a few can afford the price. This is how inequality develops and sustains itself.

Hence, supply and demand equations are simultaneously idiotic and calculated. They are stupid because they promote inequality, but they are calculated to satisfy greed. Seeking an advantage is not intelligent. Pursuing advantage is selfish.

The same applies to overall inflation. The desired average rate is 2%, which means that in thirty-five years, everything will have doubled. It is remarkable that we trust in inflation and unstable markets. Instability is a direct consequence of inequality. I detest the quote, "What are the markets doing today?" Market hysteria is an excuse to generate more profit and is more about influential noise than actual supply. Some sectors of government preach that we should reduce our materialistic consumption while at the same time, other sectors want nothing more than economic growth. In other words, they want both. How can we reduce demand while we compete in markets?

In principle, current global food production is sufficient to feed every single one of us. In fact, we could do even better than that. Even so, prices are all over the place, and there is more profit buried in shipping than in the product itself. Worst of all, wealthy countries waste about one-third of their food. This is beyond negligent, and another star quality of capitalism. Stable food pricing should be available everywhere, but it is not, and food is traded in stock markets. People, let me be clear: the point of food is to eat it, not to profit from it. Is that simple enough? The poor nations basically have to operate on necessities for the most part, and they don't have nearly as much luxury or choices. This is not the case because they fell behind compared to the well-developed. They were initially exploited with imperialism, and then deliberately left behind with capitalism. The capitalists think that this was smart on their part, but idiots don't know any better.

As mentioned previously, Marx spent most of his life on social mediating, though the self-serving social alienation of man from the rest of the natural earth also fascinated him. Looking at where we are today, we have to accept Marx's predictions as fact. A variety of political and social systems tried to prove him wrong while remaining content that the capitalist machine is best.

We don't have to over-analyze Marx to recognize that men like him should have influenced our principles much sooner. But we chose to miss them. Intentionally! People frequently misunderstood and misinterpreted Marx's concepts. He is not the father of communism or socialism. Instead, I call him an economist with a conscience that fathered warning signals. It was the regimes and politicians of the past that transformed his signals into new social and political ideologies and extremes. They made communism the anti-matter of capitalism.

Marx's industrialization concepts were understood by the communist movement to help sustain population growth. But when misinterpreted, the movement failed to understand that management is not dictatorship. Management requires moderate thinking instead of a strict commanding. Communism sometimes emerges as a brainwash system that converts people into clones. We have had proof of that in Cambodia and Vietnam. Where did such extremism even come from? We see Chinese armies in blue and green clothing, cheering to dull propaganda, and behaving in unison. This kind of army attitude restricts liberated thinking and limits individualism. Extremist groups emerge from a longing for equality, as everyone feels the need for equality. Think about it: equality is far more important than freedom.

A more moderate communist model can still serve us as an example to equalize on a global level. With such a model, the concept of a capitalist hoarding clone can be replaced by that of a productive member who serves in order to help restore. Such a system can supply labour and ideas and can restore the earth, which must happen. The new action propaganda for the masses should be that more sustainability is prioritized, more national parks are developed, and third world countries are not labeled as such anymore.

Eastern communism was never welcomed by western capitalist thought, despite the moderation options that it clearly offers. Community means communism, and it is a much better concept to sustain society and the earth's environment. We can learn something from this kind of thinking. Capitalists are loners and promote their isolation agendas as independence. They label others as dictators and communists. But other systems are just responses to capitalist oppression.

Regardless, all current systems combined are Neanderthals in uniforms and business suits. They simply can't get along, even though to get along would only require some basic mental decency.

I understand that Marx was in search of better living conditions and not political doctrine. He understood that industrialization and overpopulation had to be managed somehow. His time moved at a much slower pace than ours does today, yet it was not that much different as far as evolving societies are concerned. For example, labour-saving was a concern back then, while today it would be time-saving. Back then, it was the physical, replaced today by the digital, and the landowners of the past emerge today as corporations and banks. In summary, everything is about efficiencies, and a few minorities have always controlled the working class.

The industrial temptation to earn inflated profits has replaced that of trading goods at a fair level. Ever since we began to record history, money has been the real beast, even if it is not a horned creature. Money began circulating as a medium to ease trade, and it should have remained as such.

When we look at the European royal colonial arrogance of the last four hundred years, we can see it was just a free for all. They just had to get somewhere, and then they took whatever they wanted. And just because they were able to do that, does not mean it was acceptable. Where colonials stole long ago from others, there are still leftover colonies today. We should reverse the former theft and return whatever was taken. Imagine that. It would only make sense. We cannot blame native peoples for wanting their land back or for wanting to restore their culture.

Eventually, imperialists could no longer claim new territory because Earth became too small. So, they created financial territories, and wealthy nations are still hindering growth in the countries they colonized and exploited. The colonials started it. None of it was fair and it still isn't today, yet they still prevail.

We still carry this colonial baggage because we, the middle class, continue to tolerate it.

The capitalist predicament at issue here is that our situation can never get better without a complete financial reset. The Americans, Europeans, and BRICS will always compete for that one single thought: control! What an incredibly narrow-minded method for existing. And still the same as the distant greedy Romans, Catholics, and royals did: take, take, take. . . Bizarre!

Even in a fictional universe like that of *Star Wars*, the empire strikes back. We, the middle class, are actually the true empire, but we have lost sight of that. We are hypnotized by the capitalists' setup. They assured us that slavery was outlawed, but we face corporate slavery every day. Corporate slaves do not get whipped, nor are they in cages, but they pay bills and bind them with mental-health chains. Fun, right?

Again, it seems totally absurd for a single person like me to even attempt to oppose the grinding insanity of all this. And sure, a few common citizens can revolt, scream anarchy, practice jihad, criticize territorial claims, reject religious deception, and condemn corporate ambitions. But why do these things when there is something far more powerful?

Revolutions are not an option anymore because they have been done. They raise fear levels, consume resources, become violent, and are repeatedly crushed. They are a tribal reaction of desperation, like a little tantrum. And going out with a bang as a suicide bomber is morbidly ineffective. But at least it's a quick death.

Instead of a suicide helpline, we need a delete imperialism helpline.

The fundamental existential questions will never go away: Why can't we ignore imperialist capitalism? What is holding the middle class back from rising above it?

You, yourself, still continue to find solutions to reduce your stress every day. Try ignoring capitalism and realize an immediate relief from stress. What if everything came to a standstill because the middle class stopped complying and demanded to eliminate capitalism? I am convinced that anarchy and war would not erupt.

What would happen instead is that the authorities would have to suddenly pay attention to the middle class with a severe sense of urgency. And they would have to immediately regroup on what to do next. The entire society would then wait until the talking heads came up with a proposal for an actual replacement for capitalism. Trust me, they know what needs to be done already. They would simply have to manage complete financial collapse and interruptions in production and supply chains. That's all. No point in complicating things. They wouldn't be able to delay or lie anymore to protect the current organized mess. They would have to announce the devaluing of currencies, elimination of global debt, and elevating every nation up to equal levels. The IMF would regulate a common denominator trade currency that they create in digital format. There would be no more hard currency needed when we can create digital currency in an instant.

So what is the problem? Just a little reset with a few disruptions of business as usual. That would suffice.

Then there wouldn't be business anymore! And once the UN panel presented reasonable and acceptable basic conditions, we would be able to go back to work—but not to get paid, since there wouldn't be any debt anymore. We wouldn't have to pay taxes because governments would create digital trade currency. Governments would distribute the new digital trade currency as a pension. This would allow for products to be traded for, rather than being sold for profit.

Then we could work on global equalization projects and improve the UN panel with specialists from different fields. As we progress, we could make continuous adjustments. This is a capacity system worth pursuing, and any fear of such a reset is only overrated by capitalists. All other folks would finally find themselves in balanced and much better living conditions.

Yes, it would be a little turbulent at the very beginning, but if we know what the end goal is, we can handle a few disruptions. We just need to help each other! And you wouldn't be working when it all begins, so you would have time to adjust.

So come on, give yourself some credit! We are capable of striving for a common global good because we are already able to gauge what is right even now.

The primary intent for corporations should be conducting research in order to improve products instead of making a profit by mass producing them. We don't need nearly as many disposable products, and markets should be shared and improved instead of controlled. More small, local shops should be reinstated in communities, and brands like Walmart and shopping centres should disappear. Eliminating chain businesses and rebuilding with minor operations would create jobs in smaller communities. This is not only possible, but highly probable to occur. And it would eliminate the distinct, so-called "third world." Jobs could be created locally instead of outsourced to highly underpaid labour in developing countries. Environmental cleanup and recycling processes would improve everywhere. Birth rates would stabilize, no child would lack education, and every mouth would be fed. Every single economy would have time to adjust to our new restoration standards, and poverty levels would be statistics of the past.

One for all and all for one should not only apply to The Three Musketeers.

It's really not that complicated to imagine. All we have to do is remove money from the equation. From there, we could still function the same, just without profit. We could ignore money if we didn't need it. Imagine if there was no poverty or inequality anymore, how could we then define wealth?

This is how we eliminate money, so get organized:

1. On the same day, everybody withdraws their cash assets and holds onto them privately.
2. A few days later, when all time zones have caught up, none of us go to work.

Both immediate actions would be like everybody flushing the toilet simultaneously!

We already have a globally recognized environmental day called Earth Day. That could be the day to begin the withdrawals, followed by not showing up for work a few days later. Then we wait to find out what happens next.

They shut down all the airports after 9/11 and locked things down with COVID. Why can't we take this a little further, and shut down capitalist theft?

Implement this: Earth Day is on April 22. There is even a website for it (www.earthday.org). Or, pick any day and call it Reset Day. The sooner, the better!

We, the middle class, are the empire, not some clown president, king, or pope! Let us unite and pull out our cash from our banks on Reset Day and refuse to go to work on the following Monday.

What is the worst that can happen if we all did this? We could always go back a week later, right? Or would they threaten us with the loss of our jobs? But then, who would go instead? Do not underestimate the power that a united middle class can project.

Yes, there may be some hiccups and disruptions, and it will take some time. So what? Every sick and abandoned creature will welcome this and celebrate. They will wait for what the middle class can do for them. Let's feed them, help them, cry with them, and learn to laugh with them.

It's all there, right in front of us!

Or don't. You are a capitalist clone and you have the right to be stupid. Don't give anything up and call me a fool. But you definitely serve no purpose. You are the true nihilist. On behalf of those that endure daily misery, moving to another planet may be a better option so that you can make room for them. But that is too sarcastic. I can say that there is a better option: Change your mind and help.

Who controls whom?

Chomsky wrote a book called *What Kind of Creatures Are We?* where he explains the fundamentals of language development and how we can better understand a common good. However, let me ask, is a common good actually possible and attainable in a capitalist environment? How can we define a common good when inequality is a consequence of excess materialism? In my view, Chomsky gets lost in his own genius. He misses the position that the herd's average point of view is too undereducated to even comprehend him. Sorry, but I don't think that they can see his target. His ideas are idealism that the herd can't understand yet.

Now, it would be unfair to call the common herd stupid. They just can't devote enough quality time to education because they are all struggling. Despite plenty of information, the masses still cannot educate themselves enough. In contrast, Chomsky's book is for the philosophical elite. It does not have much practical application for the herd. Even so, it provides the right intention. He could do us a favour by applying his writing gifts to reducing the causes for inequalities.

To demonstrate how inequality develops, let's move on to an article that isolates how the American financial sector was set up. Have you ever read up on the Rothschilds' two-hundred-year history? You can find it on the web: https://www.donaldwatkins.com/post/the-rothschilds-controlling-the-world-s-money-supply-for-more-than-two-centuries

And this section stands out:

> In 1913, the Rothschilds established their last and current central bank in America—the US Federal Reserve Bank. This independent bank regulates and controls America's money supply and monetary policies. Even though the Federal Reserve is overseen by a board of governors appointed by the President of the United States, the bank's real control still resides with the Rothschild family.

During the Obama administration, the Reserve's board was appointed by Obama. He is a Democrat, and the three top executives he appointed were Republican. Should that be surprising? Meaning, who is appointing whom?

The Federal Reserve's main purpose is to regulate banks and stock markets, hold cash reserves, and sell treasury bonds to investors and foreign countries.

Bonds are loans (liabilities) to the government to raise cash, to fund their loans and investments (assets). To clarify further, some countries buy US bonds and US dollars to help stabilize their currency.

The gold standard nations buy gold to back their currency. US bonds are long-term debts for low interest that are traded for cash to finance investments that generate much higher earnings. The US dollar is very stable because it is backed by the large US economy. Most countries have a disadvantage by default because their currency is not as stable as the US dollar. Consequently, they often lose money due to exchange rates and fees to buy US bonds and cash. The largest expense sector in every country is energy, and energy (oil) is traded in US dollars.

The feds eventually have to pay back cash for the bonds when they mature. But the return payment over the long-term is much lower than the revenue the cash generated over the borrowing term. In other words, the more bonds they sell, the more they make. That also means that multiple profit-taking opportunities arise for moving money alone. They also collect fees, and profit yields can be invested again, followed by more interest invested again, and so on. In other words, this is compound interest accounting.

The whole bank deposit and bond market is more complicated than I've explained here in this shortcut, but it will suffice. It is why all the institutions and people with money can make more money without doing anything. They do however have to follow regulations so that their liabilities (what they hold in deposits) don't surpass their assets (what they loan and mortgage out). But sometimes that scenario does not balance, and that is when banks fail.

They can also pool and invest all the middle-class payroll deposits and savings while the middle-class workers slave away. Therefore, the slave provides not only the labour but also the very cash for the rich to get richer. It is absurd how dumb we are!

Federal inflation reports are a manipulation tool to implement fluctuating interest rates that fatten nothing but the banks. Additionally, the large pools of money that banks can compound have the ability to generate revenue very quickly. Hence, the saying: "It takes money to make money."

However, many banks and the US Federal Reserve have overextended themselves. They underestimated what defaulted loans and mortgages, cash withdrawals, and high liability ratios could do to their balance sheets. But still, they hide the truth of going broke with creative accounting. They can show losses as assets to be recovered later! Imagine you did that when trying to qualify for a mortgage. The banks would show you the door.

So, without serious intervention, this swindle at large won't end. A complete financial reset has to be put in gear!

The latest display of capitalist control to sustain inequality was COVID. I suspect the US intentionally caused COVID to harm China's economy, decrease global population, and increase their own pharmaceutical sales. A health threat is an excellent tool to create fear, which is the capitalists' favourite weapon. And, shutdowns generate more global debt, so they could print more bonds. Very savvy indeed.

However, bonds are just paper, and gold stocks are not actually gold. They only deliver value at the very moment they trade for cash or gold. Any paper treasury bill that can be traded into value at a later date is just a promise. Nothing else!

The current net worth of the US is about 150 trillion dollars worldwide—about 300 trillion is assets and 150 trillion is liabilities. But, they only say that their current debt is about 36 trillion as it relates to their budgets. However, budgets are not actual assets. They only represent the required cash flow. In that case, that 36 trillion has to be added to the 150 trillion in liabilities, adding up to 186 trillion in debt. But they never mention this.

Regardless of if these numbers are accurate or not, the dollar still rarely loses much strength, despite that much debt. All of this debt is based on a strong future economy. Again, even the international credit rating accepts that amount of debt based on a promise. In other words, it would be like you saying that you're bankrupt, but you promise that you won't be in the future. Do you think you could get away with that? And which other countries have that much debt and sustain the strength of their currency? None! The US previously claimed that they moved away from the gold standard to back the dollar, but how can we still believe that?

Simply put, we can't believe any financial information from anyone, period. And, considering that the Rothschild family, with their two-hundred-year global influence, still controls what the US feds are doing makes Musk, Bezos, Gates, and Buffet all look like they just have a little pocket change.

The US feds are broke. Otherwise, they would not ask the Big Four to bail out the smaller banks that recently failed. Remember, it does not matter how big you are; when you're broke, you're broke.

So, where are the Rothschilds and the other Federal Reserve glamour families? We never hear anything about them. These people are beyond celebrity status. They are not only rich, but they are ghost puppet masters that are untouchable. They hide their money in investment groups, gold, diamonds, and real estate. They instigate the propaganda machine that paints Putin, Xi Jinping, and Trump as the fools that parade and entertain us with their micro-deflections. Have you ever noticed that it's never about the rich? It's always about some other deviant. The news networks feast on MAGA extremism, humanitarian leftovers, and war debris, while the rich quietly count their money in the background. Does that sound like a common good? The herd misses the big picture: that capitalism is a control conspiracy that causes inequality, while posing as the world saviour.

The Rothchilds would concur that size does matter. However, having a mental range means that size and money should not matter at all. Wealth is dementia. When is big large enough, when all we really need is so little? We have to reverse our math. Instead of always adding, we need to subtract. Nobody can eat untouchable securities and real estate.

Consider also that the untouchables such as Putin, Xi Jinping, and even Trump, are not renegade idiots. They have completely different agendas that are not in the public domain. And they just won't go away! Why are they so powerful and why are they being followed to the current extent? If they were idiots, they would have been long gone. But here they are, and according to conspiracy theories, they are secretly opposing the capitalist cabal, each with their own method. Balance will be served eventually, one way or another. So, middle class, why wait?

Implement this: Ignore wealth and the famous. They don't deserve our attention.

Or not. Participate as a by-product microbe.

Consumerism

Our industrial advances have reduced us to comfort-seeking sloths in the G20, and we seem incapable of calculating what will be sustainable as populations grow. Our extravagance becomes most apparent in our inability to standardize commodities. When we allow people to choose what kind of gas to pump, then most will pump the cheapest to save money. If all gas was the cleanest to burn and the price was regulated, then the option to pump cheap would not even exist. With our current choices, the individual has the option to justify more pollution because it is cheaper. We intentionally cater to frugal stupidity, allowing for pollution to be bought for less. A wise formula indeed.

All trade for profit presents the same dumb marketing extravagance. The consumer is invited to save while creating waste and beckoned to save (waste) more when they buy more. Consequently, vendors can steal more and manufacturers can produce more. Like a house of cards, profits stack upon profits, and so on. Perpetual cheating and lying are now standard in business marketing.

Governments should regulate overproduction and over-consumption because regulating is what governing should be. Fewer choices would mean fewer problems. But why would governments regulate when regulations reduce business and taxes? They are motivated by profit as well. Still, they preach embracing global restoration and reducing resource depletion, even though this completely opposes their marketing. With abundance filling store shelves, how effective can preaching moderation really be?

Governing also means setting quality standards and labelling products for exactly what they are. There should be no fancy packaging and no underweight or overpriced products possible, but the opposite gets promoted with most products.

In addition, small operators producing small quantities should be a priority in every community. They could even trade amongst each other instead of selling. We still don't understand that Walmart and other department stores are cancers to communities. They wipe out small businesses! This may seem retrograde to a capitalist, but small diversification is actually smart, which is why most underdeveloped countries still operate in that way. Walmart could not survive there.

Small individual shops can produce higher quality products. I remember growing up in Switzerland when there were bakeries all over town. Now most of them are gone, and the department stores that stand in their places reheat frozen, pre-made whatever. It all tastes the same, and the ingredient lists are the size of novels, all to increase shelf life. What happened to fresh, tasty, new, and fun? With department stores, the flavour is gone, the jobs are gone, and the special, seasonal items that contributed so much to local culture are gone as well. We have to get rid of the cheap, plastic, trash mentality that clone consumerism offers. When we nurture the small, communities thrive. Just like corals and plankton sustain the oceans.

Chemical factories in particular should take note of reducing commodity choices. They all produce multiple products that all serve the same purpose, just packaged in hundreds of different ways. Why? If the beauty of the container is so important, then run a contest, pick one, and move on. Get real, people. Soap, toothpaste, and laundry detergent are basic stuff.

Chemical products and drugs also generate some of the highest profit margins. Another unregulated and stupid deception. Aren't vegetables more important? But no, it costs a small fortune to keep your house and your clothes clean. Simple processes that have now become high-profit opportunities.

Thousands of cleaning products parade down our shelves. Diluted and undiluted, companies mix up these nasty cocktails so that consumers can then flush them down the drain, dumping them and tons of other industrial waste products overboard to our friends in the oceans. Which we then plan to eat. I guarantee that most households would not use half the chemicals they currently do if they were simply not available. But apparently, we want to raise toxic seafood.

Extreme pollution and overfishing demand more than serious regulations. We need the military to move in to shut down these fishing fleets. Sustainable fishing is the responsibility of all governments, and preservation action is required before they try to convince the herd to eat fewer fish with astronomical prices.

We know that we waste, but here we are still loading up the cart at Walmart. And half the stuff we bought is packaging. It is the retail industry that fills these shelves, wasting and polluting the most, yet we are the ones asked to recycle and not to litter. As industrial heavyweights pump out more and more, they only fork over small fines for environmental damages when they occasionally get caught. Fines are no threat to corporations. They evade and plan on not getting caught in the first place. Again, stupid is cheaper.

The global water management sector alone offers immense opportunities to create jobs. There is a garbage patch three times the size of Texas floating between California and Hawaii. Seriously, how is that even possible? If we had some IQ as a species, then cleaning up, fertilizing, and restocking our oceans should be our number one priority. Life in the ocean means life on the ground. Nature would be grateful and she would reward us with abundance.

In summary, we cannot ask for indefinitely growing economies to satisfy imperialist demands. Instead, we need to moderate how we utilize our resources. We do not have other planets to sustain what imperialists take without limits.

Mental capacity replaces growth with moderation by default, and we need a single trade medium currency to accomplish moderation. The euro is a good example of such a medium that served Europe, or gold would work as well. This is not utopian! This is intelligent. If Europe can create a unified currency, then why can't the rest of the world? "Oh, but it's complicated," is the common response. Nonsense. It's only complicated for the rich, but it is very welcoming for the poor.

However, even the historic creation of the euro favoured the strongest economies of Europe. A global trading medium cannot favour any advantage to anyone. Global devaluation means that all become equal. The wealthy will never accept this, so consequently, we as middle-class individuals have no other choice. I repeat: pull out all your cash, don't go to work, and wait for the capitalist system to collapse.

Implement this: Think about what products you use. Volunteer in any way possible to find remedies for all this filth. Embrace small because it is personal, new, and fresh.

Or don't. Just look away. It's not your concern. Fill your bins with the trash from Walmart. Someone, somewhere, will handle it for you. And don't forget to complain about the fees—pollution is a business as well. Stupid means profit. Get by in your little bubble and be nice about it. Be like a sheep: constantly amazed by the green stuff on the ground, right up until they get slaughtered.

From micro-to macro-managed capitalism

Imagine that I get pulled over by a cop and he writes me a ticket for a traffic violation. I get emotional and think he is a tool of our stealing government doing a useless job, and I despise his military micromanaging demeanour. Then I digress and remember the Dalai Lama saying, "Forgive because we all suffer."

Well, I could forgive, not direct profane thoughts towards him because I acknowledge that we all suffer, and treat him kindly. But why does suffering exist in the first place? We're born to feel good, and there is absolutely no need for our entire civilization to suffer so much. Even the Dalai Lama got it wrong, you might say. Do we even need a Dalai Lama to make us aware of having compassion for suffering? What if the entire sequence of events in this thinking process is wrong in the first place? What if we just ignored authority and all our micromanaging laws?

I'm not suggesting anarchy, but we could stop complying with capitalism and lying about it. We could use inaction, we could use language sparingly, and we could ask questions. As mentioned, a good start is to ask "why" questions and then listen to the misguided, misinformed, and misleading noise that comes back at us. Then, wait.

In this capitalist maze, everything is a cause of something else and everything is tied to money. But nothing has any real meaning if there is no need for it (Occam's razor). What is this human need to micromanage everything? Why do we need fines to enforce traffic laws for example? We have traffic rules, and that should be enough. They should serve as guidelines, and only severe cases should have more consequences. And why do punishments for minor unlawful behaviours always involve money? We don't need officers lurking in hidden spots, writing up tickets to meet their quotas. Traffic cops are the result of unnecessary job creation in order to fill the vault of the deep state.

The same tolerance level should apply to drugs. We have drugs available, and that's enough. If people choose to use them, then that is their choice. I mean, you can drink and eat yourself to death, but drugs are a problem? Some countries finally legalized pot, which is a step in the right direction, and which removes volume from the unnecessary legal system.

Micromanaged capitalism is not freedom; it is idiot chaos. And depression ranks high because people get insecure that we're stuck in this imperialist gun show. The so-called "American dream" is based on motives such as freedom, prosperity, and independence. It's not a bad idea—if it can be accomplished without a gun.

Lately, the US has been breeding MAGA Republicans with motives that translate into domination, exclusivity, to be great again, and to be greater than the greatest. They should all get lobotomies.

On a much larger scale, Americans manipulate everything around the globe, all while they pose as the world's police. They always make Russia and China look like thugs, but they are just as guilty for all these ongoing wars. The western world even seems to believe that American involvement is what won the Second World War for the Allies. They helped, but the Russians actually won that war when they starved and froze the Germans to death. They were the main cause that drained the German war machine of resources, not the Americans.

In my view, the US got involved in WWII because it provided them with instant economy, all while they watched the Europeans slaughter each other. To get involved, they needed a major event, which they created by provoking Japan with sanctions and by choking supplies. Japan was provoked about a dozen times until they finally attacked at Pearl Harbor. And then the US staged it so as to be perceived as the victim that got innocently attacked. Roosevelt initially disapproved of engaging in the Second World War, but after the attack, the average American citizen thought it necessary to become engaged. Their culture was always built on motives of pride and heroism since they became an independent European colony. It was a government-planned setup for indirect world domination.

Finally, the A-bomb, which was the culmination of global nuclear research, obliterated Japan into surrender. The Americans claimed that the bomb saved lives because the Japanese would have fought to the death. But Japan was also an emerging industrial power at the time. So why not take the opportunity to obliterate two industrial hubs and slow down their progress, and then blame it on the war? This was organized crime on the grandest of scales, all in plain sight. They could have just dropped one bomb in a far less inhabited area as a warning and then negotiated surrender. But it was much better for business to obliterate a major harbour and an industrial education centre. Someone selected these targets based on hidden economic reasons and to set an example of domination.

With the WWII Allies victory, the US recognized that they had an opportunity to gain the upper hand on global capitalism. They intentionally made most nations dependent on the US dollar for trade after WWII. Most commodities and oil had to be traded in dollars, and Europe also had to pay them back for their war loans.

That war was an excellent investment and gave the Americans a head start on world domination. The US also understood how to strategically destabilize countries that opposed them by planting their own ideology, cash, and weapons within them to support domestic wars. Once these wars ended, these countries would rebuild among the rubble with American company contracts.

The US is the capitalist wolf in the world police sheep's clothing that undermines unstable governments.

When other countries do the same thing, it is called geopolitical coercion and terrorism. The US is smart at cheating; I give them that, but for all the wrong reasons. So, take a step back and consider who the real terrorists are out there. Are they the organizations that plan sneaky global subversion, or are they the eventually terrorized suicide bombers? Suicide bombers are only a symptom, not a cause. The sneaky terrorist is the freedom screaming, bible thumping, gun fanatic conservative capitalist of the United States. And apparently this is the best they can be with their American dream. *The Untold American History* is a documentary by Oliver Stone that exposes the US's distorted motives of the last century from various perspectives.

Still, even a superpower like the US is subject to manipulation. They are secretly controlled by investment firms that are owned by western society's richest individuals who behave recklessly due to their privileged upbringings. To them, greed is a game. Corrupting everything is a source of entertainment for them. And since humanity was raised to be greedy, right down to the individuals, they have the perfect audience. The stage is always set for them, and the Federal Reserve banks are their puppets that keep printing bonds out of nothing, without restraint, to seed more unlimited greed. Everybody wants more by default. Even the micro traffic cop.

The secret puppet masters play with the planet just for themselves. Their plan is to hide in their conspiracy shelters while they eventually exterminate everything that gets in their way. Creatures that never have enough, that think they have outsmarted everything, and that parade their scum in their castles and estates.

However, the core of humanity is aware and is waiting for something else. There is a global awakening in progress. Many of us are ready. All this waiting in mayhem will not matter anymore when us common folks simply walk away. Capitalist dementia is a disease, and you are the remedy!

Implement this: Reject being a capitalist tool. The more money the rich have, the dumber they can be. They can just buy their way out of everything because you let them.

Or don't. The rich can just go on laughing about their fortunes until they die. You can go on admiring their disease while they mess up your life every day.

Corporations and cartels

I have been watching CNN discuss Trump's idiocy for years. They even still talk about the same principles today. And Fox rambles about the opposite, resulting in defamation ping-pong. This is what capitalists do. They keep talking and mean nothing. Nor do they do anything, they just talk and talk, and the herd watches, mesmerized, wondering about these volumes of nothing and what they should fear next.

In fact, the networks don't care what side you're on. They just want you to buy the trash that they advertise with their empty reporting. It's bizarre. Hypnotized people will eventually wake up. But the herd is not even hypnotized. They are sleeping with their eyes wide open.

Yes, I slander big corporations and governments, but let me also explain what I like about them. Business and authority are about organizing affairs, and there is nothing wrong with that. But when authority is practised like a manipulating religion where greedy lies replace fact, then the herd gets confused. Governing entails organizing and regulating, but only with a refined understanding of what truly matters. Competent people manage world affairs, but democracy slows things down due to public voting. This intentional delay concept is what sustains capitalism. The herd is not equipped to make decisions that competent people have to make. Competence should not require a vote.

Voting is a sedative for the herd to accept intentional delay.

When capitalist agendas go sideways, the message is repetitive. It's unfair, over budget, too expensive, exploitative, and it is always someone else that has to be held accountable. But who actually reacts to any of it, and who is that someone being held accountable? And when someone can isolate accountability, it usually identifies a group that is protected by the tumour of law.

Old and complex constitutions protect corporations. When debating, nationalists often emphasize the importance of their forefathers and traditional constitutional beliefs, some of which are over two hundred years old. Ancient constitutions are statements of pride and lame in execution, like running a Ferrari with diesel. Maybe they could now run a Tesla with diesel to become even more outdated.

We need these people to get current and to stop asking to democratize and have trust in old pride. In my view, the middle-class worker does not even know what an idealist democracy actually means. Ideally, the purpose and intent of any constitution should deliver moderate regulation in a clear, flexible, and updated manner. Democracy is meant to address what is current and at issue, and not to select who can lead according to money and outdated constitutions. Democracy should be obedient to the basic global common good and serve as a format for conduct. But regulation gets lost in the various interpretations of the language they call law. As a result, capitalist influence can distort democratic values because capitalism primarily satisfies inequality and the protection of wealth. The middle class mistakes participating to win a democratic majority in a capitalist environment as a medium to create more equality. But this does not work.

Achieving equality does not depend on a majority, nor can it be attained through financial policy. Wealth is not democratic to begin with and is the opposite of poverty. So why do we vote for equality when the rich and poor are completely incompatible? How do we miss such plain logic?

It is impossible to justify wealth, period. If we want results from a global democratic perspective, we must first isolate that capitalism is not necessary and act on that premise to eliminate it. The wealthy will never consent to this because they would lose their status. They will insist upon and consent to a shrivelled capitalist voting delay democracy to prolong more of the same incompetency.

If there was no money, the rich would be gone, and so would the poor.

The methods by which we practise democracy cannot deliver urgency. We should have reduced global warming fifty years ago, but the present delay methods contributed little for that change to occur. The authorities enable big enterprise to indefinitely operate as they please. And our environmental preservation methods are so lame that we are literally sleeping ourselves into extinction.

Our sloth in tolerating incompetence has earned capitalism celebrity status. It is beyond bizarre that profit can override everything and hide behind idealist democratic ideas.

The herd is brainwashed into thinking that jobs are needed to sustain capitalist economies. But that is not true. Who would work if there was no pay, but everything was available anyway? The economy is unnecessary. Economy is only a word to measure profit. None of us have to comply with jobs, profit, or the economy. We can continue what we are doing and call it something else. How about plain occupation? And if all of us were rewarded the same (not paid) and all goods had the same value globally, then why would profit matter? See what I mean? This is like a relativity theory for complete social reform without capitalism.

Free enterprise is a good idea, provided it remains free for all involved. However, if markets are controlled or monopolized to entertain profit, then free enterprise transforms into oppressed enterprise, and that right there is the turning point where ideas for progress with industrialization for mankind become ugly.

The herd is conditioned to accept delusional living standard incentives and to support the corporate mass hysteria of endless production that this planet can never sustain. Marx predicted that long economic depressions would be a consequence of improved living standards. But corporations want and insist on producing even more. This obsession with production and ownership are the kindling that fire up these endless wars on territorial and mental levels. And there is no end in sight unless an abrupt financial standstill occurs.

Wars are the lowest activity mankind could ever engage in. WWII even became so obscene that it involved dropping a nuclear bomb. A capacity mind could never justify the use of such a bomb as a temporary remedy for anything. But, when war can turn into business, humans become opportunistic. Once a war is done, capitalists get busy cleaning up and instant economies and war recycling are born.

On a larger scale, the so-called allied capitalist democracies had to crush communist ideology and socialism wherever it wanted to spread, causing more war again. Our entire recorded world history and ideology is just one simple thought: lousy management to satisfy profit. Marx even gave us the heads-up to evolve beyond lousy management once we industrialized. But intelligence is obviously not as profitable. Can I reduce any further?

Still, who could have led the way to implement moderate control and effective management? If they looked at resources and demographics on a global scale, they would have noticed that our planet knows that she has finite resources. The earth is a lady, and she deserves kindness. Profit is never kind. And there is nothing wrong with production when production is applied to satisfy a moderate need. But profit is not a need! Hence, it is not too late today to apply what we should have learned over the last five hundred years.

Corporations helped to build a world that functions. What we engineered in the last two centuries is very impressive. And, competitive markets drove inventions at a much higher pace with capitalist pressure. But, did we miss out on other inventions that weren't able to secure funding and were neglected in favour of more profitable ones? What humans continue to invent is amazing, but now is the time to step back and get serious about what we can do with these tools. We have to listen to the earth; she is telling us to wise up in rather threatening ways. The earth does not need superpower nations. The earth needs super capacity adapting from humans. It surprised us when imperialism sneezed and the whole world got COVID, but it served as a good example that complete lockdowns are possible. Now we need the middle class to sneeze so the whole world can lock down for a financial reset.

How do we reduce crime?

This is actually an easy one. Crime is a self-inflicted byproduct of imperial capitalism. If there was no capitalism, there would be no corruption. We witness corporate theft, hoarding, overwhelming instability, and indecent global living conditions. In such conditions, imperialist capitalism comes across as organized crime. So why wouldn't we expect individuals to be tempted to do the same?

According to studies, most crime offenders have a miserable upbringing and may have even been abused in some way before committing their crimes. Miserable upbringings are caused by capitalist oppression in the first place. It takes twelve years of education to get a first paycheque in developed nations. And if you are born to parents without money, you most likely die without any money as well. Yes, there are some success stories that are repeated over and over in American dream propaganda, but these stories just promote the cancer of false ambition and are not attainable for the average middle-class worker.

The capitalist myth of attaining success, elitism, and wealth is the propaganda of stale minds. Even though financial power affords ruthlessness, it is also a weakness. Consequently, it needs protection, is corrupt, and invites theft as a job opportunity for the unemployed and forgotten.

When you grow up poor and do nothing but shovel misery and fail to fit in, then crime suddenly seems like a lucrative option that promises instant reward. Income and goods become available. The only curveball is that they have to be earned at a higher level of legal risk.

Capitalist mentality praises success and the accumulation of possessions. Even the richest can't stop from hoarding more, and they fear some delusion of falling behind. They circumvent laws and therefore indirectly invent crimes, all to chase more of the same. The constitution defines crime as illegal, but the same laws protect wealth and greed. The rich can even buy crime to make them richer still. But if nobody can prove it, then it never happened. Right?

How can we determine the effectiveness of the law when everything can be bought and bribed? Profit does all the taking and the tumour of law does all the talking. We pack jails, yet we refuse to acknowledge our own various acts of theft.

Organized crime and national secret services murder each other in order to protect. They say they don't kill in the name of greed. They call it self-defence. In a weak society, it appears that some law and order may be necessary to provide stability to the constitutional rights of citizens. However, the only right we really have is to die one day.

In principle, capitalist law would not be necessary if capitalism did not exist. Without seeking profit, there would be no greed. And without greed, inequality would be unable to spread. And when equality is a default, then there is no need to steal. We can deconstruct that capitalist nonsense into nothing.

Consequently, what wealth would remain to protect? There would be no need to sue, to postpone, to object, or to judge. All that legal noise that never ends would disappear.

When people are no longer hungry or homeless and instead feel secure and cared for, they will no longer steal or cheat. Nor will they need guns! Law is a capitalist invention, and it is lawyers who are the ones laughing as they load their bank accounts. And the same lawyers end up running our countries as politicians, campaigning with our tax money to load their accounts even further. Of course, I am just a moron compared to them. Their yachts and Ferrari's speak for themselves.

Most of these garbage geniuses remain untouchable for whatever crimes they commit. They fly around in planes with golden toilets, and society admires them. They build their mansions on stolen money and sleep well next to their mistresses, satisfied in their illegal stupor.

All these oligarchs, corporate deviants, and silver spoon offenders have the most prominent lawyers on their payrolls. They can twist and pretzel everything beyond recognition with legal language. Rhetoric, where the best lie wins a case, does not serve justice. And let's not mistake revenge for something as justice.

I propose that crime be punished immediately. We should simplify the conviction process by categorizing crimes based on their severity. Sentencing should be strict. But not jail! How about joining a global rebuilding troop instead? Crime would decline and job creation would be immediate. Further, jails could be converted into labour institutions that serve all sectors of the community. The government would manage offenders as a labour force and apply them wherever need be. Extreme offenders don't belong in jail either. They belong in mental institutions, with the opportunity to be released later.

It's that simple. Once societies offer more qualities, then there will be less crime. And there would be no need to micromanage with municipal bylaws. For example, stop signs and red lights could be optional when there is no other traffic. We could leave people alone and lose the security paranoia. There would be no need for police, gun ownership, or fear mongering in a society without wealth. People are able to handle themselves when they are respected as equals, so we should do so and trust them. And, when someone needs help, we should help!

Implement this: Recognize that when the host (capitalism) dies, so will the parasite (crime).

Or don't. Get a gun and don't run optional stop signs.

Irrelevant

It is irrelevant if some call me utopian with these suggestions. Their delusion is that they live in self-denial about the negative effects that capitalism has on them. Alcoholics anonymous makes participants confess that they are addicts to build a foundation for recovery. If we want to recover from capitalism, we have to first confess that we are addicted to it.

The capitalist elite exercise their influential power in secrecy, and they induce their hidden agendas like drugs to manipulate our comfort levels. They put us to sleep with over-consumption that grows our economies. The elite label factual accusations of greed as conspiracies and the people that expose them as lunatics. That is what cowards do. They always find an excuse and blame others to justify their serial lies. They force limitless finance and bone-headed leadership on us so that we self-destruct. That self-destruction will of course be later when it does not include them anymore.

They understand that capitalism and mental capacity are complete opposites. But if people are that dumb, why not capitalize on it? Apparently, we have all won the lottery when we don't live in a slum or a war zone. Capitalist temptations of materialism amaze us because they are so easily available in the G20. We take them for granted. And most of the less fortunate want to flee to the G20 wonderlands. When they finally arrive, we find that they also retreat into their own self-interests. The goal of an individual from a less developed nation is either to scrape by or to escape so that they can have more of the same middle-class misery that we already seem to enjoy. They also have a distorted craving for a higher living standard, thinking that by just arriving in a G20 country they will achieve it. However, they will experience poverty again, just in a better format.

Imagine if all countries had the high living standards of the G7. What would all the citizens want then? Would they still seek to escape? These are the mental questions that clearly border on the insane.

In our fake G7 reality, it is so much easier to follow than to form our own views. And a pseudo-vote for the best of bad financial platforms will never help the poor. Therefore, everything we view through a financial lens is irrelevant.

In addition, our specialized education systems also cause our mental incapacity. Quality education stimulates a species' development. But when a system uses financial discrimination to control and favours the privileged, it hinders our development. The costs of post-secondary education in the G20 are enormous. Their society undervalues specialized trades. But trades are where the actual skills are and that build better communities. We can't build anything with lawyers and accountants.

The capitalist lifestyle also leads to complacency, and complacency is especially dangerous because it breeds mindless following. For example, Tucker Carlson can build on sloth mentality by preaching garbage that promises high ratings and consequently more revenue. I am convinced that he's not as deranged as his messages. His crap sold until he got fired. Fox understands the importance of providing the mob with what they want. They will replace Carlson with more of the same and continue to profit from sensationalist speculating. Rational is boring and bad for sales. So, they lie to the wannabe-democratic society that never matures. Lies and MAGA democracy get along quite well.

Historically, the essence of the democratic process has failed humans ever since the first organized coalitions were formed. What I mean by essence is the ideal to help humans reach consensus and equality. Look around and you will find that today's segregated groups lack the ability to comprehend equality. How effective is the ideal of equality when the deprived cannot reach it? For them, it merely remains an idealism—wishful thinking. Equality should be represented by democracy, but how is inequality democratic? How is capitalist hoarding and stock market theft democratic? How are wrong beliefs that were accepted by a majority democratic (for example gun ownership or abortion)? How is choosing what is convenient over what is smart democratic? How are thousands of years of imperialist oppression democratic? How is a commonwealth democratic when wealth is not common at all? Should we not rename it to "common misery" when two-thirds of the global population are subject to the standards of the so-called developed nations (G7)? And how much can we grow as a species on this planet when we need three planets-worth of resources to sustain it?

Get a grip, people. The rich will only become extinct when they become irrelevant.

Imaginary capitalist freedom

Under realistic scrutiny, imperialistic imaginary freedom is precisely what is limiting the human species. Civilized freedom has become lazy and promotes waste. The comfort of capitalism chooses to ignore and consume, and we demand strong economies. But volume by choice is not freedom. The less privileged concept of survival means food, shelter, and basic services, never mind volume. So, what is freedom to them when they barely survive?

All talking heads wish for a better global civilization and are paranoid that a third world war could erupt. Well, have a look around. The third world war is already here. We are at war wherever we look. There are dozens of armed conflicts going on and domestic demonstrations are widespread. There are cyber wars, wars caused by corruption, gang wars, business wars, and military wars. Thousands perish and suffer with no end in sight. Yet this is just normal for the capitalist middle class. We are spectators and we don't do anything about any of it. We ignore, look away, and blame politicians, religions, and others but never ourselves. Apparently, our version of freedom allows us to ignore it all.

Mayhem is right in our faces, but it is tolerated because we've been cloned to accept misery as a capitalist condition. Consequently, our overall global despair never seems to improve. It does not matter how rich or how poor; welcome to the stalemate of democratic capitalist freedom.

Some think they live good, civilized lives, and they will hold on to whatever they have accumulated because it is all they have. Others desperately hope to live up to the same standards. Realistically though, their hope is not a solution and they will never catch up. Even the poorest of the poor have the same wrong mindset. They also hold onto whatever scraps they have because they are all they have left.

Man just has to have instead of thinking well and giving. Hence, everybody simply surrenders to holding onto what they have. They rule over their own tiny kingdoms, and they consider doing so an absolute requirement for their survival.

Many say that life is suffering, but barely anyone ever mentions that it is all self-inflicted. Getting mad about it is useless, and vulgar language and profanities are just words. Get it together, people. We can't comply with perpetual folly any longer. We need a reset, and I repeat, the only solution is to urgently walk away from capitalism and the democratic lie. We have to embrace giving instead of hoarding and realize that we don't have to hunt and gather anymore. The prehistoric apes and Neanderthals that did that reside in the museums.

Yes, my words are strong, and I purposely chose not to write in a milder tone. In my view, the general expectation to write with dignity and respect has outlived itself. There are plenty of people that preach within the parameters of accepted speech using overrated words like truth, rights, fairness, democracy, diplomacy, accountability, and so on. But these are delay phrases, and we only need them because of capitalism. All this well-intended, nice language has done little so far to improve our global disaster.

Pleasant demands are kind of like the pope giving blessings—what do blessings even mean? It is bizarre that we recognize religious blessings as having some kind of value. Why doesn't the pope invest a few billions into building simple water fountains and rice fields in Africa instead? That would actually do something. So, please give yourself a break from blessed democracy and civilized rhetoric. There is nothing blessed or civil about our wars and poverty. It is time for condolences.

Prisoner's dilemma

We can now access information and images within seconds on our devices. This provides us the ability to super-learn and to ask better questions. Every business book tells us to ask better questions in order to sell something. But selling is deception because profit overrides honesty. The capitalist machine acts and deceives right down to the salesperson. And we are all salespeople in a capitalist society. Therefore, overriding ethics with lying becomes a dilemma. So, we get tangled up in the capitalist "prisoner's dilemma." We are prisoners who want to escape, but even when we try to convince others of our escape plan, they will never be with us. Even when they take the easy route of remaining neutral (complacent in between opposites), they are also not with us.

So, we give up. But the point of escaping remains. Eventually, we betray each other, and escaping becomes even harder. The prisoner's dilemma is a paradox in the capitalist game. There does not seem to be a strategy that would benefit any party to the extent that they would not want to betray one another (competition). Instead, it seems that the best strategy for a party is to continually devise ways to manipulate a client into keeping interest while being betrayed. It also seems obvious to capitalists that not everyone can live off of the wealth of everyone else globally. Many others will never possess what the capitalists already have. As a result, they alone will continue to collect more.

The fear that others will pursue such a strategy (competition) is easily sufficient motivation for capitalists to protect their self-interest at all costs. Of course, no one blatantly advertises that they only protect their own self-interest. Instead, they always use high-sounding moral rationalizations: compassion because of poverty, non-discrimination, non-racism, protecting the environment, business ethics, etc. Whatever they advertise, the real intent they plan with their welfare is whether it can be translated into more profit.

The solution to the dilemma appears to be simple: there is none, and capitalists protect that non-solution with capitalist-invented law. Their rule of law, in its proper meaning, completely erases common global mental capacity because law restricts and limits with protection. But what needs to be protected? In a mental capacity society, protection from itself is not necessary at all.

In addition, the freedom of a contract is the most easily misunderstood. This is because of the principle that any agreement, which is from mutual consent, should be (is) valid. Mutual consent, however, does not mean that both parties have to particularly like their agreement. It is simply the one that, in the absence of other options, would be preferred over nothing. So, cheating in the long run will inevitably occur. Again, a contract is only necessary because there is no trust. In a mental capacity society, trust would be a default and contracts would be unnecessary.

One can naively assume that economic order and prosperity will eventually mature over any system that is based on theft or political corruption. But this will never be the case. Capitalist economies are unable to moderate prosperity because greed simply favours the uncooperative and corrupt.

This begs the question, how long can the third world cooperate with wealthy nations? They are complete polarities. The more people, the larger the inequality gap, and the more complicated it would be to establish equality. Therefore, equality is an abstract in these conditions.

Complying to something as sterile as capitalism is a dead end, and it only points in one direction: abuse and sewage! There are Twitter texts and blogs about trust and cooperation, but they are all coming from the wrong side of the spectrum. Capitalism is a compromise agreement between enterprise and the working class that neither party likes. And nothing will change because neither even considers that they could do better.

Implement this: Just because something is a predicament does not mean we can't escape it. But first, one must realize that they've actually been misled and imprisoned before they can seek escape.

Or don't. You are lucky and free to endlessly consume and to look away when others are completely neglected. Ignoring misery by default because it does not affect you is your escape.

Creation is political

When we create something, it can be politicized, and creation can change everything overnight. Declarations of war or the dropping of nuclear bombs are extreme examples.

Words are also creations, and some might think that social critics like myself are dangerous. However, I am not reinventing the wheel here. Many before me have tried to be heard by the regimes and the herds, but powerful people with money persistently dismiss and crush revolutionary progress.

People with progressive ideas get eliminated in various formats, and human rights fly right out of the oppression court's window.

Relevant improvements of various kinds have to be begged for. But capacity intellectuals don't beg. They become hermits and write books or even move off the grid. For them, it is obvious that money raises stupidity and that the rich simply buy themselves out of whatever inconvenience they produce. The rich treat the entire world as disposable and promote the delusion that the herd has to become rich like them. Yet, that calculated lie is only attainable to a lucky few.

All of this imperialist and financial positioning is like a plague that consumes people's mental health and the natural balance of the planet. The Black Death was in the fourteenth century and it was the most fatal pandemic in human history. Eventually, people learned that quarantines would put the plague into remission. What we need to do is quarantine capitalism by isolating the rich instead of aiming to become like them. This is not just an empty statement; this is a mental necessity. Our species has to comprehend that we can function very well with many other social systems. Kindness would be a good start.

Imperialism is just a tantrum, an infantile thought of boys that never grew up and needed to wear crowns and pose with trophies into their adulthoods. We are witnessing and tolerating the created kingdoms of fools. The business of fools borrows survival of the fittest from nature. What's interesting though is that nature still sustains balance, while there is nothing balanced in our male-created civilization.

Research is creation as well, and scientific opinions are continuously challenged with ongoing new discoveries. Science adapts, and the church had to agree that the earth does indeed revolve around the sun.

But our stubborn political systems don't adapt much, and this is because they are all financial clones. The exception is that they adapt to broadening corruption. Politics and religion still behave as one ideology, but they clearly have to be separated. The imperialist king used to be legitimized by the pope. Those days are finally over.

The purpose of a political system should be to regulate moderation and create better standards to implement. Their priority should be to advance humanity as a species. But that is clearly not the case. Political systems bicker and poke at each other's convoluted financial agendas and ancient opinions.

The issues at hand don't matter as much as winning at all costs. They oppose instead of forming collaborative consensus. And when they mix in partisan emotions, their mental abilities shrink even further.

The slandering media add even more noise for the sake of revenue, which opposes collaboration even more. None of this squabble helps to steer society towards consensus. High revenue ratings and winning ambitions may be good for business, but they only cause confusion.

When we then add religion to this confusion, the Middle East comes to mind. This small area is a permanent hot spot for conflict, and religion and historic revenge cause most of it. Humans have subdivided these lands as far back as we can remember. And planting a new state of Israel in the middle of it all was asking for trouble. Each of the condensed local tribes claim that they have the divine rights to these lands, yet none of them can help their neighbour. The Gaza strip has become the world's largest prison. That whole area is closed in and subject to economic sanctions by Israel against Hamas. And recently, this conflict has escalated into civilian genocide. This is what spiritual imperialism looks like. History continues to be followed, and they remain trapped in submissive divine slavery from long ago.

Most religions connect creation to a supreme source. However, why does that supreme source have to be a god or gods? Are they just misinformed? Can it not simply be consciousness? Consciousness at least has an ongoing purpose, observes itself, and is present. Are there any gods present?

Religion has no productive purpose besides building community. Their doctrines observe and control others with fear from a divine source that never materializes. It is a format of ancient herd police, built on faith instead of reason. But faith only anticipates the extraordinary and that should not make it sacred. But it is.

Do we need faith as a mental crutch to be productive? Reason and faith are simply not compatible, but here we are, obviously misinformed for thousands of years as clones of misinformation and faith dictated delusions.

Family faith and upbringing are the root causes of the deep-seeded problem of religious slavery. Belonging to family can be an obligation to unwanted oppression. Therefore, imperialist slavery delivered through financial oppression becomes a progression of the same. Consequently, all our systems feed on oppression of the same kind and squeeze us into what we don't want. Whether financial, territorial, racial, religious, or compliance, they all produce fear. And fear is not a good ingredient for mental health.

Speaking of, managing mental health issues away with therapy is not the remedy. We need to manage imperialist capitalism instead because it is much larger now than gods and kings ever were. And we can do this via the middle class! When was the last time a united middle class made a demand? Realize that we *can* unite and that there is far more creative dialogue to engage in than whining about misery. We unite without a leader and without democracy. We unite by abandoning our jobs and collecting all our funds from the banks. That will be enough.

Implement this: Retreat to help yourself and your neighbour. A united middle class can create instead of comply.

Or don't. Continue to donate to churches and food banks that don't impact anything substantial. They only hide the real problem that welfare is necessary because capitalism causes it.

Below is a quote from Heinrich Heine. You can also replace "he" with "capitalism".

> "Ordinarily he was insane, but he had some lucid moments when he was merely stupid."
>
> —Heinrich Heine

Chapter 4:

Democracy

A sly, underestimated problem we can't get away from is democracy. Capitalism represents its narrow financial self -interest with the democratic process of a voting choice. Choice creates the illusion that individuals have a say by casting a vote. But to be precise, what are individuals actually voting for? I think we only get to choose the best out of limited financial agendas. Think about it. Political parties don't represent social idealism and they never have. They primarily represent financial agendas.

Let's review what the definition of a democratic process means (from Oxford Languages on the web):

"A system of government by the whole population or all the eligible members of a state, typically through elected representatives." This definition echoes the generally accepted view that democracy's supreme power should be vested in the people, and that this power is exercised by voting. But voting only exercises power depending on what issues we vote for and against. Therefore, the content of the issues to be voted for is the hidden true power! The voter does not come up with the issues. The government in power and the opposing parties do. Therefore, they vest the power in the governing parties, not the people!

Democratic governing should suggest limits, moderation, and common good, but it seldom does. In fact, it promotes the opposite. It promotes capitalist economies that have no limits. Yet, we don't live on economy; we live on Earth, and the planet is clearly showing us to limit ourselves. So, give us something worth voting for!

Help yourself understand why we comply with a social system that has no limits. We strive for capitalist consuming and endless taking. These are not democratic values. These are profit values. If we eliminate profit from all business, what will remain to vote on?

We miss the point that consumption should only satisfy necessity from a true global democratic position. Excess is a capitalist desire, while necessity is practical. To be democratic, as in to pursue the common good, is not to pursue excess.

Capitalists also raise secret societies within democratic systems. What is democratic about secrets? And how does overproduction balance anything or promote global egalitarianism? Wealth directly contradicts the democratic process that should strive for equality. Imperialists chose capitalism as the preferred method to achieve civilized prosperity, but there is nothing civil—or democratic—about prosperity when it only includes a select few. Therefore, just because we are able to produce and vote for garbage, that does not make us democrats.

Democracies are actually capitalist systems that are run by secret societies. They are in control in the background, and what gives them their power is that their stolen money can buy influence in financial government agendas. They promote the election of democratic representatives based on their silver spoon agendas. Consequently, these are shrivelled democracies that can never produce what they are meant to deliver as an idealism. In fact, they organize corruption. Who we vote for are well-dressed narcissistic entertainers that are on someone's payroll. They don't represent you!

Instead, the only people that should represent you are various high-capacity professionals (scientists) that represent global idealist reforms. Politicians, lawyers, and bankers don't have global reforms in mind. They only protect profit.

People are screaming for peace, food, and health care all over the world, yet wealthy G20 countries deceive and delay behind a democratic veil. They believe that the middle class will keep accepting their terms of comfortable trash compliance.

But, younger generations are learning that only stupid is expensive. They are tired of living their adult lives in their parents' basements and begging for jobs. And they witness that democratic idealism does not apply to most African nations. They see daily how a continent suffers from violence, corruption, and neglect. The latest massive catastrophe is Sudan. That missed urgency to rescue entire countries continues to be carried on the backs of the poor, and not on the rich faces at expense-account fundraisers.

Younger generations hear the G20 nations call themselves developed, but the term "developed" only means more infrastructure, more money, more education, and so on. Developed is just another word for more. However, more is not smart. More is just more! Maybe they should change the term to "volume countries" instead of developed.

Not to mention, capitalist terms such as "third world" and "underdeveloped" degrade misery even further. The puppets of the rich talk and pretend to understand, never prioritize immediate support, and deliberately delay critical information. Well, that is what thieves do.

But again, without the middle class complying, none of this would be possible! The capitalist machine deceivingly dumbs everything down with democracy for the gullible. And the financial desperado that wants to escape lower living standards can't wait to participate in the deception.

So, it seems like a predicament to unnecessarily comply with capitalism to some, but that compliance only exists because the majority enjoy it. But just because the majority chooses to live like that does not make us smart.

John Stuart Mill warned us that a majority mob is dangerous and will undermine liberal mental potential. Therefore, regardless of whatever capitalist bogus the manipulated herd elects, the G20 societies will never reach the mental decency to pursue equality for the remaining G175. The current capitalist mob is destined to auto-destruct because comfort seduces them and drags everyone else into it.

So, whom are we kidding with voting in this sloth mob environment? They label stupid as smart when it profits and entertains, and many can't accept this. Am I wrong?

Implement this: Do not vote for so-called democratic corporate governments. They govern nothing besides profit. Ignore them with financial and physical withdraw, and have them reconvene to present values that are actually worth voting for.

Or don't. Go vote and believe that you matter in their financial agendas. Diplomacy, democracy, and equality are only words without substance in capitalist-dominated systems, but if you still disagree, then tell me where exactly their substance is visible?

The democratic charade

When Nancy Pelosi retired as speaker of the House in 2023, congress had to vote in a new speaker. Since the Republicans won the majority in the mid-term election, Kevin McCarthy was their prime candidate. They voted multiple times, pretending to be divided in order to prolong the public's attention. Eventually, they elected McCarthy after fifteen votes to demonstrate internal Republican unity again. However, this charade was not about voting. It was about free media exposure with staged delays, and it was about whom could get bribed internally to switch their vote in McCarthy's favour.

Get real, people. These votes are not about political idealism! They are strictly about the personal greed of the members that sit in silver-spoon congress. Bill Maher's "Idiocracy in action" serves as a reminder that voting for a silver-spoon party and believing that an individual's voice matters in this circus is pointless.

From an individual perspective, democracy should mean that individuals have various freedoms and that they can vote to govern for the common good. However, if people are not free to begin with because colonial interests oppress them, discriminate against them by race, remove them from territory, and keep them broke, then we have to accept and understand that people are not free at all.

The democratic process should be a global consensus process. Why can't we come to an agreement to eliminate weapons, increase foreign aid, and clean up the oceans?

Our current staged voting is a compliance exercise based on re-election instead of mental potential. Parties defame opposing parties on their profit platforms to entertain the public. Defamation is a viable business model to sell more trash and deepen compliance. They say whatever sells, which harbours permanent confusion and ships that sail nowhere. And when everything is unclear, then they have positioned the herd exactly where they need to be: stuck in the same predicaments of capitalist interests.

How can we get nicer music when everybody plays the same instrument? Political platforms have minor differences, but they are all lost in finance. We vote for hamster wheel financial idiocy: the recycled and copied versions of what the wealthy parties have always demanded with their sleepy democracy.

I can't stand the word democracy anymore. Everybody rambles about it, yet they do not know what they ramble about. Like they heard it somewhere, and it's something to scream for.

A capacity species would not even need any kind of democracy because intelligence does not need to be voted for. Intelligent creatures simply get along and negotiate consensus.

So, let me ask all the democracy-protecting fanatics: Is what you vote for worth voting for? What would you vote for if you did not have to pay for anything?

The media are companions to this ongoing mass charade. But what is the point of keeping the public informed? It's not as if they act on anything. It's just noise and is about as effective as what goes on in most governments. For example, the US congress mauls over issues, the senate vetoes them, the supreme court has to add their mustard, and nothing gets done. There are mountains of information and data, but how is this useful to the public, and how is any of this governing?

Governing should be about global equality, meaning global common restoration instead of common wealth. It should be about the elimination of capitalism and monetary devaluation into one global medium for trade. It should be about the capacity non-materialistic implementations of reduce, reuse, and restore instead of convenience. It should be about the elimination of imperialist theft and the return of all territories that were stolen to the original natives. It should be about the elimination of segregated standards, such as developed nations (G7 – G20). It should be about the replacement of religion with philosophy.

It should be about the abolition of weapons. If you look at the situation in Ukraine, there is no more need for ancient weapons such as tanks. I think the Russians deliberately got rid of them because their inventory is outdated and too expensive to renew and sustain. Long range drones and missiles are far more effective. And why would you need tanks if you can destroy the entire Ukrainian energy grid from long distance? The Russians are just having a garage sale, and the NATO military heads love it. They finally get to play with all their toys. If you need a tank to protect territory, you are still a boy in the sandbox. Growing up at some point will occur by default, so come on children, wise up.

None of these improvements I've mentioned should be voted for. They should happen by default if we want to evolve beyond being parasites.

The voting compliance myth

The complacent and manipulated mob says, "If you don't vote, you don't have a say." But that does not mean you have to join. Remember, the people that say this will always be looking at other versions of stale capitalist platforms. Their sheepish participation will never bring any change. They have the right to be stupid, so they extend that very right. Instead, think!

Who needs balanced budgets and an economy? Only the rich! An economy is not economic in countries where folks can barely eat. Yes, they are poor because of a weak economy. But again, who needs an economy? You vote to borrow what you and your government cannot afford. We overpay, and we can never pay it all back! All we do is rearrange debt terms to make them more bearable. Banks can lend every single deposited dollar from you to ten other customers that will pay interest. But the initial money only exists once, and they profit from your money. They earn interest, of which you get none. Interesting (literally)! And you scrape along, saving that single dollar that you can't even use because you already gave it to the bank. Is that not absurd enough to condemn capitalism?

This is why they call capitalism free enterprise. That it is, but only for the banks, because they get rich with your free deposits. And in return, they load you up with even more debt.

You vote for representatives that approve increased budgets that print bonds out of thin air. And when that does not suffice, they simply repeat the same process and raise the debt ceiling. Sure, we can always vote for more of the same.

You are a microbial working-class slave. All you will ever have is that vote, and if you don't use it, you won't have a say. What the f...? They claim to invest in your future while they run deficits, which you apparently approve of with your vote. When was the last time you declared a deficit? How about never? The banks call that bankruptcy, and when that happens, it's game over for you, little microbe. You can't just raise more revenue from your employer. But maybe you can invest that one dollar that you already gave to the bank. Ever wonder why you never get anywhere?

Obviously, the things that financial institutions and governments get away with every day are not available to you. You are destined to become the same financial slave that your parents have always been, and your law-abiding parents even encourage you to vote for the same conditions. If I tell you that you are insane, you won't believe me. But you accept all of this happening. Why do you vote for this?

As a democratic slave, you are reduced to the mediocre. This is a more accurate description of what democracy is. Democracy just sounds better than mediocre. So go ahead and vote for mediocrity. Apparently, this is as good as it gets. Democracy replaces individual potential with the obedience of the mob, and the obedient democrat watches others elsewhere starve to death. They witness failure at large and are convinced that voting for mediocre microbial compliance is a democratic privilege. Engaging in these procedures is not fertile, they are sterile!

Our children want utopia

Moving on, what do my alternative words mean for our kids? They have learned to accept COVID curfews and education from home. Mental health has now become a widespread concern, but this should have been addressed a long time ago. COVID was a delayed mental health attention trigger.

An interesting development during COVID lockdowns was that it forced society to evaluate life from a much different perspective. There was actually less pollution. Animals that had not been seen for a long time began to emerge, and people started to bake bread at home. All of this was possible because there was urgency, and it was all beyond democracy. Nobody voted for it. It simply got done!

And, because of the isolation of lockdown, our kids began to understand that they have the potential to move beyond being an adult techno-caveman. They wondered what the purpose of a capitalist job was when others wasted away on TV in their misery. My kids asked me, "How come others don't have jobs despite COVID?" Children had more time and could sense the fairy tales that our former generations were told.

At one point, I had to explain why planes had been flown into the Twin Towers on 9/11. Many are still in disbelief about who flew these planes, but the evidence suggests that the official US government's explanation is a blunt lie. I told my kids that only an American administration can get away with an epic cover up like 9/11 by leaving hundreds of questions unanswered. They wanted to know and they deserved facts. Nevertheless, regardless of whatever the facts were, it did happen in plain sight. And now, many years later, there is a book called *Where Did the Towers Go?* by Dr. Judy Wood. The book explains that both towers simply vanished, and provides convincing engineering proof. Both towers literally dissolved into dust on the way down during their collapse. There are slow motion videos where we can see steel evaporate. There is evidence that directed free-energy made this actually possible. Even more disturbing is that we know about this energy, but we have never seen it used on this scale. The book explains that it is existing expanded technology and is apparently available to some. So, who was behind it all? Most likely not people with box cutters.

After the Twins collapsed, there was barely any debris. Thousands of tons of steel and concrete, gone, like it literally evaporated into dust. They removed the remaining debris in a few weeks. To remove all the material that should have been there in that short of a time frame is absolutely impossible. Therefore, the question, where did the towers go?

The book has gained recognition as a scientific report by hundreds of international engineers. They support the overwhelming evidence that directed energy caused these building materials to vanish into thin air.

Further, looking at Building 7, which collapsed in on itself, the Pentagon crash, and Flight 93, none of these stories make any sense compared to the evidence presented. Even experienced Cessna pilots lack the ability to maneuver a jet into the Pentagon at such low angles, and where was the debris?

Still, the government gets to lie it all away with the published 9/11 report. Then they bomb Afghanistan, declare a war on terror, and can't find Bin Laden for ten years. Impossible, but all of it is allowed. Says who?

This is the democratic US world police at work, and in plain sight. It's like an ongoing project for them to test how gullible we really are. Then they finally announce the death of Bin Laden ten years later, just to circle back and give their bogus government 9/11 report some validity again.

When one calls BS, one is labelled a conspirator and gets death threats.

Sorry, but utopia can't approve that circus, and neither should our children. A utopia does not follow the dated concepts of getting a job, getting married, buying more, having kids, voting for liars, then repeating, complying, and slaloming through whatever governments and health organizations throw at us. Consuming, regurgitating, and barfing it back up. Sounds like a one-year-old about to grow teeth.

We teach kids that democratic values are what we must accept because a utopia is not attainable. But then is a utopia not attainable because it orients after community, which capitalists label as communism? Is it because a utopia does not idolize historic delusions, religions, Santa, tooth fairies, and the Sandman? Ideas and characters that are lies and that children never experience?

Why are we surprised about mental health concerns when real characters and life actually confront them? Our kids are not fools, and it is time that we teach them about characters that are actually visible. There are plenty of living examples available. Can I dumb it down any further? Mr. Greed still intimidates Lady Capacity! Not a gentleman indeed, that Mr. Greed. A fool would be more suiting. . .

Utopia simply means that we can't steal from others, and that status is unnecessary. It is an individual decision to work on oneself, and you don't need to vote for it. Nietzsche provides proof in "the will to power" when he identifies that an individual can rise above it all. When he makes the prophecy of the overman (Übermensch), he means for us to work on our self-worth and to move beyond materialism and wealth. He lived a very moderate lifestyle. And, despite the fact that he admired rulers, he already knew then that the complying capitalist herd was a virus.

Humanity has lost the entire twentieth century to burning fossil fuels, soldiers, and civilians to substantiate empty transactions. Just to get along seems utopian compared to that.

A man like Nikola Tesla proved that free energy is all around us in empty space and that mental capacity does not hinge on transactions. He was a utopian, and greed robbed and killed him so that others could fatten and pollute.

Implement this: Remove the young from the past and don't treat them like gullible fools to inherit the mediocre. Feed them capacity inspirations, and expect them to build their own futures.

Or don't. Keep hammering regurgitated information from your glory days into young heads and act surprised when they walk away.

Chapter 5:

Religion

Can we transcend religion into self-discovery?

John Lennon's song called for us to "imagine all the people living life in peace." So, what is peace?

Peace is a very broad concept, and religion should play a role in enhancing that concept. But our widely accepted religious systems have not brought us much peace at all. In fact, they have brought us more despair than resolve. However, it is not surprising that religious following that is enforced with fear does not bring peace. I am not arguing that believing in a faith concept is wrong. I just think that independent free thinking will most likely produce better results than compliance to fear.

We can teach younger generations that they can still respect their elders and religion-based wisdom, but they should be cautious with rituals, absurd customs, and some of the delusional hopes and consequences that religions promise. The utopian idea to unite is not abstract in religion. Therefore, why couldn't religion unite us all?

Besides religion, most have the mental ability to recognize what a deductive system of ethics should look like. Derrida speaks of deconstruction for literature. What we need to do is deconstruct our current segregated compliance mentality and convert to treating others the way we would treat our mothers. What if that was the case? Imagine what that would actually do to our societies. Granted, religions strive to improve living in harmony within their own congregations, but harmony should also include respecting other religions. A religion should not be based on its own faith and rituals alone. It's important to encourage learning about other beliefs. Religions should be about self-discovery, rather than obedience. If one is kind, then one has to obey nothing!

I don't have any formal credentials as a contemporary critic, but that should not matter. I'm just a man and I like to respect that we should all have enough common sense to work on ourselves. It is just like the movie *Good Will Hunting* explains: one can get the same elite education on his own, as long as he is interested in the subject and puts effort into it. Effort is the key ingredient to developing mental range. One has to seek and remain curious.

My effort with this book is to explain without fancy credentials and to take you, the reader, on a journey. I use plain vocabulary because there is no need to dazzle with complicated words. Anybody can use fancy words, yet substance matters more. I hope that you, the reader, can treat this book like an adventure of self-investigation that can lead to self-improvement. My suggestions comprise practical ideas that anyone can implement, and the story is especially for young people, to help them design their futures. Like the Swedish teenager Greta Thunberg who stopped going to school to summon attention for global warming, people need to step up and release their capitalist compliance cruise control.

But, to step up, one also needs to take a step back into isolation. Mental incubation leads to insights, and then these insights become habits. All potential emerges out of silence. Even the Big Bang started there. A silent, religious method of meditation is prayer. When people pray, they ask for help from another source. They may imagine something divine, but what they are really doing is listening to themselves. And when insights occur, they may feel that their prayers are being answered. This mental contemplation is already halfway towards self-discovery, and religions can be transcended into it.

Implement this: Complement religious worship with self-discovery and remove judgments. Remember that *vox populi* means "voice of the people" in Latin. This expression means the people's voice. Not the voice of governments, religions, education, or the herd. Find your voice.

Or don't. If dullness were not so enjoyable, then it would not be so popular.

For males, everything is like a religion

Mental capacity can't accommodate religious dogma invented by ancient males. Why is it that all religions are male-dominated? Considering the age of the planet, invented divine male delusion is only a few thousand years old. So where was their whatever god before that? Maybe lost somewhere in a brothel drinking with other males? Oh, I forgot, he was busy sitting in clouds while herding nothing.

But males did not stop there. They elected kings, organized crusades and slaughter, and wanted empires, capitalism, business, and chauvinism. And all of it was tolerated by religion and sometimes even carried out in the name of religion.

How come we have never seen women lead any of these activities?

Males took—and continue to take—and it's never enough. They believe that their formats of taking have to be followed like a religion. But males are not gods. They are lunatics, still following their Darwinian, male ape, herd control instinct that morphed into a domination and greed complex. And because they've gotten away with it thus far, they still assume that it is to be expected.

Well, times have changed. Some of us have woken up to the fact that we're not Neanderthals anymore and that male supremacy has outlived the tolerance of welcome. Men mostly acknowledge other men as geniuses because they treated women like cattle. Get over yourselves males. Step aside and let the women do some thinking as well. Learn from them. Go back to drinking beer and stay there.

As a species, we have to understand the cosmos with our minds and even aim for supernatural powers. Why not? Can we actually take a few steps forward instead of engaging in the male nonsense of worship, pride, honour, and discrimination? Would ego inflation even be necessary for a clever species?

We live on this beautiful planet, and its beauty reveals itself in nature. Nature—not males—will show us our capacity as a species and will shape our destiny if we observe it well. There is no need for the planet to observe a white-bearded male or other various gods and demi-gods sitting in the clouds. Come on, people, get a grip! The planet does not care about gods, so why should we? This planet should be our number one priority to learn from.

A good new beginning is to save ourselves from male incompetence and thirst for power. We are overdue to restore the damage they have caused, and we need to embrace forward thinking without them. We no longer need encyclopedias of rules and laws that protect their greed and secret societies. We have to abandon these morbid ambitions and replace them with what our earth deserves. Such a place can exist. However, males, and especially the wealthy ones, won't give anything up, and they will insist that books like mine are utopian baloney. That's OK, they can remain there in the space of the mental microbe. They will eventually learn how to deserve this planet so it can sustain them.

Implement this: Reduce, reuse, recycle, reintroduce, and rebuild.

Or don't. Buy and waste instead, and complain about the rich.

The male complex

Males assume control by default because of physical strength. But to expect control due to muscle alone is an undeveloped assumption. Tolerant mental capacity is not about controlling, ruling, or dominating. It does not require force to be creative or to be a mother. Try to imagine if human evolution had been controlled by females. Would there be completely different cultures and societies today? I would bet on it!

The human species is not in survival mode anymore. We reached a plateau where control via male strength is not necessary. Males still seek control by default, as they are self-serving and driven by territorial delusions. Stupid does as stupid is. Meanwhile, females are on standby, and have always been denied implementing their true capacities. It is obvious that muscle and penis limit mental evolution. Males still struggle even with that—that breeding is just a physical drive and that women are not livestock.

Males bask in their supremacy in organizations like the Freemasons and the KKK. Supremacy is a complex and rooted in insecurity. They always have to reassure themselves that they matter. How come we don't have any secret women's organizations participating in rituals and lynching people?

Male pride clubs have been discriminating ever since they sprung from the Middle Age Templars. The stated objective of the organization was to enhance societies globally. However, their true intention was to conceal riches in their early banking system and to gather classified information.

When women congregated to share intelligence and special gifts, they were called witches and burnt alive. These male extremist exterminations are further evidence of male insecurity.

Organizations like the Freemasons are an example of what many males are about. They isolate themselves in their pride and handle affairs with a narrow-minded view that is not only dumb but also rude.

The female perspective

Women had to accept that kings and leaders were chosen by men and by birthright, regardless of how stupid they were. They might as well have chosen goldfish as rulers (sorry, goldfish). Here is the definition of male tribal stupor: they inherit idiocy from their fathers, lean on imagined strength, threaten, sow fear, engage in rape, and insist that women are possessions.

Male incapacity can't be the best that a self-aware human brain can possibly filter. Animals know how to fit into the big picture among other species. With the exception of alpha positioning and mating, they behave as equals. But the human male's problem is that he does not fit in anywhere. His narcissistic, self-absorbed mental shortcomings are in permanent alpha and mating mode, and he never snaps out of it. The male attitude to use a bigger hammer when something does not fit seems practical. Consequently, war games are the widespread colonial activity that boys in their prime have to engage in. There is a relentless, delusional, patriotic need for armed and secret services to blow up, manipulate, and classify in the name of national security and bully paranoia. Only idiots can be that paranoid about threats. These warmongers will say that women are naive to keep men at home to raise children. And they are correct, because that exactly proves the point of how shallow these clowns are. We are not naive in calling them boys. We are the opposite, because we are mature enough to understand that armed conflict is child's play, and unnecessary in a mature society. These boys are a mental embarrassment.

Women would not even consider using hammers or wars to make anything fit. They feel through life instead of relying on force. J.S. Mill hinted that women couldn't have any democratic rights in a conservative male society. Females could not even vote! We can even draw the parallel that conservatism only came into existence because of males. If females had their say, conservatism would never even materialize.

Maybe us women should set ourselves on fire like that monk in Saigon on June 11, 1963. He set the example that at least some of us even have the courage to burn in public to get away from male idiocy.

How aliens would report on the male-dominated human species

These conscious humans are flying at high velocity on a marvel of a planet in an unforgiving void around a life source called the sun. This miracle rock is present in the depth of billions of galaxies, in the quantum medium called space, and is observable at the pace of time. Their short-sighted earth perspective, in their observable time dimension, is playing like a movie on the unobservable quantum canvas that they are about to discover. And remarkably, they exist! All because that rock was kind enough to sustain their carbon life-form, which depends on water. A gem rather than a rock, one could say. A tiny planet, but everything to them, and able to exist in the extreme conditions of space, covered with a few kilometres of oxygen wrapped with a decaying radiation shield layer of ozone. So fragile!

In this limited, fragile surface zone, humans are passengers, led by the male gender of the species, and they don't seem to understand that they can't waste what sustains them. They don't know that being self-aware is truly a gift and opportunity to discover what evolution with mental gifts could be. However, the male conceals this self-aware capacity under spiritual and primitive tribal conquests, because that is the best he can come up with. He wears suits to attract attention and is proud to have discovered capitalism. His primitive instinct to hunt and gather everything convinces him that species and resources are simply subject to him. Even the moon and Mars are on his radar. He forces females to obey and treats them like livestock while missing that these females are actually smarter than him. He mistakes strength for a mental capacity. Meanwhile, it was female strength that squeezed this caveman out of the uterus in the first place. And that female most likely got pregnant because she was raped instead of being allowed to conceive by consent. Again, he flexes another body part—his penis. The male thug can't get a grip on what a consciousness is for.

From a fundamental organism perspective, this planet does not belong to humans any more than it does to dust mites. But they claim and take and waste all resource chains. In fact, and facts are not optional, these humans don't even know where they came from. Males, at any given time in the past, always had to either hide or distort their origin with fairy tales. Otherwise, they would know what they are.

Their recorded history is incomplete and distorted, and there seems to be so much that was forgotten for thousands of years. Maybe the women are keeping the origin of mankind hidden somewhere in their closets to keep the males in the dark. The planet they occupy has no owners; it only accommodates them as temporary guests. And prior to human history, one can confirm that whatever other life forms have dominated that planet have never lasted. Still, these humans believe that their primitive kind will somehow last another few billion years, even while they can't even produce evidence that dates further back than a few caveman years.

Granted, they do have courage, much like cavemen had to have. But "progressively self-delusional" is a concise description of their kind at this point. They are a demented, temporary parasite that is trying to consume its host. They disguise their mystery origin with invented religions and claim to have originated from gods, or other things that never show up. They force each other to believe in such invented stories and have replaced fact with faith.

They have no idea what they are, and their social systems have now evolved from primitive to self-destructive. They create mediums called money in exchange for goods, and hoard as much as possible. Again, it must be that inbred gathering complex that won't leave them. They call this "capitalism" and share nothing. They behave like rats storing food, but they store money that is not edible. Even the rats are smarter.

As a herd, they seek comfort and sloth the most. A remarkably misinformed and greedy species indeed, believing that hoarding nothing has value in the complexities of a perceivable quantum universe. They even miss the simple math that hoarding nothing will add up to nothing.

Go visit and meet the *anencephalous asinus* (brainless donkey).

Garden of Eden

Let me point out that reducing ourselves to believing that we sprang from the Garden of Eden without an explanation of how we even got into that garden is more than obscure. That we somehow became Adam and Eve from being lizards and monkeys and found ourselves naked under an apple tree on the way to inventing sin is truly a stretch. But some males thought that this stretch of imagination could explain away the mystery of creation. Not sure why the herd wanted to believe this, but that's it.

Because of limited language and the consideration that the herd wanted to follow *something*, I give the Adam and Eve concept a bit of a break. It's at least romantic. Maybe it was meant as a metaphorical parallel to the Sumerian

Anunnaki story about the origin of man. But why not simply repeat that story as it was?

Wittgenstein's *Tractatus* states that language has limits and individuals interpret it based on their understanding. He was a man of consequence and was more concerned with understanding than believing. He isolated that one can comply with organizing and believing, even when one may not understand.

As babies, we learn with our senses, and we organize nothing. At this stage, childhood is enlightenment. There are no worries until the larger people create them. As we learn and mature, they teach us to organize, limit, and restrict, and they influence us to comply. The side effect of this responsible compliance is that it reduces our creative capacity instead of expanding it. Finally, when we have grown old, we behave like young children again. We are back to the beginning, experiencing enlightenment while carefree with arthritis and in diapers.

Quantum physics reveals that if electrons are previously entangled, they can be separated, and when stimulated, they instantly communicate with each other and react simultaneously regardless of the distance between them. This means that distances are irrelevant and there is an instant knowing. If the micro world, which our bodies are a part of, operates like this, then what could we learn?

Let's look at evolution and mutation. For example, how does a Canadian rabbit grow white hair in late fall in anticipation of blending in with the upcoming snow? From a quantum perspective, I should be able to do that as well, yet I can't. Maybe I can't because aging is not a seasonal challenge to survive. Therefore, the rabbit has superior abilities that affect matter. It creates the internal urgency to grow seasonal hair by observing and adapting to the environment. Science says that the rabbit has this ability due to genetics and instinct, but how exactly does that work? Maybe the rabbit lives more in the now, and can therefore project what it needs to change in order to adapt. Similarly, how does a chameleon make itself look like a twig and totally blend in? It seems to have an above-itself view. This is not just genetics. How would genetics observe how to fit into the overall picture of a final appearance? It's like a chameleon is aware of itself to fit within the whole. This is an astonishing ability, but taken for granted and explained away again with genetics and instinct. When we observe nature, we find amazing abilities and incredible abundance.

So, considering nature, how did humans come up with the lame story of the Garden of Eden and still have respect for it? Even if it is meant to be symbolic, explaining nature away with the concept of a Garden of Eden is absurd. A child could do better than that. I respect that the Bible may tell wisdom in metaphors sometimes, but what good is intended with a story about a Garden of Eden? Whom is it that these males wanted to convince with such a bizarre concept of man's creation? Themselves?

Implement this: Male-invented delusions held the mental ability of society back for a few thousand years. Purge that nonsense.

Or don't. No further comment. I think women understand this.

Stolen and copied, again and again

What is an actual original? Investigate how Aristotle's probably-stolen rhetoric, logic, and reasoning was plagiarized further and expanded upon by lawyers to the point where a lie can simultaneously be presented as a truth. Words can become misleading components when we interpret language.

Under even further scrutiny, there is no actual initial complexity in how we interpret language. Language is only sound, and our learned interpretations evolve that sound into various conceptual formats. If one speaks Russian to an Amazon native, then that Russian is nothing but sounds without any understandable meaning. The same applies to invented religious and legal languages for people that have mental range. Legal words are like an unfamiliar language, and religion is collectively packaged as a standard of conduct. Combined, we call this religious and legal scrabble "civilized." However, does a native Amazonian care whether we are civilized or not? It's not even relevant!

Our constitutional laws should represent, protect, and deliver a just society. Still, what is just and justice? Justice means equality and fairness, but capitalism is unjust by default. Think about it. Both justice and religious ethics are only necessary in capitalist societies to preserve inequality! That constant guilt trip to obey law and faith are what sustain capitalism.

If actual equality were already present, then unfairness and crime would not develop. We could simply nurture our families, help others, grow some food, and clean up the globe. There would be no need for capitalist protection laws or religion to repent for our sins. Why do we copy history over and over?

We must become original again and step away from the unnecessary obligations of financial and faith imperialism. Why are we addicted to this capitalist idiot theory and unable to stop? I mean, we stop at stop signs and red lights. We don't just drive through. Neither are optional. We can argue and insist that law, faith, and ethics had to be implemented to control the medieval and industrial herds somehow. However, the rich now make these decisions, and they control the proletarian herd with surgical precision.

To allow the rich to proceed like this is simply unacceptable. But it is impossible to stop this highly tuned machine unless we remove the fuel. The fuel is money, and the rich protect themselves with it. But if we pull the fuel out of the banks, that machine will stutter and stop. Remember, every single deposit and payment that you provide is fuel.

Authorities are mostly selected based on wealth and connections. This seems the natural selection process in capitalism. And this thought makes me return to primates again. Among them, a leader emerges by natural selection, which is an act of force. The others then follow, which is an act of belonging compliance. And that same compliance has been conditioned into group behaviour for thousands of years by evolution.

But we are not primates! Maybe we still follow primates because they did not have mirrors in the Dark Ages to look at themselves. Science learned to understand animal behaviour, but it still struggles to understand capitalism.

However, it is not necessary to copy or steal anything. There are always other options! Unfollowing is one of them, and our independent mental capacity must become a new trend.

I always associate churches with the features of an asylum, and identify them by their bell towers. No offence, but religions are borderline insane. They choose to replace the absence of facts with faith, and wait for salvation according to that faith. It follows that these delusions provide stability and faculty to those that indeed suffer from mental illness. When religious followers are confronted about their delusions, they are in denial of them, and insist on them simply out of resentment. Not even a primate does that. Their belief in the glorious divine is superior to finding sanity anywhere else. Therefore, delayed insanity is the actual miracle they seek, and it's still pending. At some point, we have to agree that asylums can't provide an environment for mental potential. But, let me try to help you understand why these faith individuals surrender their mental potential.

They may feel like they are suffering because their religions prioritize obedience over addressing individual sensitive feelings. Religions hammer on about what to do, and faith is a form of sterility. The fear of a judgment day is instilled in a follower's very core. This judgment day especially defies logic and is only a future threat.

Granted, there remains some communal quality to religious practice, where one can contemplate in silence and perhaps find hope in moments of self-talk called prayer. However, the morbid delusions of going to hell or heaven, and to kill in the name of their god simply misses the point of sane education. Yes, getting together in progressive communal development is a capacity, but it does not require religion. Why shroud this friendly capacity with blind faith, futuristic judgment, and heavenly promises? Just call it community and let that be enough. Religious institutions got away with their threatening nonsense for a long time, and the popes of the past even blessed imperialism. All religions are processes of community activity and self-reflection. But what is the use of blending copied and stolen misinformation with those processes and giving them different labels for each religion?

There are capable minds out there. Demographics are more complex, former colonies still want to be liberated, and the herd is the most educated it has ever been. Why is that not enough already to abandon copies of imperialism and religions?

Implement this: Recognize that the religious community model does present an opportunity. This model could be a medium to start reforming stolen and copied information into progress towards learning without faith. Everybody could attend, and it would serve a global mindset.

Or don't. Just go on sinning, fearing scriptures, and confessing about nothing.

Hope is a limit

There is a fundamental difference between believing something that is rationally understood compared to believing something that is rationally not possible. Believing without understanding is a form of limiting hope for the weak and delusional. Understanding is the concept of evaluating facts and asking better questions to find ways of fitting human understanding into something we can accept or even call truth. It is irrelevant that some don't want to believe what can be rationally understood. Let them be.

When we consider that the quantum universe has the potential to exist beyond what can be observed, we must insist to evolve from hoping towards actually knowing, and we should welcome this process. Mental capacity is to provide clarity to narrow things down. Looking through the lens of alien clarity, it seems evident that humans are lost out there in observable space as nothing more than a temporary necessity with potential. Rational observable consciousness suggests that it is necessary that we do exist, otherwise we would not experience it.

To be able to exist and to observe is a gift. And to observe and feel good about experiencing awareness is a joy. But we miss that we exist to enjoy! Instead we dwell on suffering from invented delusions provided by imperial males with visceral fat-inflated torsos.

Our history admires these people that built empires, like Caesar, Napoleon, Gates, Bezos, Buffet, and so on. The herd recognizes them as giants, but I recognize them as leaders of the blind. None of them ever had the capacity to introduce global decency in any of their empires and to see a target worth pursuing. The target, and the only empire worth admiring for all of us, is Mother Earth. I mean, we can respect some male ideas, but not the empire kinds, and not just because males think they can demand it. Because of our male-instigated suffering, there are demonstrations, blogs, shrinks, and self-help books that exist to ease our suffering. But, they all mean nothing to capitalists, and nothing ever changes.

When I was six years old, it was said that the continent of Africa needed the most help in the world. Over fifty years later, it's actually worse. All these talking heads ramble on and on about their good intentions while nothing, more nothing, and never-ending nothing to improve persists. The capitalists' grind deceives over and over. Talking, talking, and more talking, but very little doing. And hope will fix none of it!

Wayne Dyer said, "If you change the way you look at things, the things you look at change."

Here is how we can change how we look at things: We can stop participating in capitalist herd opinions, stop watching bad news, stop working, withdraw all our money from the banks, and meet ourselves. Let's have some fun and let's go on strike against capitalism.

We can do this on Earth Day instead of just turning the lights off to save power. Then we can assemble in our communities and fix our environment so that we have an immediate impact. Once momentum builds, our collective mental health would improve, and global good news of rebuilding, planting, saving livestock, reducing, recycling, and reusing would be on the media instead of the usual. All of us would work towards fixing the planet and sending people to places where they are needed so that everything can rebuild and flourish. There would be no need for borders, currencies, or hoarding anything. With a new equal reset medium, we could trade and rebuild the planet. This is not a utopian hope or anarchism. This is just smart! Everybody knows that desperate times require desperate measures. So, wake up, people. We are already desperate enough, and we can do this! Let's turn off that capitalist business sewer, drain all the feces, and disinfect.

Implement this: Understand that hope for a better planet is not an option, nor is it a job that will get done by others. Find yourself involved.

Or don't. Ignore mental potential and just keep going, talking, and blaming others. Maybe move to another planet.

Fear is unnecessary

Kant has a grip on detail. Occam's razor removes the unnecessary.

Historical religions are only opinions about reality's absolute and transcendent parts. Where is the detail necessary to substantiate them? Kant's antinomies are about contradictions that arise from attempting to understand transcendent reality. He thought that certain theses of his antinomies (God and Freedom) could be resolved by postulates of practical reason, but some could not be resolved and his attempts to conceive the transcendent produced unsolvable contradictions.

The predicament to the antinomies is that we cannot know how to resolve them because God never speaks up to explain. We must therefore suspend judgment in the matter, and so they remain. This was also the recommendation of the Greek skeptic Pyrrho of Elis, who stated that concrete knowledge about anything was not possible. Therefore, we can interpret Pyrrho as Kant's transcendental idealism. Still, transcendental idealism is only a thought and completely thought-dependent. All knowledge is just thoughts; they are not consciousness in itself. That should solve the problem. Right?

So, if we are basically unsure of what can be truly known (thoughts), then why do we replace what is unknown with belief? Belief is also just another thought.

For religion to preach that we have to fear punishment when we don't obey the gospel is not only rude but also quite absurd. Religions replace what they don't know with divine stories and threaten with other thoughts of divine punishment that they don't know to exist either. Therefore, religions are about multiple unknowns, and they expect us to fear the wrath of these unknowns. Follow me?

Therefore, I highly recommend religious disengagement. Faith and fear obstruct intelligent development. They accuse anyone that does not comply with their bogus unknowns as profane and blasphemous. Meanwhile, I don't accuse them of anything. With the exception of maybe needing a mental evaluation.

To their credit, I understand that religious practice can train the mind to develop civil conduct with deep devotion and contemplation. This can be interpreted as a spiritual practice and a deeper connection to life itself. But please lose the guilt trips and the worship complex. When we move into the province of spirituality, which is the nature of consciousness, we need to expand our capacities beyond what the scriptures tell us.

Spirituality means that the quantum universe also resides in our heads, and once we step out of our heads, we should obey the progress of science instead of long-forgotten scriptures. Today's science model tells us that space at its smallest is a subatomic (dark matter) canvas, and that consciousness may even be that dark matter, invisible, as a force, and holding everything together. If we conclude that these properties are the background force that makes the perceivable matter in the universe possible, then we must see the universe as an infinite, invisible "it" canvas with an infinite potential to be perceived as "is" within a measurable timeframe.

Following that, we are both "it" and "is." And if this is the case, then there is no room for a third-party god at all. We would be god. So why should we be afraid of this? It would mean that we would have to obey and be afraid of ourselves. Why would this cause anxiety? Is it that overwhelming to be alive? It can be, but only if we're constantly told to be afraid.

Implement this: The present now is actually "it" and infinite, and we experience the now as "is," second after second. That is all that ever exists and will be. Why be afraid of the present?

Or don't. Fear others' thoughts and your own, even while these thoughts are all empty.

Why do we believe?

Religions are belief systems that are respected by billions. Even though there are various customs in practice, a fundamental concept unites all religions. That concept is to take advantage of personal insecurity and anxiety. Capitalism does the same. It takes advantage of the insecurity of poverty and the anxiety of not fitting in. Some join groups of people in churches and others in secret organizations. There is a need for collective comfort—a sense of delusional group relief from the troubles that torture individuals. Consequently, clinging to hope emerges as a self-inflicted fiction. Still, having hope is a more positive approach to life than proceeding without it. The final outcome may be the same, with or without hope. Faith invites one to believe in the future possibilities that one wishes for. But why rationally hope for wishes to come true? Practical thinking in the present is a much better approach.

If we want a sense of well-being with practical applications, we have to apply plausible scrutiny before we believe anything. Believing is simply not practical. For example, if there was nothing to fear, would it actually make a difference to believe in a god or not? Most reasonable beings would probably rethink what they would choose in that case. Believing in fairy tales may entertain children, but it should remain entertainment.

Even philosophers have gotten caught satisfying the existence of all sorts of beliefs just to satisfy the authorities and even avoid prison. Again, Nietzsche said that God is dead. His open-eyed analysis is more accurate than being a blind subject to an all-knowing imaginary belief. He meant that man himself eventually killed his own concept of God. Man evolved, and consequently he began to challenge both God and belief, because neither actually exists. Do you follow? We are in asylum territory here. According to Nietzsche, God slowly emerged as a schizophrenic phenomenon to man, instead of remaining our absolute. Still, and no matter what calibre any philosopher may be, we can recognize that the desire for a sense of belonging to something, whatever that may be, and the desire for unity among the masses is present. So, no need to take this desire away. Let it be.

Having said that, people are now used to believing, and we can use that to our advantage. Humanity could write and present a mental capacity bible with new options that would invite us to move beyond both religion and capitalism.

Another belief problem is that political views should never include religious views. They should be completely separate. The political process revolves around making decisions, and they should be based on reason. In contrast, the religious process does not require any decision-making, and cannot be based on reason. So, politicizing religion is absurd because it distorts focus and doing so should be removed from any political platform.

Governing means to build and maintain sustainable infrastructure, regulate food and shelter, and provide education and health care. That is enough. It should never matter whether you have any association with any religion or are an atheist.

Implement this: In terms of religion, believe what you want and let others believe what they want. Even an atheist believes that there is no god.

Or don't. Insist that only your view is the right view and be on a lifetime crusade against others. Stay offended in the name of religion. It is apparently your right to be so almightily serious.

Chapter 6:

Psychology

What are you in all of this?

The self-awareness that consciousness projects identifies with a self, and we are quite opinionated with our own self. However, our opinions are mostly derivatives of other opinions. And practically, opinions do not get much done. We opine on ideas and react to causalities.

One of these opinions is that a capitalist compliance society demands that we all participate in it. Yet, compliance and participation should only apply if they are for mature choices. What we are currently expected to participate in is not even mediocre, never mind intelligent.

The socialist and communist models are not valid compliance options either. The only difference there is that the state and a few complicit oligarchs keep all the revenue instead of the rich, and still, their intentions also revolve around profit. All systems are simply opinions, and they all compete for larger economies and profits.

Profit-seeking, even with moderation, remains just selfish greed. We are generally of the opinion that we should be profitable and effective, and that we should get a deal. All these factors are about winning. Why are we so obsessed with winning? Winning is not a capacity, it is a delusion, and the materialistic goals that are associated with winning limit society's ability to progress beyond hoarding. Yes, winning is limiting! We, as individuals, reduce ourselves to winning because we've been brainwashed since youth to not be losers. Yet, what is in between winning and losing? Is it the mediocre, the communal, the being at peace that comes with neither winning nor losing? The grey instead of the black and white? What is wrong with being in between winning and losing?

We can't all be billionaires, but the delusional capitalist dream makes us secretly wish that we could be. What most of us really are in the G20 is middle class. There is nothing wrong with that either, provided that it also applied to every single non-middle-class person on the globe. We have the luxury of forgetting about the inequality part of this equation because we can. So what could we change to help us remember?

When I read Fred Alan Wolf's book *Mind into Matter,* I noticed that there were no practical capacity applications mentioned. His book is a report, whereas I see applying conduct recommendations to such a book as an opportunity. The opportunity is to ask people to pay more attention to self-discovery and to implement attainable actions in their daily lives. Reading a book might be entertaining, but acting based on a book is quite a different concept. Acting requires the mind to shift to doing. And doing has to have purpose.

When we analyze Kafka's main character in *Metamorphosis* who woke one day and found himself transformed into an insect and Dostoevsky's characters in *Notes from Underground* and *The Idiot*, we learn what they suffered from: feeling alienated from society. They wanted to explain rather than complain about their concept of existential understanding. They found relief from the absurdity of experiencing existence within a herd with no purpose.

I feel similar, but we have a purpose, and that is to evolve as a species. However, when probing daily, I see many talking heads and witness endless reporting of not just the absurd, but also blunt lies. No wonder some feel that they have no purpose. We suffer in this noise and not much ever seems to get better. It's like Groundhog Day, every day. We retreat into our small private spaces, expect bad news, and switch channels because it does not affect us. And then we continue to care about our own microcosms at our own leisure.

We all do this every day, and because we do, it may feel like this is nihilistic (meaningless). And simultaneously, we still wish and beg for global change. So, it's a predicament, and we can all judge and blame others for what we don't like. It is easy to say that other people are idiots—many philosophers have said this as well. But what is an idiot?

Idiot

Definition 1: a person affected by intellectual disability and the inability to function competently.

Definition 2: a person affected by denial to participate in intellectual capacity and the inability to function competently because the majority of other people follow what everybody else does.

Since I am convinced that you would agree that we live in messed up global affairs, I will use the previous Definition 2 as a metaphorical example.

If I asked random people in society if they were idiots, they would of course deny. However, if I asked each person independently if society has been messed up by idiots, they would concur. If I then asked again if they thought they were part of the cause for the global mess, they wouldn't give me a straight answer, but basically, they would deny again. This would mainly be because they would claim that they can't do anything about the global mess. Apparently, it is not their fault, even though they may have the intent to help change the mess.

So, what is going on here?

The problem appears to be unintentional following despite denial. But how does this happen? Following is mental self-deception, and it is rooted in defects of self-disciplined will power, such as:

We should, we could, we would. . . but we don't. (We don't have to.)
We should not smoke, drink, eat junk, etc.. . . but we do. (Sometimes we have to.)
We don't like to work, pay bills, etc.. . . but we do it. (We think we have to.)
We recognize global poverty. . . and we look away. (Because we can.)

But why?

In some cases, it is because we individually think that we can get away with anything for a while, and we can. This is deceptive self-delay! However, as a majority (herd), we can't delay going to work. This is because the herd expects us to show up at work by default. It is also an expectation to fit into the herd, because if we don't, we isolate ourselves as misfits. But most of us still don't want to go to work, right? Yet we go, again and again, despite denial.

Now, we have to be aware that personal conduct and herd compliance are fundamentally different, but due to the involuntary fear of not complying with the herd, they become highly related. Therefore, we become mild idiots, but not by choice. The reason why is because we are expected to comply. And when we comply, we become part of the idiocy, regardless of whether we choose to comply or we are indirectly forced to fit into the herd. We still comply by default! Therefore, you may now have discovered that you are a mild idiot as well, but not by choice. (Bear with me, and I apologize for the insult—but I probably got your attention.)

To emphasize, the result is at issue here. You have become a mild idiot. It does not matter why, when, or how. Even your potential denial would prove that you are an idiot already. If you were not complying, then you would be living off the grid, gone from the herd, on your own, and without an excuse to comply to anything.

So, by definition, as an individual you are not an idiot, but by complying with the herd, you become one. Mildly said, but a problematic fact. I repeat: it remains very common and easy to say that other people (the herd) are stupid, but I have now theoretically proven that you are as well. So, idiocy actually unifies us. This is circular self-deception.

As a result, idiot phenomena are happening to you because you let others indirectly make decisions for you. When you comply, you do not decide for yourself! Therefore, to decide for yourself requires a mental shift to disengage from the herd and embrace your own mental destination.

You now have to evaluate if you want to remain a mere compliance individual, or become a mental capacity person. If you are rational, then a serious decision needs to be made here, and this is your personal decision. The right decision for if you expect a better-performing society is to not comply with the herd. So, decide! Even Yoda said, "There is no trying".

Rest assured that the herd will continue to collectively demand to decide for you, because the herd is too broad to focus on anything this serious. They are deeply conditioned to remain entertained by financial temptations. This herd-following is also why the myth of majority-governed capitalist democracies will never work for us to evolve. Capitalist oppression, greed, murder, destruction, and resource depletion are not democratic values. Besides profit, this myth delivers nothing but division and trash.

Instead, consider a capacity operational system that eliminates finance and is not political. This would be far less fatalistic by default. To be clear, a capacity system does not mean socialism, communism, or nihilism. It simply means a system that operates as a global platform without profit, primarily focuses on rebuilding equality, and learns from the planet as it restores itself. Mother Earth will do this with us when we give her space and time.

Lastly, and to emphasize even further where we surprisingly stand today, there is a term now called indirect quitting, which describes when a person remains in their position of employment, but only does the bare minimum to stay employed. This is a very current and widespread symptom of delayed idiot compliance. People want to quit but don't, because they fear that they can't. It can't get more morbid and sterile than that, and yet we still tolerate it.

So, try this: don't listen to the news, don't congregate with religion, turn off your devices, turn off the TV, and don't watch movies. Wait, sit back, and yes, now you will be bored. And now that you've stopped doing all these things, notice that it does not impact your immediate presence at all. So, leave it all behind for a while. Yes, quit, and take time to reset. You can enjoy entertainment again, just later.

Now begin from scratch. This is where mental improvements start. Get past the boredom by finding something that you really like and choose an individual action that you can do for yourself, like a craft or study. And then take it from there. Pay attention to what happens. You will begin thinking creatively and refining implementation instead of complying. You will do things that didn't used to get nearly as much of your attention when you participated in herd activities.

Are social beliefs feelings?

Exploring our mental depth brings me to differentiate specifically between morality and reason, and how we feel about them. There is a distinct difference between morality and reason. Morals refer to ethical conduct and decency. If we are good by nature, which is a feeling, then we should have evolved based on ethics first. Meaning, once we are decent, we have a foundation to make reasonable decisions.

So, let me ask, is faith more related to reason or ethical principles? The answer is neither. Faith is like a hybrid of both with selective discrimination. The Crusades for example were wars in the name of Christianity, which is a single faith. What would be the reason or ethical cause to wipe out another faith? And how does that feel?

Mental capacity individuals don't need faith, period. Of course, one could argue that various faiths may be based on whatever reason and that they were chosen to satisfy tradition. But this is exactly where we have to be careful to not discriminate against others. These beliefs influence how we feel.

What's important is, how do we react next? Do we conduct ourselves according to our emotions or according to clear thinking? Emotions will override clear thought if one is not trained to curb them.

However, regardless of if beliefs are true or not, one cannot develop compassion by reason alone. One also has to feel it! Therefore, one's feelings can have collective moral roots somewhere and apply not only to one's own belief system. Additionally, both reason and morality are tools that help harmonize our patience and steer us towards kindness.

However, capitalism abruptly ends patience and kindness. Capitalism is pure thought.

This is why we haven't been able to find any peace for centuries. Both capitalism and religion always promise that their ideologies will lead us towards some kind of peace, but so far, neither has proven to even have the potential for our salvation. Still, their deceptive idealism is contagious enough for the middle class to remain gullible and continue pursuing some fictional salvation that can never happen. Think clearly: ethics are only necessary because of imperialist theft, capitalism, and religion. Therefore, ethical conduct remains a choice for capitalists. In contrast, when a society has range, there is no need for ethics.

Unfinished, defined internally

Imagine that it is 7 a.m. and we are part of a group of fifty-six individuals waiting for a bus to take us from Lhasa, Tibet to Katmandu, Nepal. This is a four-day trip, and the bus should be here by now. It is late October, and the sky is clear at early dawn. Suddenly, an orange glowing light appears in the distant sky. It is hard to tell how far away it is. It glows like a diamond and moves right to left, up on a forty-five-degree angle. Someone says, "What is that?" We all watch it for about ninety seconds, and it seems like a long time. Eventually, it disappears in an erratic corkscrew pattern into space. Later, some of the group write in their diaries, "Waited for the bus and saw a UFO." None of us will ever forget this.

This is a real experience that changed me, and it left me with an unfinished and surreal feeling about an event that I could never have anticipated. But it happened.

Now, how does the feeling of unfinished feel to you? Have you ever noticed that there are some sensations and experiences that are particularly difficult to describe with words? This is why I want to isolate how unfinished feels, and what awareness is. Awareness is always unfinished at the very moment of now, and then it is gone, impossible to grasp, and every new second presents another opportunity that is unfinished. And these temporary present seconds just keep coming, relentlessly.

Now, close your eyes and imagine that you can feel yourself breathing fresh ocean air on a beach and that there is a slight breeze on your skin. Feel it, and remain there for a bit. . . Now, open your eyes. What is the very first impression that you sense now? Is it a thought, a feeling, or simply a presence?

What actually happens is that you have to collect yourself first, and the very first moment is blank.

Recalling these past moments when your eyes were closed, how do they feel to you now? Is there a connection, a difference? You most likely don't recall having any thoughts other than imagining the beach scene while your eyes were closed. What's interesting here is that you can only think one thought at any given time. You were not thinking about your liver functioning or what you had for breakfast. And, in imagining the beach scene, you were trying to feel those moments, not think them up as a constructed thought. Therefore, you can only feel moments when there is presence. And this presence is awareness, which springs from pure and undisturbed consciousness.

We often have internal moments like the beach scene conjured during holidays or during breaks from activities. We call this relaxing. And then we return to society, coping with it by necessarily reacting to it and handling it with thoughts. We don't feel society.

Now relax and sense for yourself if feelings or thoughts are more enjoyable to you. I prefer feelings (like joy and bliss), because having no thoughts at all is what freedom is to me! Therefore, a sense of freedom is also a feeling. This does not mean that I am dull about everything, it just means that I live more in the moment and wait for what the future will reveal. How we deal with our unfolding lives is far more crucial than where we have been.

We all want to move more freely, live in broader equality, be understood, and have purpose. But why do we anticipate that capitalism can help us with these longings? Humanity desires progress, but capitalists cannot facilitate its realization. They misinterpret talking for acting, and hope is their delusional future drug that offers no concrete solutions. So, the question is, how can they move beyond talking and hoping?

Well, they could, but they won't. So, we need to proceed on our own! This all starts with you, because only you can measure yourself. This is where mental discovery has to begin!

Forgive me, this is not another beat-yourself-up mantra that I am releasing here. Instead, I now ask how you feel about what you are. I'm not asking what you think you are, but rather how what you are actually feels. When you look in a mirror, you see your image. Yet, seeing this image is not feeling at first sight. Do you actually ever think about how you feel when you look at yourself?

See what I mean? There are these slight nuances that we don't even seem to notice. What I am isolating here is what our thoughts actually are. Thoughts appear like an image in a mirror, and initially there is no feeling attached to that image. Only later, after we start to sequence the images into coordinated thoughts, do we begin to feel associations with these thoughts. These associations reveal themselves and consequently progress into other associations and various emotions. Eventually, we become a product of these combined sequences and identify them as our self-identity.

Upon closer examination, it becomes clear that identifications, associations, and emotional attachments don't truly exist in themselves because just about everything depends on combinations of previous occurrences. When we digress and deconstruct this process, we often don't even know how and why we make these associations or where they began. They are all a bunch of individual, mentally self-projected events, and they feel like this is what we are. However, these thoughts are only the surface of our full being. This is confusing and unfinished, yet we are still expected to handle it all. As a result, it should not surprise us that our mental health needs far more attention than it usually gets.

Mental health

What does the definition of mental health look like? The broad definition of mental health from the Brain & Behaviour Research Foundation on the internet is: "a person's condition with regard to their psychological and emotional well-being." (https://bbrfoundation.org/blog/everyday-mental-health-tips).

To clarify, this means a person's condition with regard to thoughts and feelings. This is exactly my point. Societies get lost in surface noise. We learn about things, tweet on, and even become specialists. It becomes irrelevant where that noise came from in the first place. Yet we comply and follow.

How we un-follow and un-friend directly affects our mental health. And yes, to withdraw requires a shift from instantaneous following. Just like when driving a car, once in a while we have to return to neutral when we change direction.

Let's assume that we choose liberal thought as a neutral mental health foundation. Liberal root qualities strive for balance. J.S. Mill is the father of liberal thought, and he wrote that conservative ideas are not necessarily stupid, but that a lot of stupid people are conservative. This single profound statement explains quite a lot.

Now the conservatives will obviously not agree, however, I will dissect that his statement is very accurate.

Let's define what stupid is according to Mill. He mainly means following history, being complacent in entitled laziness, being disinterested because of plain ignorance, and lacking the true capacity to un-follow. In other words, to be stupid means to be gullible with an absence of intellectual competence and to be borderline sterile.

The fact that incompetence is quite common and can easily be influenced is a force in itself that can be taken advantage of. Meaning, once there is momentum in convincing the incompetent to support a cause, they will insist on these beliefs because instant gratification is pleasing and occurs before thinking even begins. So, they will reject the potential of thinking and replace it with belonging. But, belonging eventually tends to collide with self-identity. Therefore, when the momentum of rejecting thought grows into a herd mentality, it can further evolve into a false democratic majority. This is dangerous!

It is not that the herd is actually stupid, but gullible belonging and instant satisfaction make them less competent. As a result, the masses evolve into a following mob, and consequently they not only undermine the democratic process but also their own mental health and potential. Democracy was intended to promote balance with truth and equality, and to find the best options for the benefit of all. There is nothing wrong with that. But mobs lose the ability to return to neutral viewpoints. Even socialists and communists follow these same rabbit holes. The wealthy understand that they can still manipulate and misinform the mob to form a majority that favours them. So, the original democratic value for common comfort fades away.

In addition, conservatives tend to become borderline radicals. They are a group that not only stays stagnant, but even evolves backwards. The crab walks backwards because evolution demanded it to. Conservatism limits potential and is not globally minded. When a majority voting process lacks subject competencies, it will only sustain limits, and limits produce dividing forces against social unity.

Our idealist, unifying democratic principle of consensus is constantly divided by participating political parties. We lose the purpose of consensus to politicizing stubborn agendas. All democratic countries today fail to reflect a true consensus model. They are imperialist capitalists first, fake-news pretending democracies second, and never for the people. Long live division to profit with a democratic halo.

The word democracy is much overused and very inaccurate compared to what it should actually represent. We are simply not smart enough yet. We even claim to be civilized. Here is a definition of civilized: "Having an advanced or humane culture, society, etc. polite; well organized, must fight ignorance, easy to manage, and refined relating to civilized people."

https://www.collinsdictionary.com/dictionary/english/civilized

There is no mention of choking each other with wars or financial oppression. And where does it say that civilized people justify slaughter by looking away from it instead of looking at it? Maybe our problem is as simple as not interpreting language for what it is meant to describe. It might be a better idea to distribute dictionaries instead of bibles.

To actually act civilized is our mental health issue. One must wonder when human evolution can actually occur. The stench of colonial residue still lingers everywhere.

Mental health requires mental capacity!

So, we have to convert into capacity and recognize that talent and genius can develop at any time, including later in life. It is not only subject to our early interpretation of children. We don't control how flowers grow. Why do we need to control anything? Learning happens all the time, just like growing does. It may seem absurd to compare the mental ability of a five-year-old with a teenager. But why? Everything is a matter of exposure and conditions. A teenager may not be interested in a study subject but may be forced to take it, while another teenager who is interested in the same subject is rejected. Therefore, what is the best way to begin learning? I am convinced that what

I learned up until grade twelve could be learned in half the time. I am not saying that kids should not be kids, but once I isolated the basics, I realized that there was a lot of wasted time spent on repetition. Volume is not learning, concepts are!

Hammering facts doesn't promote imagination or the abstract. Writing truly is imagination and can be abstract in action. Even more importantly, one can expand infinitely on what is to come and beyond what one has learned.

Nietzsche believed that writing should be treated like an art, and that it is in the writing environment that maturity develops. Good literature springs from quality reading and incubated thought. As one broadens their horizons with intellectual capacity, one can eventually write well.

I chose to write as a healing activity because Nietzsche's psychological depth and belief that the motivation to better oneself is an art in itself inspired me. People did not appreciate his finesse and enthusiasm about human capacity during his lifetime. My view is that this was because the mediocre dominating male was not ready to handle his thought.

Nietzsche did not isolate the mediocre male in particular as the root cause of herd mentality. He only labelled the herd as mediocre and never mentioned how women fit in. This is where Nietzsche limited himself, and it may be the case because women had disappointed him deeply. He got sick with incurable syphilis, which caused his mental decay and which he most likely contracted at a brothel. He was a highly educated loner addressing males. I am convinced that he would have been a much more content individual if he had understood women. In his defence, during his time males were very much in control and borderline absolute, while female neglect was a default. Considering all of this, we have to move beyond the male dark ages and its delusions and aim to inspire women, children, and teenagers to make a difference. There is no doubt in my mind that women and the young would have built much better global cultures. J.S. Mill and his wife also hinted long ago that we should all demand much more recognition for women. They have not only been limited but also deprived of their opportunity to plant, grow, and even flower their thoughts. A wise species would never limit any gender.

In summary, our problem is that we miss that mental health has much deeper roots than we admit. When we learn to address the causes, the symptoms will decline.

Begin with "Why?" and "What is it?"

The big question of why we do what we do remains entertaining. Nietzsche believed we should be more concerned about the why instead of the how when we approach anything. I agree, and this means we have to pay more attention to language.

What use do words have if they don't move you before they move others? It is important to note that language has its limits when it comes to expressing certain things. For example, why do we sense bliss when we meditate, and how exactly can we explain this? Einstein could not prove relativity by equation yet his intuition felt it was there, and the physics community proved it later by following his lead. This is the kind of new and uncharted capacity that springs from why questions.

Sages may be recognized by their decisive words and their behaviour—they often only elect to explain what is necessary and nothing more. Why do they explain their views with such scarce words? They do it because well-evaluated coherence seeks balance, and balanced capacity can only develop in present-moment (now) clarity. Sages also abandon most information that others claim to know. They have no attachments and carry a kind of no-thought, "gap" demeanour during the day. To them, less is more, and they patiently wait for insights.

Wisdom takes time to unfold. Socrates said that there is nothing to know, but never mentioned that nothing can be something as well. That nothing becomes something when observed in quantum physics. Nothing literally means the space within us, all around us, and especially in between thoughts (the gap).

Quantum physics tells us that empty space is actually not empty and that energies and dimensions exist that are not visible. We can't explain what these entities are, but they exist and seem necessary for perception to occur. The news that it appears to be necessary for the universe to exist and observe itself is in itself enough to recognize it as the absolute. However, what is the medium that observes itself?

Consciousness is that medium and without it, nothing would exist. The human mind insists and claims to know because our awareness sorts thoughts based on empirical experience. And when we deconstruct these thoughts, we find that every thought depends on another thought. So where did all our accumulated knowing begin? Where was that first thought? Regardless of the answer, whatever is declared as knowledge and faith is all man-made in thought. So, Socrates was right: we actually know nothing.

Under even closer examination, most of that information is still incomplete or may not even be true. Arnold Arnold wrote a book called *The Corrupted Sciences*. He conveys the message that both thoughts and science can be corrupted. Why was he inspired to write such a book? A lot of incomplete knowledge still becomes widely accepted, but only because we don't know any better. Inaccurate knowledge confuses the herd, and that disables the herd's ability to focus.

Have you ever noticed that society's manipulators are always missing in action? Yet, they are present and in plain sight; we just can't recognize them. They talk in code in the public domain and have false identities to pedal their agendas for all their wrong reasons. On the surface, they call themselves Freemasons, cabals, and investor groups—tribal clans of regurgitated wealth that never found any value in truth and decency. It is almost impossible to undermine them as individuals, because they always exercise their influence as a group. Thanks to slippery cults like them, it has become common to dismiss truth as an actual quality. Truth seems neither relevant nor entertaining. It may even come across as boring or delusional.

Religion even chooses to ignore generally accepted facts. It represents a format of fake truth until proven otherwise. For example, nobody ever comes back with evidence of hell, but religious followers still fear hell. Apparently, the lack of evidence does not matter at all. According to them, having a fear of hell is far more plausible than evidence. Trumpian Republican extremism is another ongoing example of serial lying. Making America great again provides us with another dose of Neanderthal pride, and news networks like CNN and Fox increase the volume of lying. Both claim to be better than the other. And? It's all noise, and that's it. One can ignore it all, and nothing will change. They only report what happened, not what can happen. Why do we even want to know the current news? What is the point of analyzing lies? If it was all good news, there would be a point.

But let's turn the volume up even louder with social media ego platforms where people lie as well and pose. Look at me, I did whatever today. How grand! Parading legends everywhere. Another epidemic is the status of being cool. But what is cool? When you pretend, is the next best thing to act cool?

Forgive me, people, but get over yourselves. Thought is far superior to well-repeated or well-posed. However, well done is best!

Personal range requires contemplation to stay focused on our own abilities, even when it is simply to rest in silence. To the sages, silence is important. Still, what's even more important is their decision prior to commit to silence. One has to tame the mind first to approach calm abiding.

Nietzsche reminds us also that creation happens in the consecutive present moments of the now. This is the spontaneity that is necessary to realize art. His art is to inspire us to be as art! Compliance is not art. It is dullness. If more of us start to understand these principles and actually act on them, then society can abandon most of its incompetent limitations. History clearly proves what our limitations were and still are. It should not matter what male supremacy wants because none of us should be subject to anything. To be precise, only a fraction of people misinform and manipulate, and they know who they are. All we have to do is isolate them to themselves. Necessity demands it!

Implement this: Ask why. You will be confused with what to do next, but then think again. What is it for?

Or don't. Why questions are too much work. Just vegetate, regurgitate, and repeat.

Mother

From a moral perspective, I've accepted my mother since I was a baby. The natural connection of her having given birth to me does not imply that I should believe in her views as I grow older. But whatever any mother's views may be, most of us will comply. Why is that? We do it because we have learned to love our mothers, and this may even be a mutual expectation for some. We interact with our mothers with respect or even fear and comply with their views until we eventually build our own perspectives. Therefore, when it comes to our mothers, our instincts don't favour mental capacity. Instead, they simply favour mutual compliance. I could just remove myself from these mutually expected values and move on, never thinking of my mother again, just like some animals choose not to stay dependent on their mothers for life. Still, most of us continue to sincerely care. Not only because of the naturally nurturing bond we share, but also because we make that free choice on our own. Therefore, why and what we choose to sincerely care about is never objective unless we have more information.

I am using this mother example to point out that we behave similarly in regards to religion, social behaviour, and leadership. These topics are in a sense like our mothers as well, because both society and our mothers expect us to comply with them. And so we obey and follow instead of finding our own calling. These influences begin very early in life, and it is easy to stay with them and get caught in opinions instead of potential.

According to Buddha, the purpose of life is to meet and find yourself when sitting in stillness. Most would say that life is not as simple as this. But it actually is! Once we depart from stillness, there are all kinds of noises that distract. Perceiving and living our daily lives means that consciousness is our true mother because it is a given that we never question. Therefore, every other creature we encounter also has the same mother, consciousness. Yet how do we treat all these other creatures? Our compassion is hardly ever as far-reaching and reassuring as it is with our own mother. Any creature will stretch their patience for their own mother, especially when she is ill or in need. Emotions though are much different; they become more careful and more intense.

Still, maybe some of us don't get along with mother anymore, and there is no further conformity. But regardless of what happened to any mother relationship, there remains a choice of how we interact with all other beings. There is something unusual going on here, and it's a lack of intelligence that causes us not to treat every being like we treat our mothers. Obviously, there are historical and emotional issues that make us handle mothers distinctly from others, and the preferential treatment and invisible ties remain. But we discriminate against most others.

Since consciousness is also our mother, then that would be like discriminating against our own consciousness. Our affection to mother is an invisible tie of self-created thoughts, and affection and emotions develop over time as we interact with others as well. But does deeper affection and emotion only develop because of repetition and more time spent with mother? And is the quantity of information and an extended timeframe more essential than the quality of information? When we dig deeper, we can observe that the longer we have known the information, the more likely we are to comply with it, irrespective of its reliability. Or, like Heine said, "The blind can lead in a dark room."

So, we mostly don't trust others because we don't know them. The same is the case with ourselves. In fact, most of us don't even take the time to meet ourselves.

We usually don't trust new information, but again, we trust some ancient information even if it is of very low quality. As a formula:

length of time = compliance

I think this is directly related to fear. Since imperialism and religion have conditioned the masses to be afraid for two millennia, we still comply with the masses today. So rather than asking you for non-compliance, I will suggest not being afraid instead.

In conclusion, personal information under the microscope is made up of blended bits and pieces of opinions and facts that have been compressed into our own stories. How we trust these pieces can become a problem. Therefore, we need reliable stories to build on. Since we are at the mercy of the other story's accuracy, that given information is not necessarily reliable. Therefore, we have to do a much better job at fact-checking information for accuracy.

Consider also that information generates feelings for both genders. Females tend to feel more than what they know, whereas males claim to know more than what they feel. They both differ. Although, when mom tells us something as kids, we run with it, just like when we think something ourselves. We assume what we think is correct because we think it. But that is not always the case either. This is only the ignorant self. Remember, consciousness has no self and is the mother of all.

Implement this: Evaluate information and others like you would evaluate a menu before you order. Take your time to select. Understand that the menu is the same for all.

Or don't. Consume information like music. Don't think about the song, just sing along.

Chapter 7:

Philosophy

Mind to matter

The most advanced mental activity that can help us remove ourselves from compliance and fear is to engage in philosophy. Philosophy is the bridge to understanding our minds and invites us to become more reserved and cautious about our conduct. The philosophic message is that we first have to evolve as individuals and then society as a whole can follow. But we do the opposite. We follow society to evolve as individuals and we comply because of others.

However, studying or even reading philosophy is not a priority for most. Cash, sex, drugs, and defamation are apparently more entertaining and lucrative. Capitalism overrides philosophy. Philosophy is also not useful if we don't intend on applying it. So let me help explain where we could apply philosophy.

Nietzsche was one of the first philosophers that built his philosophy around human psychology. I became familiar with him because he was a university professor in Basel, Switzerland, my hometown. There he had a reputation for unconventional thought. He was the one that named society a "herd." I think he was more than unconventional and that he was ahead of his time. He challenged the herd to work on themselves with education and art, and he did this with language. One of his precise insights was that writing is far superior to reading. He also gave advice on how to become a better writer. He understood that sentences are mental calculations and that one is only as good as one's next sentence. His gift to us inspired me to write, which I did over the years, jotting down a few paragraphs here and there.

He also inspired me to read more, because I wanted to understand where his thought processes came from. I mainly read non-fiction, and what continues to surprise me is that there are hundreds of books that try to explain what consciousness is. This subject is the ultimate mystery in philosophy, religion, and the health sciences. They approach the phenomenon from various angles, and some have shed some light on what is going on. However, the mystery remains.

During my younger days, it was my goal to spend time travelling the world, and I lived for many years with all of my belongings in one bag. I was content with so little, and I met a few profoundly spiritual people along the way. Some were street people, others were Sherpa or monks. They all had an amazing energy and serenity about them that is difficult to explain. They seemed connected to every instant moment, like they were almost transforming the ordinary into an immediately clear and precious presence. This may sound bizarre, but when I was near them, it felt like I could feel their energy. These encounters and learning from them convinced me to meditate more often than I already did. They emphasized that their daily persistent practice was the most important part of their day.

As the years passed, I wrote more and more about the depth of consciousness. Eventually, I compiled my notes into coherence. When I researched, I could not find much reporting that connected the scientific with the spiritual. So, I thought that I was onto something substantial and kept working on explaining my experiences and how they related to what I had read so far. Then one day in 2022, I found Fred Alan Wolf's *Mind into Matter* in a used bookstore. My first thought was, let's see what this is about. I flipped through the pages. Then I thought, this is the kind of book I am working on. After checking its publication date, which was in 2001, I thought to myself, not only has a book like this already been written, but it was also done decades ago. I bought it, read it, and wondered why people did not pay more attention to such a fascinating book.

Wolf also wrote a number of other books, and I started to dig deeper. What I found was that there were quite a few new authors that wrote about the same subject of consciousness from a quantum physics perspective. Regardless, this kind of knowledge does not seem to expand the human mental radius. But it should! The message is that we are consciousness in action, and not bodies that produce consciousness.

Despite Wolf's book and others, society does not seem ready for this kind of information because not enough people make it mainstream enough for

Nietzsche's herd. As for myself, I found more or less the same information by studying theoretical physics, philosophy, and Buddhism, and mostly through engaging in persistent hours of daily meditation. I remember that the most profound people I met advised me that "there is only practice."

Another reason why this information is not mainstream is because even science has difficulty explaining what can actually be felt during meditation. And that is because feelings are not thoughts. You don't think of pain or joy. These sensations just happen. So, if science struggles with this, then it is also too complicated for the herd. To help society understand this as a herd, we have to simplify it down first.

Anyway, Wolf's book and mine are similar. His book is more of an alchemist fact and curiosity report based on his training in science. He also understands meditation, though he does not mention that he meditates daily. In my case, I arrive at my views based on the people I've met, my reading, and the insights from my daily meditation practices.

Wolf explains a perception loop, though he does not call consciousness the source of the loop. His loop describes a present-to-future awareness, and asks for an observer. Once the observer observes, the loop closes, which results in present perception. His observer is there as in a person (him or you).

My view is that consciousness in itself projects independently from a person and that consciousness is also the observer simultaneously. Our chosen body is like a filter that identifies with consciousness through awareness as perception.

Wolf also identifies a soul, but I don't. The soul to me is awareness, the self that is our most private entity. Wolf's soul could be described as an aura, which is an energy field, yet he does not say that. He also refers to a god, which may be to satisfy his religious beliefs. In my case, I would call god consciousness. Therefore, my view is very similar to his but differs in what the source is.

Grind it over and see what you come up with. Furthermore, I think that all matter in space-time projects simultaneously from the same universal consciousness. There is no loop. Consciousness is simultaneous, everywhere, and infinite. Perception is our format of recall experienced as time. Our mental problem is that we can't grasp that we actually experience infinity and that we are an eternal energy source. It seems too fantastic. This is why it only appears that we all have an independent experience, but we are really all one collective, self-observing, simultaneous entity. And, because we can't hold onto anything, nothing actually exists in the mental dimension. Most Indo-Asian religions confirm this as well. So, this is how we become something out of nothing, or how we go from mind to matter.

What do we know?

When we wander in thought, we dance with bits of information. When we read philosophy, we are invited to wonder what truth factually is so we can reason with truth. Philosophy engages in the practice of dissecting information and investigating language. It separates the metaphysical from the physical and welcomes the scientific. Consequently, this particular system should be supreme in how we measure what we can believe. To define truth is a capacity, and truth can be both boring and surprising. Through a philosophic lens, nothing is as it seems. But what is it that philosophers want us to see? Is it action or is it precise thought to opine?

Philosophy is a rebellion because it asks questions and conquers opinions. Even so, how often does philosophy ask for action to be implemented? We can't become wise by knowing what wise should be. Becoming wise would be to do wisdom. For example, doing can be something as simple as reflecting into this very moment of being.

Deepak Chopra said, "Treat every moment as a gift, that is why it is called the present". When we experience the present, these gifts just keep coming, relentlessly. Yet, what makes each moment appear? Leibniz asked in his cosmological argument, "why is there something rather than nothing". By "something," he meant a necessary being, or god, that caused and sustains the universe. His argument points in the right direction, but in my view his god is actually consciousness. Marcus Aurelius wrote to himself to find himself. Why does an emperor have a need to find himself? This is what philosophy represents. Seeking the abstract, even the surreal, can only happen in that very next moment. And in that moment, when insights appear out of nothing, we realize that we don't know what we don't know. Schopenhauer was right: "The genius sees what others can't see."

Implement this: Verify how you define truth.

Or don't. You are already busy with listening.

Learning how to learn

Learning is the science of obtaining new understanding, and it can be influenced. How we learn should include knowing the difference between respecting historic influence, accepting current influence, and imagining for the future and in the abstract. We mostly accept the current conditional forces that form our communities. But we have to do a better job of filing away our historic incapacity. Existentialist capacity requires complying less to self-proclaimed historic authorities. Who declared religions and imperialism as authorities? Thoughts did. Religion has robbed us of fearless freedom, and imperialism is theft in plain view. Religion even authorized imperialism as a war tool to enforce divine thought. What is divine anyway?

In principle, there has always been the aim to control. If divine control is to promote well-being, then imperialism is not a fit. Control words such as faith, patriotism, duty, and prosperity have nothing to do with learning. They mean and represent disabilities as far as I'm concerned. Yes, capitalism is a disability. But the herd is not handicapped! We have to unlearn the historic systems that we still follow and change how we learn to move forward.

Financial and religious control are just formats of territorial behaviour worthy of Darwinian apes (no disrespect to apes). Are we apes? If you're not sure, go look in a mirror. Then circle back and contemplate again about how we should learn. We should learn how we learn because of what we learn! What we will learn today is about control, but tomorrow it has to be about moderation.

What does education mean?

A challenge or an obstacle is usually mastered with some education and ambition. But ambition can interfere with education because it can easily be confused with pride and greed. It is a psychological event to develop a healthy level of ambition, and it is vital for managing present and future matters.

Moderation is also important in terms of language. We have to proceed with less scientific, political, and psycho jargon. When we teach children with plain language, they will have an easier time comprehending. Adults need to be taught in the same way, because language plays a big part in how we approach anything.

Education will result in progress. But what are we progressing towards? If the goal is not clear, then the message can become distorted. Confusing messages can be dangerous. Messages are information, and information is everything in regards to how we build mental value. However, education depletes in value if it cannot be applied. When not applied, it simply remains as information. We have become over-educated in the capitalist elite and under-applied in the middle class.

Imperialists embrace sophistication to sustain superiority over others. This sophistication also creates an elite that is driven by desire and ambition and that does not comprehend the concept of moderation. The elite are not interested in cleaning toilets. Someone else will do this for them, just like all the leading capitalists demand other nations to harbour all the dirty jobs for them.

The rich build their own private schools, and they promote who they know instead of what they know. Kind of like the blind leading the blind. These silver-spoon people promote from within at their private universities and then they choose our leaders. So, one can be an idiot if one has funding and still end up at the top to make key decisions. In comparison, a capacity system would demand that the silver spoon principle be eliminated. Class and wealth cannot matter if we want to provide equal opportunities as a mature species.

Global equality seems out of reach because capitalists cannot get over themselves. Their highly praised—and priced—education is not smart enough to implement moderation over individual gain. Their mantra is "multiplication and hatred until everything explodes."

We have to believe that most people will actually develop superior skills provided that they can grow up in reasonable environments. So, to enable only the rich with superior skills is not only unfair, but it is actually limiting by sheer numbers. It also favours the stupid that can afford it. This limitation then compounds into broad incapacity. We will remain disabled as a species as long as we are led by the rich. They corrupt our education systems all the way up to the university elite and industry experts. They are so polite and reserved with their research and advice for addressing our capitalist symptoms of decay, but they never take the abrupt stance that we have to find remedies for the causes.

If we want improvements on the education front, we need to include more philosophy. This education concept is superior as it prioritizes psychology over profit. Philosophy helps us recognize ourselves. Both philosophy and education should not be valued as high-end destinations or distinctions. They should be ongoing all the way through life.

The process of writing is a recollection capacity that reveals how educated one is. When writing, one frequently discovers that a subject will invite fact-checking and referencing other information. And as one learns, one can be inspired by something totally different. One can discover areas one has never wandered through before. In my view, self-discovery is the very best education. Yes, there are benefits to signing up for some learning package from an institution. However, most of the things we learn from institutions revolve primarily around remembering what was previously taught. Education is the environment that grows around us and with us. It should be fun and loaded to inspire curiosity and implement action.

Furthermore, we must get children involved in abstract thought much sooner. For example, right now we teach them that they were conceived (without explaining sex), became a fetus, and were born as a body. We tell them that because they have a body, they are conscious, and that both body and consciousness expire at death.

But, we don't help them understand when exactly life becomes conscious. Is it in the mother's egg, in the male's sperm, or at conception when both combine?

What if we told our kids that we are infinite consciousness, which, according to quantum physics, observes itself as it creates itself? We could tell them to assume that we may have chosen to be born into our particular bodies. That would be an unusual approach to the origin of our being. What would kids say?

What if we told our kids that if we could travel faster than the speed of light, then we would not be able to see ourselves in a mirror. Therefore, travelling beyond light speed suggests an event horizon (like at the edge of a black hole) where visible perception changes into another dimension. So, does the velocity at the final light speed event horizon speed up or cease completely like a neutral infinity (dimension zero)? We could tell them that once light speed slowed down again, perception would be visible again. This could explain why we observe the universe as infinite and as expanding, because we are within the limits of observable space-time velocity. What would kids say?

These are just some examples of questions to ask. What would kids come up with if we taught them such things? Why don't schools recommend reading books about quantum physics such as John Schwarz, Michael Green, and Edward Witten, *Superstring Theory,* or the book by Sir Roger Penrose,

Stuart Hameroff, Henry P. Stapp, and Deepak Chopra, *Consciousness and the Universe,* at a much earlier age? Children have amazing abilities, and I think we are holding them back with infantile Santa stories and fairy tales.

Post-secondary education is also a business. It teaches as much as possible in the shortest time frame. Its priority is profit, and most of it is overpriced. Since educational institutions should be a priority investment to build the best possible societies, they should be free to attend, and they could teach at a reasonable pace. Our current privatized institutions stuff a ton of information into every semester, and students are constantly under deadline pressures. Prior to post-secondary education, kids are bored until they finally arrive at graduation. As a result, the post-secondary information overload does not develop our kids' IQs. It develops revenue.

Granted, deadlines and pressure measure performance. But performance does not equal IQ either, just as practice does not equal talent. At the top, the so-called sophisticated provide suggestions to do this and that, and then they sink into research that has to be financed. Students that graduate from the universities then join research teams, and suddenly time seems unlimited again. These research teams try to do their best, but they are highly dependent on funding and changing opinions. Again, money is limiting to the development of higher accomplishments. If we took revenue out of education, where would we be?

Imagine an educational system without private funding and where everybody is welcome. Imagine institutions that raise overall global human performance instead of profits. When everything hinges on funding and limits participation, then how educational can we be? Not very. Global education with government funding would not only accelerate our development as a species but also result in a much faster restoration capacity for the planet. High-level education for the select capitalist elite is like clothing a whole body with a sock. We need more than a sock; we need a survival suit.

It is not that we don't have the capacity and the tools to progress more effectively. We simply reduce ourselves to subjects of the rich at far overpriced rates. Additionally, we get bombarded by the opinions of wannabes that post millions of blogs and selfies. Kudos for effort, but still very limited in scope. Entertainment is not education.

So, who can really help us all accelerate our mental progress? The next guru? No, it's actually you! Instead of engaging with self-proclaimed gurus, you could be asking what the poor and the minorities need and then engaging with their demands. This way we work from the bottom up, instead of from the top down.

Implement this: Nothing is as it seems, and kids especially are interested in all kinds of abstract topics. Education should be free and available for all. It should not be a business.

Or don't. Teach kids our history so that they can think about what we should forget.

We are addicted to tragedy

A movie generally evolves from an introduction that escalates to insurmountable odds and then, under suspense, leads to a conclusion. From this movie perspective, our species constantly lives in the never-ending suspense section with no end in sight. The cause of the suspense can be narrowed down to the question, what do we want to be?

According to Darwin, we are some kind of hybrid ape. The hybrid's territorial claims resulted in permanent oppression and wars. They believed they were not animals anymore, and they learned how to deal with information. Consequently, information replaced their instincts, and information became everything. The tragedy seems that Darwin's apes actually can't handle information, but they are now addicted to it.

In the Middle Ages, people had limited access to what they could explain, understand, and believe. Then, Gutenberg invented the printing press, and that revolutionized information. The Christian church recognized that the formerly limited access to information created a unique opportunity in that moment to instill control with the written word. So, the first books that were printed were bibles. These were powerful tools to help faith take over society and induce fear. As a consequence, the Christian tragedy became gospel and replaced reasoning with faith for a long time.

Once electricity was available, electronic transmissions took over. These increased noise levels far beyond what books had done. Today, society craves social media, loaded with fake information to entertain. The press claims that there is a right to know in a free society. The right to know what, exactly? Just information, or what is going on behind closed doors? Where exactly do we draw the line? Or do we report just for the purpose of reporting? See what I mean? We never developed the capacity to manage how information was to be handled. Information has become uncensored opinion without prudence, and the appetite for defamation is relentless. It's all noise, but noise is not information. Noise is just noise. Information has to be of plausible value.

In a mature capacity culture, defamation would not exist. However, some milder versions could be classified as satire to entertain in healthy doses. People mistake news reporting for an opportunity to expose. Sensationalist defamation and opinions can be presented in the name of freedom of speech, but people fail to consider that the definition of freedom of speech is still subject to the interpretation of language and conditional views. What does freedom of speech actually mean? The media do not welcome profanities, but they do politely smear anything on anybody. Their politicized smear campaigns are not subject to censorship. And there is no common capacity IQ present. Instead, they shovel garbage all day to the gossip- and product-loving herd. Where is there value in any of it? What have we become? Contortionists of information?

We are so hung up on information that we even forget what the point of information actually is. Language evolved to clarify our actions, and information is a language. So, the point of information is to clarify, not to confuse. As a priori, information is a medium for the growth of creatures, both physically and mentally. But our current format of information does not help us grow. Instead, it has become our limiting dimension.

The colonials installed bibles and constitutions. None of today's mess would have been possible without these scriptures and their resulting abuse. Can you follow this with a neutral mind?

Back then, the colonialist takers completely missed the opportunity to provide social capacity, and it is still missing today. They continue carrying on and think it should be acceptable that they stole whatever they wanted. Colonialism was theft in plain sight, a tragedy that we're addicted to. Universities still teach about this factual theft of the past as if it was an accomplishment. To evolve as a species, we should teach something else. How about forgiving our screw-ups and returning that stolen land and treasure? That would be a capacity move in the right direction. But they won't do that until the cauliflower in their heads is replaced with brains. They do kind of look the same.

The details of doing

Plato, Hume, Kant, Schopenhauer, Marx, Nietzsche, Cioran, Arendt, and Wittgenstein provided us with tools to help us understand how to question society, but Krishnamurti, Aurelius, Ramana Maharshi, and especially the Tibetan sages suggested that we have to meet ourselves first before doing so. Once we practise meeting ourselves more often, we can develop the capacity to understand the absurdities of mankind. And doing things well requires a kindness that can only spring from understanding. The so-called educated continue to ramble, yet only actions have actual consequences. What will you do?

We've dissected what information is and that even the past also had a beginning. Even so, our past needs to end now with a new mental reset. The honeymoon of acting like primates is over; it is time to refine our development as a species. First, we have to seriously tame and even remove capitalist interests and second, we have to shift our primary attention to nature. Nature will show us the way; it has an incredible ability to bounce back.

It is time to clean up, provide room, and allow time. We can start by doing our part by restoring our neighbourhoods, consuming less, reusing, recycling, and restoring. The three *R*s are essential for every individual. They are the very best things that we need to *do*, and not just talk and report on to be done in some hypothetical future. Results will never materialize without action. We learned to understand quantum particle physics because we cared about the building blocks of matter. And now we need that same interest and scrutiny to fix our planet. A parasite will eat its host, just as capitalism will eat the earth. Science and the Tibetans won't.

Chapter 8:

Capacity

Inventing mental capacity

There is nothing more precise and powerful than a well-thought-through formula. Einstein's $E = MC^2$ is the most famous. His story is that he followed the standard scientific physics models until he reached a dead end. He isolated himself, conducted tests, and assumed that the speed of light was a constant. He felt in theory that his assumption was accurate, even though it meant that it would change the standard physics model. By persistently working, he explored uncharted territories for the benefit of others. The theory of relativity grew out of his intuition and it earned him the status of genius. Tesla was also considered a genius, and he refused to accept the theory of relativity because he believed that mass and energy were not equivalent. Quantum physics is now adding other factors such as dark matter, dark energy, and string theory to the physics of energy. Hence, there are many established physics standards, but we still continue to research further.

We can learn a lot from the concept of studying physics, because it is the best example of where only intuition can stretch beyond limits. When we spend more time developing our intuition, we will become a capacity species.

Physics research is a process where trial-and-error experiments result in data. The data is then analyzed, which leads to conclusions that are within reason compared to other reliable data. We then establish generally accepted formulas that guide us further, and we call this process research. Hence, research increases our understanding capacity as it helps us reach for the beyond. Without research, we cannot evolve.

If we compare these same principles from science with social behaviour, we discover that our formulas are based on opinions instead of research and proof. There are some formulas that societies mutually respect, such as law. Laws mainly serve to protect, but what are we protecting? Why is protection necessary in the first place? Does the necessity to protect confirm how stupid we are, or how civilized we want to be? This is a simple question. Can you answer it?

Some people will think that I'm a dreamer to suggest removing capitalism. But maybe these people are dumb, and it is up for debate who the dreamer really is. According to my earlier theoretical proof (chapter 6, under Idiot), people must be idiots to think that I am the dreamer. And why be nice about it? I only provide examples and offer to help.

What does idiot capitalist compliance do? We know that political opinions override what actual scientific proof recommends. Dumb and dumber can opine themselves with stubbornness and resentment into their invented micro-realities. Still, from a mental capacity perspective, that should only be possible if we let them!

It's rational to say that our capitalist society finds itself hanging at the cliff edge of insanity. But hanging out there, exposed over the abyss of mental incapacity, does not have to be a suspense that we have to endure. Mental capacity is mental health in itself. So, let's address capacity!

Back to the formulas. Newton learned that when that apple dropped from the tree, it fell to the ground. It did not travel sideways because it was subject to vertical gravity. He learned that every other apple would fall at the same speed, no matter where it was on the globe. This is a basic thinking formula, and an example of sanity.

We need formulas like these for us to step back from our insanity cliff, involve our best contemporary scientists to think anew, and file our history away. At some point, logic, intelligence, and reliable sources will replace incapacity. Facts will be validated, and reason will help us establish sufficient proof. Moderation will open new doors instead of closing them. What are we waiting for?

Capacity individuals understand that genius is not always a gift. Genius can also be realized with effort and balance. We don't even need genius to reform our social chaos. The solution is that the middle class can simply unite, just like any union does, and then we can negotiate better terms together. Only idiots declare something as simple as this to be utopian nonsense.

How do we measure genius?

The mysterious William Shakespeare had a vocabulary of about 66,000 words. He knew about 35,000 words, used about 31,000 different words in his writing, and he introduced about 1,700 new words to the English language. The proud English and theatre-goers praise this as monumental, and rank him highly. Meanwhile, Johann Wolfgang von Goethe had a vocabulary of about 93,000 words. He is actually ranked number one, before Leonardo DaVinci, on the top ten genius list of all time on the internet; https://listverse.com/2007/10/06/top-10-geniuses/

Shakespeare is ranked highly by the English, which is biased.

Goethe is ranked highly by the Germans, which is also biased.

Both vocabularies are extraordinary, but who is the genius? They both are. But Goethe wrote *Faust* during his entire lifetime, and he brought the German language single-handedly to exhaustion. This is an example of how genius was measured in the past in terms of art and language, which is impressive, unique, and very creative. However, what humans need today is the genius to reform our social mess.

It is important that we appreciate the paintings in the Sistine Chapel, and it is important for them to be protected and preserved so that society can go on admiring them. It is now time that we apply this same kind of capacity mindset to protecting and preserving against global exploitation.

Another example is remembering Neil Armstrong's first step on the moon. It was basically an impossible feat for the time and may have been filmed in a studio at Area 51 according to conspiracy theories. Either way, it happened, and in this case, we have to ask if this moon landing represented the intention to demonstrate human capacity or if it was simply a political space stunt between the US and the Russians.

Regardless, we all watched the earth float weightlessly in space for the first time. Everybody that witnessed this live remembers exactly where they were at the time. I watched it in elementary school on a fuzzy black-and-white TV with an antenna. It made me wonder how they were able to send these live pictures all the way from the moon to this tiny little antenna. I understood what I was witnessing, but I missed what it meant and how it all worked. It was amazing though, and that was enough.

Landing on the moon that day lifted the human capacity bar to a higher level and inspired humans to imagine an even further space potential. Since the space race was also a political contest between the US and the Russians, it makes me wonder what else could have happened? From a science perspective, both superpowers could have worked together and taken their time to make that space project even better. And from an engineering perspective, they only conquered space with a firecracker that was slingshot around the moon, and the landing was a controlled crash. Amazing, but still primitive in execution.

The broadcasting of it seemed to prioritize the US global propaganda machine rather than acknowledge the science and equality of the Russian space program as well. If the intent of the moon landing experiment was to further scientific capacity, then why was it politicized and turned into a race? The space race was a tool to further extend the gap between capitalism and communism. It was a hidden format of war in plain sight. Much like how 9/11 was covered up and how COVID was planted and is still mutating.

Think again, people. What is really going on? Is genius to be found now in the sinister?

Global inequality is why humans continue to embrace a hostile and self-promoting, self-serving model. Nations claim to participate with other societies, but they will protect their own self-interests first, no matter what.

Aggressive and hostile attitudes emerge in all kinds of formats. Regardless, whether it is cyber, strategic, positional, financial, unionized, or whatever, it's war. And somehow, we have these united human plans to fly to other planets in our solar system and develop space stations. To do what? To conquer each other there and unload more trash? We can't even unite here on earth. We want interstellar global cooperation even though we continue to simply neglect African starvation and abandonment. On one side, we deserve to explore space, but on the other side, the Pink Floyd song *Pigs* should be our global anthem. Put some lipstick on that pig. (I mean no disrespect to this highly intelligent and highly slaughtered species.)

Still, there is more bad news. Our deceptive ambitions reach even further when we teach our kids to admire images of the earth in space, taken from the moon. These images serve our future capacity to challenge space, but the millions that starve don't care whether we fly to the moon or not. Where can we find genius in a species like that?

Mental capacity is the genius of philosophers

In the past, there were some individuals that understood our mental potential, and we can still learn from them today. I will mention a few historical examples here that are still important to existentialism today.

Avicenna's theory of essence posited three modalities: that essences can exist in the external world, associated with qualities and features particular to that reality; that essences can exist in the mind as concepts associated with qualities in mental existence; and that essences can exist in themselves, devoid of any mode of existence. He wrote this about 1,200 years ago, and we are still confused about how to separate them.

Seneca was a master of making a point in his stoic morality letters. His style was to set the stage not only for his plays, but also for clean and captivating paragraphs. The examples he used were from observations in life and how to learn from them. Another reason to write!

Marcus Aurelius was a ruler, but he struggled with his fortunate situation. To ease his struggle, he wrote to himself without asking for recognition. That is far more evolved than reading what others wrote.

Erasmus was kind, and that was enough. They labeled him a humanitarian.

Leibniz, an underrated genius, was a polymath (a person with wide-ranging knowledge) and panpsychist. He believed that everything is conscious, including plants and inanimate objects, and that everything has a mind or something analogous to a mind. More specifically, he held that in all things there are simple, immaterial, mind-like substances that perceive the world around them. So, he described consciousness over three hundred years ago, but most did not pay attention, and they still don't.

Hume had an appetite for life and the unknown. He was definitely not a lawyer.

Kant was the most interesting, but not entertaining in style. He provided the most detail in describing consciousness itself (the thing-in-itself), even to the point where he admitted that he could not know himself. He could have expressed more and perhaps would have spent more time with meditation and personal isolation if he had the ability to access to quantum physics at the time. Kant wrote *Was ist Aufklärung?* (*What is Enlightenment?*), an essay on how to think of yourself. It is also about Genesis and how Adam and Eve eat from the tree of *Verstand* (understanding). His key questions remain: What can we know, do, and hope for? Comfort and freedom are reasonable desires. But what is freedom? In my view, freedom is to have no thoughts at all! He searched to find himself and to be the very best that he could be.

Schopenhauer was influenced by eastern philosophy concepts and donated marvellous style in explaining consciousness. Pessimistic or not, he insisted on the very real. Most opinions, whether written or oral, steal previous beliefs when analyzed in particular. Even Christianity appears to have emerged from the Upanishads. Schopenhauer clearly identified that our inner ideas and the vast mysteries of what lies beyond empirical experience are far more important than reading others' books and concepts. He believed in a steady routine of writing, reading, walking, and adequate rest (so did Kant). He was the philosopher that planted the seed to find and invest in new ideas from our deepest inner selves.

Marx's *Manifesto* and *Capital* warned about overproduction, yet his methods to combat capitalism were misinterpreted. He did not ask for military style revolutions by extreme regimes. That would be too radical a mind shift and too abrupt an approach. When revolution is necessary, it has to be introduced as a personal mental adjustment that an individual is willing to make. Once one understands the logic that springs from Marx's depth in economics, then one has to prosecute capitalism. Marx also declared that philosophy must become a mandatory education tool. One could no longer be content with interpreting the world; one should be concerned with transforming it, which meant transforming both the planet and each individual human's role in it. He was right then, and still is today!

Nietzsche made music with his words. He wanted to create a moral monastery. The wordplay of poetry also influenced him. He liked Horace and Heine, which becomes apparent in *Zarathustra*. For me, Nietzsche is an artistic Socrates of the nineteenth century. However, he thought that Socrates offered no solutions to many problems. He both admired and despised him. He was a professor of Greek mythology and developed some extreme views, such as becoming an overman. That he specialized in teaching about gods and demigods could explain why he expanded towards an overman. This was his expression of a character with capacity. He admired the strength of rulers because they earned what they ruled with their will. Equality, moderation, mediocrity bored him. I think he confused individual desire with what humanity as a whole (the herd) needs, though. Life is not about individual will and strength (his overman). Striving for power is just a desire (a thought), whereas mental capacity is about discovery (a feeling). Not everybody can be an overman / overwoman, but he evolved in the right direction.

Jung is Nietzsche's disciple who he picked up on the psychological elements of his philosophy. He was also close to the self-reflecting stoicism of Marcus Aurelius.

And there was Cioran, another remnant of Nietzsche, with some sober and current stimulation of self-reflection.

Emerson was the American father of language, and well-balanced.

Krishnamurti abandoned history for mental depth and truth in the present moment that reveals the beyond. It seems that Nietzsche also influenced him.

Mother Teresa said that one can be poor, but that the greatest poverty is to be unwanted, unloved, and not cared for. Let's put that into perspective with capitalism. What did Mother Teresa insist on? Doing. She washed homeless children in the streets of Calcutta.

The Dalai Lama represents liberation, but remains tangled up in political distractions. Some see him as an example of freedom in exile. But how is he free when he constantly has to beg for freedom?

Sartre, Camus, Heidegger, and Arendt were influenced by Nietzsche and focused on existentialist psychology and the absurd.

Wittgenstein developed the *Tractatus* for the interpretation of language because he questioned what could actually be expressed accurately.

Derrida's deconstruction of language also followed existentialism and the footsteps of Wittgenstein.

Chomsky intended to socially unite. He taught respect but should have used simpler language to help the herd. They were not ready for him.

Bryan Magee was a guy that also found that Hume, Locke, Kant, and Schopenhauer were the threads to follow. He understood what made them profound and recognized that they all asked the same question: What is the "I"? Some (like Schopenhauer in *The World as Will and Representation*) called it will. But is it actually unidentifiable? How can it be characterized?

And then there were characters that wrote about superintelligence, like Nick Bostrom. But people, please take a step back! Superintelligence may be a gift, but the sheep in the herd primarily need grass and shelter. If we become anything close to superintelligent, then we will run away from the herd. Superintelligence, compared with the mental decline of the herd, is like looking at humanity from a black-and-white perspective. We need to look at the grays and all the colours in the big picture. The herd may seem narrow-minded because gullibility degenerates potential. But we can turn the herd around if we simply promote gradual philosophical self-development.

Philosophy is an investigative activity, and it points us in the right direction. The predicament, however, is that philosophy wants us to reason in capitalist environments. But reason cannot flourish when inequality surrounds us everywhere!

Vox populi is the people's voice, not the voice of inequality institutions, and the people are the middle class in this capitalist chaos. They are the most powerful force of all! But we still don't seem to understand this yet. We often say that society is manipulated, but we can't really isolate how that manipulation works. I think that comfort and convenience are the mediums that allow for this manipulation, and our laziness and lingering apathy may even come across as human stupidity. Still, people are not stupid, but they sure are lazy when it comes to becoming smarter. Therefore, people remain disinterested in anything that does not concern them; it is their self-claimed democratic right. And when people insist on the right to be lazy, then they have lost intellectual capacity. Consequently, they feel manipulated.

To conclude, it is interesting what the aforementioned philosophers did and wrote. Still, it is far more interesting why they chose to care.

Implement this: Mental capacity springs from the very present, has a vast range, and is all unfinished! Read, write, and do.

Or don't. Watch and talk.

The Dark Ages

Prior to the Greeks' rise in science and philosophy that they stole from others, there was the Dark Ages. It was a time highly influenced by the sea people, who were a mysterious blend of Mediterranean pirates and coastal tribes. Then, suddenly we found ourselves recognizing a character named Leucippus. He was a contemporary of Democritus that started to educate about atomism. How could the Greeks have possibly invented atomism without hearing about it from somewhere else?

Prior to the Dark Ages, we had archaeological bits and pieces that dated back a few thousand years. But, recently, additional ruins dating back hundreds of thousands of years were discovered, and academia must now slowly admit that the scientific knowledge they claimed over the last two hundred years is now incomplete or even incorrect. So, we had bits and pieces for hundreds of thousands of years, then the Dark Ages, and then a sudden information explosion that is only about six thousand years old. Therefore, the Greeks could not have invented much without stealing information from other sources. In addition, there is barely any information prior to the Dark Ages. It almost seems as though information has been deliberately covered up by some influence, for whatever reason.

Let's move on to what suddenly appeared. It was science and education, and it was the Greeks that claimed credit for most of it for a few hundred years. Does it not seem suspicious that most information of scientific consequence came primarily from the Greeks? There were some contributions by the Romans and the Egyptians before them, but not nearly as much.

Eventually, Plato emerged with the story of Socrates the Wise. Socrates was a character seeking clever capacity with arguments of truth to challenge incapacity. The art of the "Socratic method" to isolate underlying presuppositions with constant probing had serious psychological consequences for humanity. If one reverse engineers this method, one can accomplish underlying presuppositions as well. Consequently, manipulation was born.

Plato recorded some of the probing truths of Socrates, then Aristotle isolated the fact that truth can be distorted by persuasion, and Christianity adopted and twisted the process. Religions even managed to become the new delusional laws for humanity. The result was that we wasted away in religious dogmas, deprived of mental progress for over two thousand years. Not very wise!

So, "Back to Socrates, we must go," as Yoda would say. But who was Yoda for Socrates? That would have been Prodicus. He taught Socrates the correct use of language, which became the prerequisite for him to leading a decent and truth-worthy life and to make precise arguments.

Prodicus was a contemporary of Democritus and taught by Protagoras, who was one of the original Sophists. Protagoras isolated that language has to provide clarity, like a fine art. Therefore, the word "sophisticated" represents him to this very day. He was also the founder of the paradox. For example, "the more we manage something, the less we learn from it." He also stated that a protagonist is the primary agent of a cause.

Socrates, regardless of how he was invented, should be acknowledged as a giant in philosophy because he initiated the search for truth and prudence. Consequently, a "Tractatus of Prudence" or a "Capacity Manifesto" seems necessary to aim for mental capacity.

So many have led the way towards finding "the way"—as in the Tao—to get us out of the Dark Ages. But to find the way, we have to think clearly and express ourselves accurately. When thinking produces solutions that still include one's original intent, then that is precise and accurate. This is what Wittgenstein would have liked. People should also present language in this way.

To create wisdom, philosophers filter truth, often surrendering to the basics, and combine it with self-criticism.

If we circle back to the philosophers that I mentioned in the previous section, we find that almost all are males. Could you tell me why? Women are just as capable or even better at advancing humanity and science. But society never credited women! Even though they must have stood right behind most of the males that have been taking credit ever since the Dark Ages. Society has always limited women's contributions, and it still does today. In some societies, women are viewed as possessions, like livestock. Man's exclusion of women has hindered the advancement of humanity. If women had been in charge of decisions, we could have avoided wars and famines would not even exist. We have to give women the opportunity to design our future moving forward. It is simply their turn.

Can we design a future where knowledge can be unfinished and leave the historic remnants from the male perspective behind? Socrates insisted that he knew nothing. He just asked questions. That is not much doing, but it is at least thinking.

So many questions. Clever capacity is not finding the genius in the herd. Instead, it is finding the genius within each of us. Wisdom is a timeless art form that Nietzsche suffered so much to defend. His wisdom recommended becoming an overman. Yet, he forgot to mention the overwoman. I won't.

Unfinished beyond

What is beyond capitalism? Can society find a new formula like physics found the theory of relativity?

Democracy is optimistic idealism, but the capitalist process limits its realism. G20 leaders insist that humanity has to follow this ideal, while they comfortably neglect the other 175 nations.

It is absurd to assume that the capitalist concept can somehow unify and equalize us as a species. According to capitalist principles, the economy has to pay for development in countries that are struggling. But poor countries can't crank up their economies, so they will remain poor. Also, how much is a democratic voting process actually worth in these poor countries? What is the majority voting for? Slightly less misery?

Capitalists imagine that compliance with their system promises progress for everybody. But when the poor have no money, then this delusional promise becomes submission to an unattainable goal. Competing for profit with the rich G20 does not apply to war-torn and corrupt nations. Bankruptcy there is not even a problem, it is standard. To assume that 168 nations should follow the G20 is an idea, but what for? To become like them, which is impossible? So, here we have an impossible global idea that gets discussed over and over at G20 meetings. They meet to expand their self interests and to disguise their permanent thievery. To be blunt, capitalism is deliberately taking advantage of consumers that are still unequipped to comprehend what life on earth actually requires of them. And under the democratic veil, the unequipped can be influenced to form majorities in capitalist societies. Consequently, we have a mob complying voluntarily to greed. It's like the blind supporting the blind.

Ouspensky, Gurdjieff, and Blavatsky already told us that society is somewhat asleep, even when it is awake. I agree, and I interpret that sleep as capitalism and that being awake is to challenge capitalism. Once we recognize capitalism as a possessive condition of the tribal male ruling complex, we can reason its limits. But stubbornly, we never even attempt to move beyond it. We bask in it like it is an accomplishment. And a desire to eliminate it is completely absent among the sloth-worthy. So-called economy experts are especially holding us back with their narrow, profit-seeking mindsets posing as authority. Along with them, self-promoting, greedy academia sticks to their titles, free enterprise, and shrivelled opinions. Their fat stupor prevails because they don't want to know any better. They already got their grand diplomas from their universities, so why bother with thinking beyond? Everything is narrowed down to profit, growth, and comfortable discrimination at large. Sorry, but there is no polite way to state facts sometimes.

I now encourage the young to think clearly, because I wrote this for you. Ask yourself, what reliable sources can help you mentally to reach a beyond? It's definitely not the diabetic Baby Boomers. Neither is it the Darwinian primate evolution called history. Please accept that we cannot possibly have evolved from primates. Looking at the biological and chronological evidence, there appears to have been alien content in human evolution somewhere. Here is why I say this: if humans evolved from apes, then why did all the other apes remain apes? It follows that we should consider Darwin's mental capacity equivalent to that of an ape. But, in Darwin's defence, he could not explain otherwise because he needed more information. He could also have imagined an evolution that reached beyond the animals that are still present today. No disrespect to apes.

Maybe Darwin imagined the beyond secretly but had to protect his reputation and what was generally accepted at the time. Or, his mission may have been to misinform and confuse deliberately to hide what was really going on. Who knows? Well, some thought they did for sure. Off the educated went, adopting Darwin, just like the church adopted crucifixion and Aristotle. Their excuse was that they did not ask what they did not know, and so they continued with what they wanted to believe. A truly wise choice, right?

Further, considering the unexplained and bizarre architectural ruins all over the world, one should ask if these structures are also evidence of alien content in human evolution or simply that of Darwinian primates. I think the pyramids were there before the Egyptians even evolved. They just painted their history on them to claim them for themselves. Moving and pouring giant stone blocks with copper tools and lifting them up four hundred feet was simply beyond the Egyptians. Archaeologists don't consider that unconventional construction methods could have been used. I think the targets to pursue with pyramid construction are the use of levitation and kinetic energy. It seems obvious that we have to think out of the box when something does not fit.

Is potential alien influence really that obscure a possibility? Would it be better if we called questionable human evolution and architecture "beyond ordinary" instead of "alien"? The term "alien" seems to frighten academia and the herd. They cannot seem to get over themselves.

At least Plato's Socrates invites reason to help us contradict these lies. Socrates was a documented first step towards existentialism. However, the

Socratic method to contradict is only a mode of critical thought that does not provide many solutions. Still, contradicting leads to asking better questions, which can in turn lead to the beyond solutions.

Let me be crystal clear: a concept of beyond knowledge is not alien, foreign, or an assumption. It is simply something new that we do not know yet. New is where capacity begins!

Granted, some have better resources for beyond knowledge in the form of access to better or even secret information, such as the strange secret in plain sight called Area 51. This area is an example of the fenced-in mysteries of the privileged. But does not hiding such information undermine the intelligent progress of a species? According to the Americans, they don't belong to the global species. They are special, and proud enough to miss what mental range actually means. Only the paranoid and stingy make their discoveries secret. They assume super status because they can hoard secrets. But what is the point of protecting an advantage just to disadvantage others? Is it the assumption of control over weak minds? Regardless, the United States of the recently un-united must be great again, along with being the leader of all the superpowers. How grand and polar. We want to evolve as a species but reduce ourselves to hoarding secrets.

When we look at science and education, we find that there is an intent to actually solve secrets. They leave the doors wide open. But, when we get to the top of governments, we find hoarding behind closed doors. Not knowing and having secrets kept from us are fundamentally the same; would that be equivalent to stupidity as well?

When the masses don't know, they are left behind and raised as a mob to follow. This is what manipulation is, and the process of manipulating is far more damaging to society than intended greed. Still, manipulators know this and manipulate anyway. Consequently, stupid is what stupid manipulates.

Because of these manipulators, we can't seem to identify what is actually good for us and the earth. We have sterilized our potential with capitalism that continues to limit our future with territorial fussing, petty little secrets, and ignoring how we should fit into the global food chain.

Does this nearsightedness even remotely demonstrate intelligence? Do young people want to inherit this Neanderthal rubble? Do you intend to dumb yourself down to fearing compliance and fake information, burning the earth, ignoring acid oceans, and exterminating more species?

To summarize in one paragraph: We need rationalism and existentialism to eliminate and replace possessive financial extremism, and we need to lose the delusion that democratic capitalism is a remedy for its own, self-inflicted problems.

Merely discussing these issues won't suffice, and thinking that we can't change is correct. What we need is urgent intervention and elimination rather than change.

Implement this: We need a beyond approach. Capitalism is not the remedy for the problems that it causes in the first place.

Or don't. Carry on like you always have.

Overwoman and overman

How can a nobody like me bring the imperialist species grinder to a halt? It seems ludicrous to even approach this. However, think again. Everything is connected, and the middle class has the most power when applied properly. When we all dig deeper, we can discover that none of us have to fit our current human herd profile.

There is room for overwomen and overmen. Our minds need to be like the core of stars that produce nuclear fusion, not like the surface of stars where turmoil and flares constantly erupt. That core fusion is what makes the star what it is. The surface is the eventual progression of what the core generates, until it collapses on itself (Supernova). Once we remove ourselves from that capitalist surface mindset that instigates fear and compliance, we can retract and approach our core capacities. Look for them!

Implement this: Imagine that day on the coast of North Africa again that I mentioned at the beginning of Chapter 3 Capitalism. Use it as an example to create an environment where you can share, dare, and consider your options.

Or don't. Self-improvement is too much work. Be content with capitalist sloth and waste.

Intellectual capacity

Intellectual capacity asks why, what, and how questions, and it demands to ignore compliance within the human hamster wheel that we apparently love to stress in.

Let's take a closer look at existentialism and phenomenology. Existentialism is the study of how the human condition affects oneself, and I am convinced that this kind of self-study has a healing quality. Taoism is a good example of existentialism that simply intends to understand nature and living in harmony. If one needs some basic direction, then Taoism is enough.

So, where is existentialism today? The short version is that the human condition has morphed from the private and individual (you) of the twentieth century into the mass public (the herd) of the twenty-first century.

We keep losing ground in finding what we truly think ourselves and sharing our deepest thoughts in person. We still share, but we mostly do so on devices now, so that one-on-one experience often becomes a one-on-many experience instead. Consequently, we have too many influences, and our ability to function as individuals becomes distorted. We take instant information gratification for granted and may even feel a need to participate in it. But what is important? When everything is important, then nothing is important.

Yes, what we choose is up to us, but trends are often chosen for us. We drift along from one thing to the next, surrounded by surface information from others that lacks the depth to push us to reflect more deeply. As a result, devices have reduced what individual existentialism invited us to consider, which was to isolate what is going on in our own heads. We remain so severely engaged in the noise of and about others that we often neglect to catch up with ourselves.

Surfing the web means tapping into endless information that is available at our fingertips within seconds. This presents benefits, and I think it's an accomplishment that everything is so available. Still, what are we actually doing with this massive availability? There is so much of it, and because we can't handle it, it becomes disposable. We surf entertainment, post on social platforms, and drool for news. We are free to decide what we want to follow, although for what exactly? Is all this information necessary?

If we apply Occam's razor here (not multiplied beyond necessity), we need to turn down the volume. Is it not the case that once we look at something, there is always something else, somewhere else, that is newer? Then another thing, then the next, and on and on? There are all these talking heads and blogs everywhere. The sheer volume makes us numb. Report after report, war after war, and more and more global abuse. It's like we are heading for a concrete wall on rented time and can't find the brakes. But we just have to know.

Here we are, on our couches, with our treats and our appetites to consume more of whatever we can't practically afford and process. Most media formats are circular info rides that never have a destination.

Mass information availability should actually increase our evolutionary capacity, yet this is clearly not the case. The science community initially developed the internet to share information more efficiently. However, the global community now primarily competes for advertisements and subscriptions. We are at a point where the quality of the information has become secondary. Surprised? Capitalism can't even leave information alone. The intent again is profit and not quality. Availability is now hijacked for sales and consumption that amounts to garbage instead of intelligence. The most developed nations insist on their garbage-generating ambitions and promote never-ending growth. But there is no intellectual capacity in this whatsoever!

Simultaneously, we hope that our global condition will someday, somehow, magically become better. But hope is not a solution. Hope is stupid. Capitalists claim that their living standards lead to a better civilization, while the underprivileged and impoverished report, beg, hope, ask, demonstrate, strike, or even self-destruct. Yet, almost nothing ever improves. Thanks for showing up for another dinner party, G7. Just keep talking us to death.

It appears that perpetual global misery has become a negative information problem. But to be precise, reporting misery is actually intentional, because it makes the G20 look better. As mentioned, imperialists manipulate the masses with information. Their propaganda for the middle class is to identify the poor as victims. But poverty and misery are only a deflection for the herd so that the rich can go on to count more money, unnoticed. We never focus on the rich—we just focus on mayhem.

Some of us may remember the days of using encyclopedias. The times of accruing intellectual information in person. Gathering information was a much slower process even only fifty years ago. One had to read books, attend presentations, listen to the radio, or hang out in cafes at North African beachside hotels (mentioned in chapter 3). At that time, TV censorship chose what information was important and suitable for the public.

Today, overload is streaming all at once. Everything is instant. But viral entertainment volume overrides content, and trends people into idiocy. Here is a cat doing a handstand—1/2 million hits. Or, here is what all the critics have to say about the Barbie release. . .

Intellectual capacity comprehends that overindulgence in entertainment is overrated. Volume is just volume, and this kind of entertainment is mostly followed for a sense of belonging. Let's have fun, be cool, and look nice. Everyone is so self-important with their device advice. Look at me and my blog, I must be heard and subscribed to, I have the freedom of this and that, I present opinion over opinion, and then what do I do? Nothing, nothing, nothing.

Belonging is not a bad desire. But let's belong to something that has intelligent content.

The herd is seriously misdirected due to the misuse of information, but it is right on track when it comes to the deviously calculated capitalist brainwashing. Therefore, my phrase "dumb it down." But nobody is actually dumbing anything down for them. The herd does it by itself, in itself, to itself, to entertain. It's like herd consciousness. The collective general format of the herd selfie is a phenomenon of a capitalist society that will never mature. Capitalism is not an intellectual concept. It is an oppressive compliance concept that breeds followers.

Without independently thinking minds, societies will linger on as compliant groups that choose dumb ideologies and dumb leaders. What is the business community's highly praised leadership anyway? Perhaps an overrated sales pitch at best? Capacity people don't need leaders. They lead themselves as a collective and by default. The demand for leadership is only a requirement for feeble minds. Compliant people will always look for opinions somewhere so that they can sing along. Being led is an escape from intellectual reflection. It's easier to bypass the concept of discovering an individual, existential view.

So, the fundamental challenge is to help every individual understand that they have to wait first (rather than comply), and then think about what's next from their own perspective. And yes, thinking is work, and it takes convincing to help people begin the process. But if anyone wants to claim that they are intelligent, I invite them to prove it.

As mentioned before, Nietzsche declared that God was dead over a century ago, and that was symbolic. It not only resulted in a decline in religion, but it also meant that other absolutes could die. He meant that humanity killed God, and I now declare that existentialism has become borderline extinct as well. Existentialism is dying because the herd dumbs everything down and influences the individual. Herd mentality is mental decay, and this is dangerous.

Jon Stuart Mill declared that even democracy is dangerous. He explained that if a majority believes in the wrong intentions (I use capitalism as an example), then that is a threat to society. Herd intentions present that same danger by complying to unreliable or even wrong information. From a capitalist perspective, complying is easy and quite comfortable. What's wrong with having nice, shiny things and more of more? Nothing is wrong if you're a manipulated copy of a follower. Capitalist compliance contradicts intellectual capacity, and it is an underestimated existentialist threat. Intellectuals understand that our problem is simple: global inequalities are caused by some gaining more over others. Nothing else creates hate, revenge, and wars.

Therefore, instead of addressing hate and aggression, which is what we always do, we have to address gain over others first. If we didn't steal, cheat, or enslave, and if we were content with our food, shelter, and basic care, then why would we hate or discriminate against anything? Even war would be unimaginable.

This sounds utopian, yes, but only because the conditions to steal, cheat, and enslave already exist. In comparison, animals can get a little territorial, but they balance each other by default. Are they utopian? This is what we don't get as a species. The imperialist capitalist machine is so sly that it always blames the conditions instead of the causes, meaning it surely never blames itself. Similarly, the Church preaches that we're all sinners, yet the only cause for sin is the Church.

It is absurd that reform to a point where humans can live in relative comfort and in a completely sustainable global system seems impossible just because we have to overcome capitalism. Only capitalist conceit insists that such reform is utopian. That same conceit looks away and moves on from misery.

And so we continue, grinding along for the sly capitalist mill. We accept that lies can override fact. So what? Let's lie. Facts are boring. Since we follow idiots, there is obviously no difference.

The Murdoch Fox network opinion cult is a prime example of how to drive misinformation rather than facts. Their fake concepts attract extremists at large. What Fox spews, sells. Rational creatures should not buy into it, but they love it. How do they become that intellectually dull and traditional? What is it that does not spark any sense of enlightenment towards progression? Is it boxed-up religious hatred that still lingers from the Middle Age

Crusades? The point of Fox is to fan the flames of decay that serve capitalism. It does not matter what Fox releases; they just have to get paid.

In comparison, the existentialist seeks information that is reliable, eye-opening, and seeds progress. The existentialist recognizes that we misinterpret the sly capitalist experience as an improved living standard because it stands out compared to countries that drown in severe conditions. The existentialist realizes that the herd relishes in the gossip and trends of capitalist technology and are so self -assured that living in their narrow-minded paradise is the ultimate.

Granted, having all this instant technology is an admirable capacity, and we could use it for many applications. Devices are great tools for converting information into immediate action. For example, we could go viral for drawing all our cash from the banks and not going to work anymore, all together, on the same day, simultaneously, out of nowhere. That would be a real awakening. It would force global capitalists to pay attention, guaranteed. So, on behalf of nature and the poor, let's all flush that financial toilet. This would be an intellectual move!

In addition, intellectual existentialism also exposes that religion is irrational because it exposes why individuals are being threatened with fear from a divine source. Why would following such a doctrine be more beneficial than fearless thinking? "Thou shalt not doubt" is relentlessly limiting. And since we follow religion, thou shalt not doubt capitalism as well. What is wrong with us? Everything is following!

We always seem to need a messiah or something to fill our empty insides. Following is all the same, just packaged differently. We are somewhat conditioned to hope for some kind of salvation by default. But salvation from what? The delusional hell, poverty, ourselves? Thanks to Nietzsche's existential residue, religious following is finally on the decline. Even so, why do we even need a Nietzsche when all one has to do is think?

For the interpretation of language, the word "religion" should maybe be replaced with "community." And, the religious process should be practised without relics and with less ritual conviction. In essence, community is maybe what religion was meant to be. It was a gathering whose purpose was to get together and share. Or let's call it a party—there is nothing wrong with that. But to worship statues and rituals, to live in fear of eternal hellfire, and to repent for sins according to scriptures are all meticulous chores that are unnecessary to build communities.

New generations are now ready to reject the following of religions to satisfy their parents. But this may not be due to a wish to oppose parental guidance. It may instead be because they have found a new religion. They have found their sense of community in their media-loaded devices. They still follow, but on a device and without having to wait to congregate in a church at a specific time. Individuals now have the ability to completely isolate while still having access to instant exposure.

When we wanted interaction in the past, we had to step outside. This new phenomenon of social mass exposure while in isolation is a concerning polarity because it becomes a handicap to expanding one's social skills. It is not surprising then that online dating sites are popular, and that obesity is an epidemic. Is there a lot of online dating and obesity going on in famine-troubled countries?

Healthy existentialism demands in-person interaction with others and to find social capacity together with conversations and actions. Humanity has to mature into kaizen mode. Kaizen is the Japanese concept of continuous improvement, and improvement requires reliable information. What we have previously absorbed into our lives will shape what we choose to believe. However, this prior information may not be accurate or even necessary at all. For truth to be verified, we either need reliable sources or we have to independently research information for accuracy. This sounds like common sense, but this fact-checking loop is often not followed, so it's actually not common.

Our beliefs will shape what we become and how we behave. But what we secretly believe may not necessarily be related to our actual conduct, because becoming also involves fitting in. To fit in, we have options, and we can mask our true beliefs with false behaviour. We can act, pretend, or even lie, and this is where the downs in life develop: when we believe something, yet do not act accordingly. That is intellectual stagnation! So, one should consider where their current beliefs come from and if there is space for fresh becoming.

From a mental capacity perspective, there are three primary wise concepts to remember for spontaneous, fresh becoming. Reflect on them:

1. Practice - Meaning consistent daily meditation practices.
2. Kindness - To all creatures and matter, and also to yourself.
3. Fasting - Meaning food fasting to help the body repair itself. And mental by isolating and staying off devices.

Again, some may think this is a boring, look-in-the-mirror reminder. But boring or not, how we cope with the sequence of events in every single moment defines what we become.

When we evaluate the depth of all the complexities that we seem to drown in, one has to wonder how we will ever deal with all the volume. We don't want boring, but we can't handle volume either. So, we are overwhelmed and we begin leaning on others. Consequently, the herd mentality is born and it leads us away from our intellectual capacity.

What if I told you that the capacity to live life well depends on simplifying what we do? Emphasis here is on *what* we do. If the three previously mentioned concepts had been more respected, then no colonial, religious, or business practices would have had the ability to fester into global boils.

Many repeat that empirical experience has only one constant: change. When investigated, there are many layers to change. We can't grasp the past, the future, or even this very moment. So, even change has to be understood as a phenomenon that we can never hold onto. Consequently, why do we need to hold onto information? Or onto anything at all? How valuable is anything when it constantly changes?

Change is also the only observable constant in the universe. This is why I named this book *Unfinished*. When everything is always changing, nothing is ever finished. Even when we think some things are complete, like someone's life or a project, they are only components of something else.

The scientific community confirms that the perceivable physical universe is mostly empty space where matter reveals itself as bundles of particles that are held together by energy. Still, our perception experiences objects as physical, despite them mostly being empty space. So, how small is the smallest divided again? Eventually, we should end up at nothing. The mental domain is not physical and is therefore like nothing as well. I mean, I just reduced both the mental and the physical dimensions to nothing. But there is still the mind-body connection. Even when the physical is reduced on an atomic level to mostly empty space, it is still connected to the mental dimension which is not physical.

Simultaneously, the entire cosmos is also infinitely changing. Not a single particle will ever be in the same location ever again. There are now new dimensions that we attempt to imagine, like dark energy, dark matter, black holes, wormholes, and string theory. These are all concepts beyond perception and that touch the infinite.

And so, we are self-aware, and we exist only within the perimeters of our perception in this ever-changing all. We assume that we intelligently control our destiny with our self-invented ideologies, but if we did, we would not bother with imperialist capitalist materialism. We are so much more than financial debris.

In conclusion, intellectual capacity is the ability to put all these components together and to reason for a future without limits.

Youth is capacity

We condition the young to believe that the poor and the common middle class have to comply with the trickery of the wealthy. However, wealth means wasting resources that only fools care to enjoy.

We don't need to raise more fools. We have to retire the fools.

I proceed to inspire you to search for unfinished capacity in your young and fresh minds. Only fools and sitting on a couch while spacing out into a device can hold you back.

Let me dumb it down for academia: young people don't need to follow tribal imperialism just because universities deem it imperative. Their future careers should not see them as cavemen in suits and uniforms. Instead, we should be teaching them how to recover society and the planet.

Imperialist education is littered with judgments that are often incomplete and even wrong. For example, political science merely analyzes past events instead of suggesting social tools to improve our socio-political potential. Why bother studying historic wars, failed extremism, dictators, and false hopes such as democracy and capitalist delusions? Yes, it can be educational, but to what benefit? Can we not isolate what can be summed up in one word "idiots" and move on?

Political doctrines inspire far too much emotion. Consequently, people react like nuclear fission (starting with a singularity, escalating to critical mass, and eventually exploding). What we need instead is nuclear fusion, which releases far more energy than fission and is the opposite of splitting the atom. Even think-tanks are confused about critical mass. They mistake that capitalist confusion can be turned into global fusion.

So, where does thought-produced emotion begin? It is most likely a judgment call, where a previous thought was labelled and then progressed further. This progression can then become dangerous when emotional intelligence can't keep feelings at bay. Contemplate closely and discover that emotions are actually feelings, and not thoughts in themselves. These emotions are feelings that can erupt into delusional thoughts and then transcend into actions. For example, there is no stress in itself. Stress is a feeling that is caused by thoughts. These thoughts are dependent on entangled labels and processes within the dimension of our personal awareness. In other words, they are imagined sequences of events. When dissected even further, in between every entangled process event is a gap. It can either be an empty gap that invites us to stop the process, or the binding gap of reasoning and the stress to connect the pieces. Hence, the duality of pure consciousness (the gap) and mental awareness (the binding gap) mentioned earlier appears again. You young people, remember that you can always choose to not attach yourself to any sequences of events. You can literally eliminate the process. Gone, just like that. . .

Once you realize that consciousness remains without our thought entanglements, you understand that you can move beyond what the educated claim to know. When we consider that we are now in a position where quantum physics confirms that the universe seems to observe itself, that spooky relations at a distance are a reality, that photons can appear and disappear into observable reality, and so on, then unfinished capacity is wide open and right in front of you. It is effortless, without stress, and of abundant potential.

Implement this: Youth potential is capacity. We have to set youth free to explore wherever they want to go.

Or don't. Remain asleep and accept what the educated claim to know.

What is a capacity motive?

Business means competition, and we praise this like a religion. We seem to recognize value in this because it sustains our chosen lifestyle. We want, want, and want. And we pay, pay, and pay.

Does the painter paint to express or to earn? If the painter paints to earn money, then the motive is gain. Consequently, it is highly doubtful that gain provides a meaningful condition to create quality art. But creative expression is valuable and deserves recognition too. However, to pay millions for a collector's item is a prime example of how distorted our values have become. Is recognition and modesty not worth something as well?

Why do we measure value with money? We can't eat money. It's the savvy capitalist medium that provides the opportunity to inflate values even more.

I agree that top athletes should make a decent living for their entertaining careers, but do they deserve millions? I agree with TV networks charging for advertisements, however they are billion-dollar enterprises. The spending numbers for these advertising spots are staggering, just for a few seconds to promote trash. Supply and demand are the delusional factors here, and these high capitalist values distort what reason would define as adequate.

Is all this cash for advertising necessary while others are still living with cholera? Such extreme contrasts only exist due to the capitalist values that come from intolerance, and low tolerance is a condition of lacking intelligence. Capitalist greed even relies on artificial intelligence (AI) to cheat even faster. By expanding AI, they've created a new mystery dimension that frightens the herd. They already fear that more lies, data, tracking, and deception are on the horizon.

Think about it: deception in exchange for limitless growth seems smart to capitalists. But deception and secrecy are also conditions of low IQ. Rich people governing should be a method to apply intelligence to our species, not to add more secrecy and AI to cheat the financial markets. And, replacing the labour force with machines and AI is not sustainable for growing populations. Instead, the wise, long-term priority should be non-profit global equalizing for all governments. This means primarily jobs and services. Non-profit equality is in complete opposition to profit and AI. The earth is not interested in AI. AI can't get food into the ground or roofs over our heads, nor can it clean up the oceans.

We need self-sufficient, small, local communities that can regulate the fundamentals of trade without money. This would be possible if we had one single global denominator. Currency conversions would no longer accomplish anything.

Everyone would get to start from scratch, which would instantly create mutual and equal global trade. The emphasis here is trade and not profit. In a global trade community like this, everybody could contribute and have a job. Previous financial speculators and inside traders would have to find real jobs. The capitalist system of money earned from money traded would not serve a purpose anymore. The rich would be done with stealing, and inequality would vanish. It is actually simple to tip that scale! We could end it by making all money, debt, and securities worthless.

We could build up the underdeveloped nations to catch up to the standard of the so-called developed nations. We would do it by treating everybody the same. Work would be work, and it would not matter what one's work is. Yes, that would mean that a few people would earn a lot less, but simultaneously, it would also mean that a lot of people would earn a lot more.

There was once a development called the Venus Project that is a good example of a previous attempt to build a capacity society. Their operation struggled because the project tried to convince society of their aims with conventional education and fundraising. No wonder it did not work. Everything hinged on investment, and capitalists surely wouldn't invest in their own demise. We need a global attitude to adopt such a project. Fundraising would not be necessary because trade would mean not selling for profit. Trade would mean that all countries would rebuild also with trade. Our global motive should be to trade goods and labour and replace greed with goodwill and volunteering. This is how we become capacity-builders instead of disaster-managers.

Implement this: Understand that a capacity society is actually possible because we have the technology and massive labour potential available to rebuild every continent from scratch. Do not comply to capitalists. They've had two thousand years to prove their capacity. What do they have to show for it?

Or don't. Watch mayhem unfold and deny that you should be ashamed to be human. Capitalist encouragement, empowerment, liberation, democracy, freedom, and diplomacy are a bunch of sounds that mean and have accomplished nothing. Obviously, the stupid are in denial and stupid is convenient.

Facts and questions

Mankind has evolved into something. But what?

We have evolved over millions of years from lizards to monkeys and then progressed in only a few thousand years from tribal cavemen to machine-riding, self-destructing parasites.

We know that there are various human blood types, including type O. This type can be a universal donor, and we don't exactly know why this is the case. We share about 90% of our DNA with monkeys, but we also share about 50%

of our DNA with bananas and the viscosity of our blood flows similarly to that of sheep. Therefore, something seems to have interfered to result in only one human blood type being capable of being a universal donor. Blaming aliens would refute Darwin's monkey theory. Maybe blood type O is just a mysterious coincidence, or maybe some religious rubbish can explain it away and save the day. Fact is though, we don't know.

Since the mutation from monkey to flying human leaves a lot of questions unanswered, alien interference seems like a valid option. But humans insist on denying alien involvement and even choose to cover up the possibility. We find comfort instead in insisting that monkeys are our great-grandparents.

Why do we continue to want to somehow confirm our origins through both science and religion?

Nietzsche branded science as the evil enemy of holy religion because science has no tolerance for faith. For me, religious faith is like expecting Santa to relieve global misery and then having nothing happen. Maybe Santa could do charity work instead of delivering presents. Believing in Santa is as plausible as believing in a prophet that spoke the words of his god and then disappeared to an angel-tended heaven after he was morbidly nailed to a cross.

Apparently, this prophet abandoned earth and its creatures to sit in heaven and do nothing but enjoy his presence there with his father. In the meantime, millions of religious people here on Earth believe and hope that some day that prophet will eventually get off his butt in heaven to save the abandoned and relieve global suffering on Judgment Day. And they believe that if you live an obedient life, you too can sit in the clouds and join in on doing nothing as well. Why are mentally advanced individuals expected to respect this?

Mental capacity recommends that humans can only save themselves from themselves with ideologies like this and that the Christian kind of faith is not a reasonable saviour for Mother Earth. Christianity is still the largest religion with about 2.6 billion followers. That means that about one-third of the world's population follows a mild form of insanity. When we pile a bunch of fake news on top of that, we may even approach a democratic majority to vote for insanity.

If there really was a divine source, why would it not present itself, or at least release some satisfying facts so that we could move on?

All religions have their own versions of the same concepts that were stolen, copied, and copied again. In summary, a prophet who was a moral teacher produced miracles, was executed or died, and then was resurrected to save us one day from the miseries that we had brought onto ourselves. Their disciples are then expected to hope for salvation to occur in the future. May all power rest in hope!

It does not seem to occur to that Christian one-third of the population that hope is a broad word for unpredictability, and that there is a fine line between what is possible and what is probable. Probability is a condition that predicts that something may happen with a higher degree of certainty than possibility does. So, for the interpretation of language, which one is worth hoping for? How about neither, as there is no factual evidence anywhere to justify religious hope for salvation. None! So why hope anyway? Because we can?

If there was a single religion that I would be willing to respect, it would be one that strives for harmony with nature and does so without gods. Taoism fits this description. The number of other varieties of religion is astonishing. There are hundreds of Christian denominations that are all very similar, but faithfully segregated and un-united.

The herd connects such opinions with politics, and some even become extremism. Mentally, this is not much different from becoming mild terrorists. Terrorists confront opposition by instigating fear, assault, and force, and they connect this opinion to a belief and a cause. For them, opinion morphs into fact. Whereas religions sheepishly won't use force until they are threatened. Their former crusades are now less violent, but they're still active. And to be accurate, both terrorism and faith connect their opinions to their beliefs. Therefore, are not both extremists? But no, religion claims that their extremism is holy. Is holy just another word for devoted?

Terrorists are devoted to their cause as well. Consequently, their actions could be considered holy as well. However, we could not just call terrorists devoted people. See what I mean? All people are devoted people; it does not matter what we label them.

Capitalism is also practised like a religion. The capitalist's devotion is believing faithfully in higher living standards. Still, these living standards don't include everyone. Consequently, they are extremists as well, and their use of the word "standard" should be replaced with "oppression." So, capitalism is oppression extremism. But it is not sold as such!

That humans had to evolve into something was inevitable, but that something does not necessarily represent better or best. Better is not capitalism, and best is not extremism.

Capitalist extremists also glorify fame, according to Nietzsche. His book, *The Will to Power*, elaborates on the human desire and will to strive for control and fame. However, fame does not necessarily represent mental capacity.

Nietzsche had a desire to become an overman. His statements called on us to become existential individuals that can breed genius, not sloth. His overman could only be realized with detailed personal self-improvement, and not with faith, money, or fame. He wanted us to unite as a high-mental-standard species from an individual point of view.

But, as a collective, humans mutated into familial, tribal, territorial, royal, political, religious, corporate, organizational, and even cult-like groups; groups that have always been segregated to themselves, by themselves, for their self-serving interests. And when threatened, they tended to resort to stricter isolation or even violent behaviour to protect their turf. As a result, segregation and isolation now exist by default. Both are not just opinions—they are actually inbred delusions. Eventually, all these social groups grew larger and claimed to be civilized. But they are all extremists! Most of them don't get along, and as our populations grow, it will only get worse. There is just more of the same unrest. Division, segregation, and opinionated stubbornness are not intelligent behaviours that a high-IQ species would engage in. Neither would they want to defend party extremism with a democratic majority voting system for fools.

Here we are, screaming, "Get along. Don't judge, discriminate, or isolate." But that is like asking fish to move on land. It won't work. Instead, we have to remember that fish thrive in water. It is the environment that sets the conditions, not us. And capitalism is our environment!

Another discriminatory concept is that family is always priority. Granted, family is important, but why is it always the most important? Why is protecting your own more important than protecting your neighbour? I get the privacy piece, and the natural drive to protect your own offspring so that they survive. But from a mature capacity perspective, choosing favourites should not be overemphasized. When we look at all the extremist business families out there, we will find nasty examples. They only seek their own growth and steal from each other. Me, me, me is quite civilized extremism indeed. And to govern, the same business families ask the ill-educated to elect puppet politicians as leaders. They fool us with these leaders. People don't see that the real decision making targets hide behind these puppet leaders.

To remove those targets we have to wipe out capitalism first! This is an attainable and simple fact. We only think that it seems impossible.

Are you content with what seems impossible?

Implement this: Neither faith nor hope offer any solutions to replace facts. Yes, one can pretend that delusions have value, but this is self-limiting. When delusions are not kept on a short leash, they turn into extremism.

Or don't. Continue to replace fact with whatever salvation makes you feel better. But consider this: why do you need to feel better in the first place?

Why are we here?

So far, my story might seem repetitive, but I've done this on purpose so that I could explain from various perspectives. Each perspective leads to the same outcome, and that is to acknowledge what we want to be as a species—and that being is to simply exist first.

There is no need to question why we are here or to sink further into an abyss of uncertainty to explain the meaning of life. The better question is more about how to justify life. Why do we always assume that someone owes us an explanation? We knew nothing before we were born, and there is nothing to know now. We always live in the present, and then we pass into the nothing of not knowing again at death. Literally all of it exists within nothing, so it is absurd to question one's being. We just are, and so it seems necessary. If it was not necessary, then it would not be happening, and that is enough. I am content with that simple proposition.

The quantum universe wants to exist, and because it observes itself, we exist recognizing ourselves.

Everything in the very present is connected, and life will always find a way by itself. It is time to enjoy and decide what we want to be as a species.

Implement this: Adopt the certainty that existence does not occur to employ delusions. Our history proves that we waste time instead of building a better time.

Or don't. Continue to believe in male fairy tales of origin and judgments because they are so inspiring—especially the one where high-capacity women were burned as witches. Truly inspiring. At the same time males believed in wizards and druids. How come they did not burn them?

Extinction

It is obvious that humans don't respect all other species on earth as equals because they harvest, exploit, and exterminate them. But humans underestimate that they are also an existential threat to themselves. Self-aware humans claim to be more entitled than any other species. And, as mentioned earlier, the males especially seem to believe that leadership manifests itself by means of slaughter and possession without limits. To them, planting misinformation and digging landfills are accomplishments. It's ironic that all other species on earth seem to have a collective understanding of how to share and maintain balance in their immediate environments. They have this fundamental intelligent quality by default. This must be super-intelligence to humans. Some humans—especially the religious kind—even profess that there are no other intelligent life-forms beyond earth.

The odds point towards absolute certainty that there is some other life-form out there, and that there are obviously more things going on than us little earthly humans are able to observe. NASA really stands for "Non-Available Space Aliens." But they are at least working on it.

Only ignorant humans can imagine that they are alone among infinite galaxies. How bizarre that we exist on this single planet, squeezed into a limited oxygen belt, and some can't seem to expand their shortsighted egos any further. Leading, silver-spoon educated capitalists most likely hide alien evidence from the slaving herd in plain sight. I mean, if they did not hide what they knew, then we would know. Plain and simple: some know! Ah, the great mystery. Let's produce hundreds of TV shows to keep the herd guessing in the dark.

The elite are borderline alien. They can overproduce debt to hoard even more, fly unidentifiable grey planes into buildings, evaporate steel into fine dust, collapse buildings onto themselves, and incur plane crashes with barely any debris. Surreal or alien?

"I saw this; therefore, I reject this," is what Descartes would have said.

If I was an alien, I would stay far enough away to not get noticed by humans. Why would aliens want to attend disaster management? Aliens may even exist among us and observe us unnoticed. They may be giving us room to experiment without interfering, until we blow ourselves into nuclear oblivion. I suppose they would most likely interfere then though, because it would affect them and the quantum environment.

The one thing we humans are good at is extracting and burying all our material simultaneously. Like sophisticated moles, we float along, at least until a meteor's trajectory precisely matches collision coordinates with earth. Then, out of nowhere, oops, the next selective biological extinction will begin. The concept of engaging in false capitalist transactions and religious delusions will be irrelevant then. The slaughter will have ended, and all that garbage will finally decompose. May all resources rest in peace.

After a few million years, earth's nature will have recovered, humans will be gone and forgotten, and there will be room again for something capable. Not a big deal. Get over yourselves, incompetents, and learn from the earth if you want to remain a passenger.

Implement this: Don't just watch. Clean up and rebuild the planet.

Or don't. Remain addicted and keep sleeping. Everything will get better by itself. You won't be disturbed.

The abuse of animals and nature

A species can only develop its full potential when it can control disease and predators. We as humans are no exception. Besides our greed, we have no predators, and the diseases that we experience are a consequence of our own lifestyles. We treat all other living creatures as totally disposable and think that we can decide their fates however we want.

I declare that animals should not be used for testing, nor should they be slaughtered in excess for food and harvested from.

Yes, animals eat each other, but the cycle of evolution demands this to keep harmony among all species. Humans are now at the top of the food chain and they breed and eat whatever they want while they simultaneously starve their own kind. So where is the harmony at the very top of the food chain?

Wonderful forces are at play when Mother Nature evolves. But our species, with the little biological knowledge we have accumulated, already assumes that we can mess with those forces. Recent developments in microbiology have brought us much closer to understanding the DNA of nature. Some say that it is unethical to mess with the building blocks of life. However, exploring DNA science has its applications, and the ethics depend on what it would be used for. If we clone better seeds so that we can grow better produce, grains, and synthetic protein, then what's wrong with that?

Still, we have to be very careful when we experiment with living cells and viruses. We may assume that we know what we are messing with, yet COVID-19 did happen (or it was deliberately planted by the sinister). Common sense recommends that we set limits, but how do we limit what we don't adequately understand? Are potential gains worth risking our potential demise? If disease is to be our end, I am sure that the remaining life will find a way to bounce back. Planet Earth will recover and the rest of the universe will not care. But until then, we can care.

Implement this: Respect and protect all creatures. Eliminate disease with the principle, you are what you eat and drink. Yes, planning better nutrition requires willpower at first, but consider that if it was all you had ever known, then you would not mind at all.

Or don't. Snack on and consume garbage that can stay on a shelf for months because it's convenient. Suck back sugar and cheap carbs and develop diabetes, then blame it on genetics and burden the health care system. It's definitely not your own fault.

How much do we need?

I mentioned earlier that I travelled and lived for years out of a bag. This time in my life taught me that the less I have, the more I am. Life is very uncomplicated when everything is in one bag. When I accumulated extra clothes and gifts, I sea mailed a box to myself. The buddies I travelled with did the same. We all loved cheap and tasty street food, and we hardly ever got sick. When it was raining, we read and wrote more, and when it was nice, we explored. We had no careers and truly enjoyed life. We saw people making a living with a single soup stand, and they were happy. When you spend time in G175 countries, you discover what street food and small business is all about. The food is delicious, the goods and garments are high quality, and man is it fun to get around!

After about ten years, I thought to myself that I could not live like this forever. On second thought now, this might have been a mistake. Why couldn't I live like this all the time? Regardless, I have no regrets. I was longing to raise a family, so I met a nice girl and together we raised one in Canada.

Then things started to pile up, and freedom without responsibilities became a memory of the past. Shopping became a consistent activity because capitalist families consume from shelves. Through this, I became more aware that large department stores and malls are truly a cancer to humanity and culture when I compared them to my previous frugal travels. The capitalist consumer has so many choices at every price level, while in some parts of the world I could not even find fresh drinking water or a clean glass of milk. I am experienced in living in both of these drastically different environments for extended periods of time, and I despise that the capitalist herd still bleats "survival of the fittest" and worry about the millions it will cost them to retire.

Most people in the third world don't have these problems. They survive, are hungry for many comforts, and don't get that old. Sometimes they have even less than a bag's worth of possessions, and when they have a serious health issue, they die somewhere.

So, let's recap. Who has a better life? Me, the former traveller, or a wealthy stockbroker? There is not much of a difference besides the volume of and the price tags on our individual goods. We both exist and we both try to make ends meet. Both of us are being manipulated by minorities that we don't even know. Yet, I did not comply back then, while the broker always complies, trades, and hoards so that he can retire early.

I was squeezed into capitalist compliance due to raising a family. I understand how we all get there. Still, I remain frugal and make time to write about a better future than this. I want to retire our species from capitalism.

Chapter 9:

Mental Capacity Chess

Let's use the game of chess metaphorically again, and this time, we will use its strategy to navigate through life. Our lives and how society should adjust are like a game—a consciousness game. As the game unfolds, we have to make adjustments. We understand the game as a whole entity, and the purpose is to not out-position ourselves. If we lose, we can think that our playing partner has mated us, but really it was up to us to avoid the traps that resulted in loss. So, in essence, we always play ourselves. We evolve our mental game as a species by recognizing the traps that we create for ourselves.

There are no consequences if we lose a game of chess. We can just play another game. But as a species, we can't just move on to another game. We have to make adjustments to at least save a draw. Losing is not an option!

The opening game is rooted in philosophy

When we look at a chessboard, we see that all the pieces are lined up. The objective is to control the centre of the board and develop our pieces. Our first moves build a coherent, strong base to develop a strategy. So, let's begin with David Hume waking up Immanuel Kant with his empirical philosophy.

Hume based his principles on empirical thought, which involves drawing conclusions from experience. Kant woke up from his previous, famous "association slumber" to a new thought process. He explained that thought experience is not necessary to conclude that we empirically exist, meaning that one can experience consciousness and become aware without relating it to any thought whatsoever! So, when does one begin to reason, and how?

Kant's *Critique of Pure Reason* is exactly what the title says it is. It was written to seek truths and to limit confusion. This is precisely what society needs, and even more importantly, as far as I understand Kant, it expanded on his fundamental question, what is the thing that thinks in itself? In other words, what source becomes aware of itself and exists in itself regardless of eventual thought experiences or even reasoning? What is this "eternal priori" that exists without an explainable cause? And, how do we perceive all phenomena from the thing-in-itself? Is it actually more of a feeling, and not a thought at all, like a thoughtless source? Further, are objects things-in-themselves? We perceive and identify objects with our thoughts. Thoughts exist; therefore, things exist, and even without thought, things continue to exist. We think that we are separated from things. But what if we are not?

It is obvious that we perceive phenomena within the pace of observable time. We think that when we cease to perceive and observe, we also cease to exist. But what causes that observable perception in the first place? We could then ask in theory, would things continue to exist if they were not observed by all creatures and matter collectively? If time stood still, we would simply perceive a single frame of consciousness in time, like a single frame in a movie, which is actually an instant moment of a previous now. Therefore, each individual frame would be the exact divider between the past and the future. But how many frames are actually available at each now moment? Would these frames be infinitely divisible?

Science seems to agree that time is a condition of space, or vice versa (spacetime). For now, let's agree that without observable time, we would not be able to recall what was observed within this space dimension. However, does time cause us to observe, or does observing make us perceive time? I think the latter. Either way, we can label time as a dimensional format of perception that passes at a specific and consistent pace on earth.

Prior to Kant, Aristotle hinted in *De Anima* that there was something he labelled as "a this," as in a presence. It may be possible that Kant picked up a seed from Aristotle. Still, both Aristotle and Kant clearly confirm a "this" and a "thing-in-itself" as absolute, meaning entities that cannot be defined but seem necessary without an explainable cause and reveal themselves as perception. They both clearly isolate a presence, but that presence is not time. It is consciousness in itself that we perceive at the pace of time. Think about it: if that presence was only time in itself, then time would have to be conscious. That would mean that time could think.

However, we could still be conscious as infinity without a concept of time. The standard physics model suggests that time and consciousness are dual entities, but what if they are not?

The fact that it appears to be necessary for us to experience perception as this entity (a this) provides sufficient reason for Kant to separate and isolate "being" from "becoming." He means that being requires no reason to exist whatsoever, whereas becoming is only a consequence of being.

Moving forward, we can now argue how to interpret these facts, and if there is a cause for being or not. It simply remains a valid fact that we are indeed a presence.

Considering what "a this" actually is or could be can help explain how our delusional religious faith systems developed. Since our mysterious being source cannot be explained, it becomes an option to invent that god(s) caused "a this" or "the thing-in-itself". Gods, by the way, cannot be proven either. They are just a collection of imaginations that people combined to form the core of religions and then mixed with arrogant imperialism, leading our species to historical confusions like war, segregation, and discrimination.

However, let's rationally narrow things down to the bare minimum: all these imaginations are nothing but thoughts. Confused thoughts, like the made-up rules of a chess game. We can ignore these rules moving forward in the game of life. It would be easy, and we could just stop playing according to these rules. But we can't just step out of life's expectations. Instead, we are numb from this ongoing noise and unrest about which delusions are best and which ones are to be rejected, accepted, or even followed. These delusions become our widely accepted beliefs. I write this in the present tense because this is all still the case today. It seems that the longer we delay deluded nonsense, the more likely we are to believe it.

Extended exposure to delusions will progress from the absurd into the bizarre. When it doesn't matter that something is strange and we just blindly accept it anyway, we can't rationally believe that our self-awareness still serves us. Therefore, it is still important today that we learn to recognize that understanding the difference between being and becoming can provide us with actual answers for how we should proceed as a civilization. Kant taught us to understand this, but we are still not ready to receive him today!

So, these are the rules for a plain beginning that opens up into potential and range.

Strategy, expanding on initial positions

Now we have to come up with a strategy, and this means that we have to isolate the pieces that are important to implement a coherent system that can both attack and defend. All the pieces are important, but only one can completely transform into another piece, and this is the pawn. It is the least valued of all pieces at first sight, but it can advance, shield, protect, and recapture. It is most effective when it is connected to other pawns. The pawn's most underestimated quality is that it can turn into a queen when it reaches the opponent's baseline on the other side of the board. No other piece has that ability. The pawn is you, and it means transcendence in the game.

Transcendence from the thing-in-itself is what Immanuel Kant made us more aware of. And post Kant, many philosophers have argued whether the thing-in-itself can be explained.

Still, there may be no point in explaining something that would actually have to explain itself. Time could be spent more productively in moving on and elaborating what could be possible from the thing-in-itself and seeking its potential (the transcendence). The thing-in-itself is a beginning, somewhere, and Kant's point was that there is something that does indeed exist, regardless of whether an explanation can be established or not. But what is that we want to become? This is the strategy we have to have in mind. Life does not happen to us; we project it.

Consider the opponent and all the pieces

We also have to look at the positions of our opponent's pieces. What are we facing? This is where all the questioning begins to occur and where we cannot forget the basics. We can now progress to considering the implications of the question, what are others projecting that we perceive simultaneously? And, how do we all deal with an infinite that can also mean "simultaneous" instead of an always, endless, or larger than the greatest?

Again, this (literally) begs the question, what is time? Also, what if there is no such thing as time in itself? Meaning, if we project our future simultaneously, then we only recognize perception as time. Since infinity must be aware of itself (because that must be a condition of infinity), then infinity in itself can only be consciousness because this is the only medium we can experience as existing. And if infinity deems it necessary to project itself into a format that is observable perception (awareness), then it must be necessary. Consequently, the principle of necessity, as in indispensability, would then also suggest that it would be absurd to ask why this is happening, because without our awareness, we could not ask that question at all. We are simply experiencing necessity (infinity). So, out of the depth of infinity as it relates to our species, why would we find imperialist capitalism necessary? Capitalism is our opponent.

Spooky

If we remember that Einstein finally admitted that there is such a thing as "spooky action at a distance" among particles, we must investigate what he meant. By "spooky," he actually meant instantaneous, which is also simultaneous from a non-dualistic perspective. So, if particles can communicate instantaneously and we can observe this in a research environment, then we must assume that linear time, at the very precise moment of spooky action at a distance, does not exist and is not measurable or relevant. Therefore, we can also confirm that we both exist within and without time as a duality, because we can observe the instantaneous coming and passing of time simultaneously. Otherwise, "spooky" could not be realized.

Following this, the non-duality of duality would be infinity. Therefore, we are infinite or eternal (as in being), and we experience this as conscious perception in a linear format (as in becoming), which we project ourselves, simultaneously, as a spooky action at a distance.

Further, remember that this perception does not require thought at all. Thoughts are only mental adaptations to the environment that consciousness projects and finds itself in. Thoughts can only develop as a consequence of previous thoughts, which begs the question, where and when can an original, very first thought be found?

The answer is when consciousness becomes aware of itself and perceives itself as a thought within an environment (bodies, creatures, objects, dimensions). Then everything else progresses from there. So "spooky" is an important piece in the game. Why would our projected causality result in imperialist hoarding?

The mystery of gravity

Since time is only somewhat of a linear format (as in pace) of our projected perception, I conclude that gravity must be a force format of perception as well. For example, if there was no time, like in spooky action at a distance, could we observe gravity? Most likely not, because instantaneous could not imply force as there is no space-time for force to be experienced. Would you agree that using the term "format" is far more descriptive than "time" is? As mentioned, the concept of time does not exist. We experience perception at a dimensional pace format.

To describe this is difficult, and it is an example of how language presents a challenge. Science cannot physically explain gravity completely, and intellectually we cannot describe it with language. We can feel its force within the format that we call time, and that unfolds in perceivable space. But where is the mind-gravity connection? If feelings and thoughts were subject to gravity, how much would they weigh? This brings us to the mind-body connection, and since we can't explain this piece in the game either, then why would we just explain that away with religion?

Visible space

Since I hinted that gravity can only be observed as a force within the format called time, then observable space containing infinite galaxies and nebulae would not exist without the format of time either. Neither would there be measurable light speed, and consequently our universe would not be visible. Therefore, a Big Bang theory adds up to some degree.

The standard model suggests that suddenly, something became visible. It also suggests that light speed only applies to the physical, observable matter in space, which, according to current science, only represents 4% of the activity in our cosmic energy model. The other 96% is dark matter and dark energy, which seems to provide the energy canvas for the observable 4% to unfold on. Therefore, the unobservable 96% must include immaterial space such as the metaphysical (consciousness), which is an energy force as well. And this unobservable format, independent from the time format, provides what has been measured as spooky action at all distances. This is instantaneous consciousness, and it would then also conclude that space is consciousness, and that this is why space looks infinite when we look at it. Otherwise, what would infinity look like? Is this piece in the game convincing enough in theory?

Given all of this, I believe that what we experience is mind over matter, and not matter over mind. But we let matter control our minds by wanting to hoard and own matter (as in things).

Eternal

It is now clear that the physical (material) cannot exist outside the format of time because it cannot manifest itself or be experienced. We must also accept that the metaphysical (consciousness) can simultaneously exist both within and without time because we observed and measured spooky action at a distance, as in instantaneous and simultaneous action. This suggests that consciousness must also be eternal as an always now, and that consciousness is that eternal essence of being. Eternal being is without a self, without a body, and present in all matter as a force. This force is simply energy. So why would eternal beings become so obsessed with finite things, such as temporary control over others and hoarding objects?

The Tibetans and the book *Mahamudra* help explain what I am trying to say, but from another perspective. They say that what philosophy and science try to explain to no end can actually be experienced when silencing our mental activity during meditation. There is the thing-in-itself within you. You can feel its bliss, and regardless of infinite potential thoughts, there remains a gap in between every single thought. In that gap, everything dissolves, including time, but one is still aware and present in effortless concentration.

This is what freedom is to me. Effortless presence without thoughts.

Psychologists recognize a subconscious and consciousness. I suggest that their subconscious is actually consciousness, and that their consciousness is awareness. The psychological subconscious primarily regulates body senses and functions and processes previous empirical experiences. I call that consciousness. For example, we are not aware of our organs functioning, but they do. Consciousness also records everything because its source is infinite. However, consciousness retreats and presents itself as awareness. Consciousness is still there. We're just not aware of it as the source. We are occupied with our awareness which is just the recall of what consciousness already projected and reveals as residue. So, a rather important piece in the game. If we project our residue, why can't we project a mental capacity species?

Combining options and putting it all together as a rationalist

We now know more—we understand our position and some key pieces in the game, and we have the upcoming end-game in mind already. We need a plan to finish well.

Reading Parmenides, Spinoza, and Leibniz, one could say that they are rationalists. They can explain theories by method of ideas and reasons. Compared to empiricists, who explain from experience, rationalists raise the bar of imagination. They suggest levels of clarity that are based on reason and assumptions. Monism is just such a rationalist theory which suggests that everything originates from one substance (the Greek *monos*, as in stand-alone). However, this is still a dual perspective because one is more than zero, and therefore has a cause. In my view, Monism does not explain zero as a non-dual capacity prior to one. But maybe they meant that zero was actually the one stand-alone substance. If that was the case, they should have called it zero. Do you follow?

Besides zero, there are many other thought processes that philosophy makes us aware of. Parmenides claims that the universe has one unifying substance, though he can't name it. Spinoza developed ethics built on geometry. It is a systematic construction of the universe, but highly metaphysical and not physical. Not metaphysical in the sense of a God, but in an infinite source (substance). He asks why we would expect that God would love us just because we love God, just as it would be absurd to expect that nature loves us back just because we love nature. Now, if I understand Leibniz correctly, then his rationalism includes an interesting thought process. It parallels with Tibetan Buddhism in the Mahamudra tradition and asks, how is it necessary to identify anything if we can't hold onto anything ever? And, why do we need an explanation since it is all happening anyway?

I mention these questions because Leibniz expands on necessity to the point where he says that eventually, there needs to be no reason to explain necessity any further, just as the tiniest particle will eventually not be able to be divided anymore. Therefore, is necessity finite? If necessity is not finite, then it would be infinite, and if that was the case, then particles would be infinitely divisible by necessity. Right? This would beg two questions: Where does matter end? And where does the metaphysical begin?

Still, both the physical and the metaphysical appear to be necessary because we can experience both simultaneously while we exist. They co -exist with each other. But can the metaphysical continue to exist after the time format expires from being perceived with the body and can it continue to exist without a time format (infinite) as an eternal force? We know that our physical bodies decompose into other forms of matter when observed within the format of time. Would it be necessary for the metaphysical to separate from the expired matter? And would it prevail as eternal, or simply remain within the soup of expired matter as it changes form and progresses in the time format? I think that it won't matter, because if there is no perceivable format of time, then there would be nothing to decompose because nothing ever existed. It was only projected and is already gone.

Based on the logical assertion that the necessity of the mind-body perception appears to be a constant, and that this particular necessity is an occurrence within the phenomenon we call time (format of perception) that occurs in sequences of connected individual moments, we would have to ask again: How many moments in time are there? Are there infinite moments, or are there a finite number? This then poses the possibility that time can be both finite in a present instant, but also infinitely filled with moments within that present instant. Do you follow?

So, do we experience eternity in a single instant but miss it because perception is linear?

We experience perception as a continuum, and can't seem to be able to stop or grasp it, and we can't go backwards or forwards from any given now-moment. In other words, assuming we could break down time into individual moments that are never finite, we would have to begin pulling an Einstein here and imagine close to an infinitesimal moment of time. What would that be like? It would appear that time would have stopped! Now, imagine how that infinitesimal moment of time relates to the constant of maximum light speed, which is about 300,000 kilometres per second. In infinitely small moments, we would not see any light at all, because infinite moments would be too small for light to even appear. Light speed would basically be standing still compared to infinity. Yes, way too slow.

So, we've defined infinite moments of time as stopped (constant) darkness. But it still exists in itself as the source of everything, because it simply is. No wonder even the Bible says, "Let there be light, and there was light." Therefore, in infinite moments of time, and in constant darkness, there it must be where we find dark matter and dark energy, which form the underlying substrate energy canvas that makes our perception eventually possible within the parameters of the speed of light. This underlying substrate must be consciousness by mere necessity, so that it can project and perceive an event horizon. Regardless of whether my theory is scientific or not, language is the gift to allow me to ask these questions, prior to even attempting to prove anything. This is how abstract this end game can get. But we don't think this way. We hoard money!

Further, does the metaphysical separate from the observable 4% and remain as a partial in the unobservable (also called the Akashic, or all enclosing) 96% of the universe? If it does, then the metaphysical can explain karma, reincarnation, recognition of previous lives, and so on. This means the metaphysical can change form, and it could project itself into another body or object. That would conclude that this would still be a duality universe of division between the metaphysical and physical within the format of time. We recognize this as our standard model. However, in essence, both body and consciousness are one and the same in infinity without time.

A non-dual universe would not distinguish between observable universe (matter), dark matter, and dark energy (metaphysical). Karma, reincarnation, nirvana, and all other phenomena would be instantaneous, simultaneous, and infinite. Even duality and non-duality would coexist as one. To conclude, the absolute is consciousness in itself! You can call it God if you like.

My apologies if the previous section was hard to follow. Maybe read it again.

Now, let's digress to the previously mentioned perspective of necessity. Our standard view assumes that the metaphysical separates from the body, and we call this separation soul or spirit. What happens to the soul or spirit if there is a dimensional entity possible after physical death? In my view, there is no soul or spirit, because I anticipate that this entity is consciousness and that it could also exist in dimensional absolutes where there is no time. Consequently, consciousness could still cognize (not recognize) itself as a body in a universe without time. Now this is just an assumption on my part, but we have to begin to understand infinity as infinitely dimensional, and infinity by necessity would have never had a beginning. Therefore, necessity is infinity and vice versa, otherwise it would not occur.

Also, if time is a finite format of consciousness that flows constantly, why does it move at the pace we experience it? Physics tells us that our pace is because of our revolving solar system and the galaxy we find ourselves in. But the big picture still requires that everything be balanced for our solar system and the Milky Way for them to exist as they do. So, this balance can be viewed as a condition, like stillness. Maybe this is why the Taoists say that there is stillness in movement, and movement is stillness. Without that balance in our Milky Way, everything would fly apart. So, how is this balance found? Does balance eventually occur, or is it a priori constant in the universe that makes everything possible? What is holding everything together and providing equilibrium for energy to form into matter? It seems to me that without balance, there can be no order. And whenever we measure something within our pace of time, we discover balance-related constants such as gravity and light speed. We can measure these constants in the laws of our standard physics model, but what we measure in quantum physics is random. There we know that all particles will never be at the same spot in the universe again. What we observe is never specific.

According to Heisenberg's uncertainty principle, the subatomic world becomes unpredictable. There is this infinite process of constant randomness that somehow relates to constants, and the subatomic eventually emerges as a coherent form in visible perception. So how does this randomness in subatomic space transform into organized and balanced matter? What is the organizing source? It seems that finding balance is the most important of all, and I think that consciousness is what provides that balance.

Also, we can assume that the 4% of visible universe must be below the speed of light value because if visible perception was above that speed, then we would be faster than light and light would not be visible anymore. Consequently, everything would be completely dark above light speed. But is it?

The other 96% (dark matter and dark energy) that is above the speed of light or below absolute zero speed should be invisible. In other words, light seems not only the medium but also the balance for perception to occur at our pace. So, is it actually light that we experience, or is it time? In addition, because at absolute zero speed nothing would be visible, we would indeed need a "Big Bang" for anything to appear.

Here is a teaser: imagine below absolute zero speed! A dimension before absolute stillness or any light speed even starts. As mentioned before, light would not be visible at absolute zero speed. But could it progress below zero speed, as in with negative speed or in another dimension? Would we then experience time reversal?

If we think outside of our human box and enter these micro-dimensions, a second seems like an eternity.

So, we can assume that if light stood still at absolute zero speed, then the light wave function would collapse. But does that mean that the photon would cease to exist, or would it just change form? In my view, the photon would only cease to be visible, but it would not cease to exist. It would change dimensions!

Again, God in the Bible says, "Let there be light, and there was light" which is the same as the Big Bang. But if the Bible acknowledges light, then it could also refer to its source. But there is no mention of the source. And how could the people that wrote the Bible have possibly known that light (or the modern Big Bang) had to be the very first source for life to evolve and to be observable in the 4% of observable cosmos? Back then they could barely even write, and yet, they basically wrote, "Let there be a Big Bang." So, who told them? Let's also mention that the Bible says, "the earth was formless and empty, darkness was over the surface and the deep, and the Spirit of God was hovering over the waters". But the Big Bang would have happened prior to an earth even forming. And if the Bible meant that the light was the sun, then that would not make any sense either because the sun is much older than the earth. In addition, that the Spirit of God was hovering over waters would mean that those waters would have had to be ice without the presence of sunlight. So the Biblical light source is very obscure, but is still present from the very beginning. However, the statements of "the formless and empty, and the darkness over the surface and the deep" are interesting, and they could mean quantum dark matter, dark energy, and consciousness. Why would the Bible even begin like this unless there was some valid information already present to make these statements?

I believe that we can find the mind-body correlation in the quantum environment. Since we can measure that the speed of light is a constant, we have to respect the word "constant" as being relative, meaning that if light can't go faster than 300,000 km/sec, it could most likely also not go slower than absolute zero. Meaning that it is limited by its own measurable limits. Therefore, visible perception could not perceive itself beyond that speed or without any speed. This would then suggest that there would have to be at least two kinds of existence (dual): that in the visible (within light speed limits) and in the invisible (beyond and below light speed limits) ranges. But, as a whole, both are existing in the non-dual dimension we call infinity, which we experience as consciousness.

Again, I propose that time is actually perception within the parameters of light speed. Therefore, physical matter must dissolve into the metaphysical at the beyond and below parameter thresholds of light speed.

Now also consider that atoms stop moving at about minus 272 degrees Celsius. Consciousness cannot be physical because it feels independent of temperature to us. In other words, living matter, such as the brain, cannot produce consciousness, even though the brain experiences it. Think about it: our awareness of our hot bodies sweating during a workout does not cause our consciousness itself to heat up. It feels the same as when we freeze.

In conclusion, what I propose may be a reach, but can you see it? Think about it.

My abstract formulas and summary look like this:

> Consciousness is represented by absolute zero in the ever-present now. There is no value below and no value above, yet it still represents a value of necessity that simply is.
>
> Therefore, absolute zero = $-(E = MC^2)$, which is consciousness.
>
> Below absolute zero is anti-matter (so we assume), and above absolute zero is $E = MC^2$, as in perceivable matter.
>
> Anti-matter mirrors matter = non-dual projected infinity (which is perception). But, consciousness as in absolute zero is also situated in between anti-matter and perceivable matter. Also, gravity becomes obsolete at absolute zero because there is no perceivable moving matter that can cause it.

Another interesting fact is that my source of thoughtless consciousness feels the same at six years old as it does at sixty years old. $E = MC^2$ is relativity, which is perceivable energy, but the observable body is aging and does not feel the same at six and sixty years old. All of my cells have been replaced with new cells again and again since conception. I learned how to skate a long time ago, and despite all my cells having been replaced numerous times over, my body still knows how to skate at age sixty. How does that work? Therefore, my invisible consciousness is not subject to $E = MC^2$.

However, the specialists explain this away by saying that mental memory has trained physical muscle memory. But since all the cells have been replaced, that incomplete assumption is not enough to explain this. They don't know!

From a rationalist perspective, there is a lot we don't know. But we still have to continue playing the game.

The end of the middle game

After all this, we are at the end of the middle game. We have to deal with all the potential we have from our position to line up a capacity end game. So, tell me, is it reasonable to ask why we bother to sustain our current caveman style as a species? As mentioned, our options are numerous—especially from a non-dual infinite perspective. We still argue about male-invented tribal imperialism, opinions, racism, religion, education, qualifications, and personal pride.

I explained mental capacity and what we could be as beings—something somewhat alien compared to our current human behaviour. The serenity and kind essence springing from silent and infinite consciousness allows us to recognize that we have this precious gift of self-awareness. But what are we doing with it? We can do much better than primitively submitting to greed. Instead, we can use this gift to practise decency and tame our delusions. All that noise eventually fades away at death. Delusions are imaginations of weak minds that never live in the ever-present now.

The end of the middle game means that we come upon the never-ending mental cause-and-effect process. We arrive in situation after situation, influenced by individual thought moments, yet we will always exist and live in the now that requires no thought at all. We know this, but we barely even notice it. We dwell on becoming, subject to our delusions, wrapped up in getting new things, and then spend the rest of our lives fixing them. We suffocate in evaluating others' opinions and ramble phrases such as, "It is what it is," without realizing what "it" actually means. The actual "it" is to exist, and it is unfinished.

The endgame—implementing the unfinished

The endgame is the hardest to finish well because the board is wide open, most of the pieces having been exchanged off the board. But, there may still be an insignificant pawn that we can advance all the way and convert into a queen. We may have forgotten about that pawn in the middle game, but there it is.

Be that pawn and become that queen. This is transcendence from the ordinary into the extraordinary.

In summary, we established that we may not fully realize what we are because we have become lost in the game of what everybody else is. We claim to be intelligent and use words such as "consciousness" and "gravity," but we still can't explain what they actually are. We are a life format in the process of experiencing self-observing infinity—and what are we doing with that gift? At this point, our species behaves like parasites invading a host. So, let's ask a few key questions.

What is our end goal in the end game? Is it high demand economies with finite resources? Logic clearly suggests that this is unsustainable. We need new rules! Bill Maher, the comedian and social critic, loves new rules. So, what should these new rules look like?

We will become something next. What will that something be? Historically, we have been tangled up in male-invented imperialist beliefs and religions. Their power trip delusions still override facts and breed herd compliance. They label their outdated dogmas as absolute, they preach fear with gods, and they call pride patriotic. These are the fantasies and residue of primitive tribal thought, like the smoke stains in a caveman's cave. In contrast, something as ancient as Tibetan culture, and respect for a book like the *Mahamudra* will help anyone understand how meticulous mental refinement actually is in practice. That there is an advanced process available for us to discontinue acting like beasts. That there is a need to meet ourselves first before we can ever become something else, for someone else. Not only as a private mental idealism, but also as an opportunity to physically practise this daily.

Indo-Asian wisdom already suggests that self-reflection includes sitting in complete silence. During the practice of meditation, one can experience that there is just being in the moment (not becoming). In this silence, one tries not to control the mind, because control is a thought as well. The very now feels effortless, weightless, and eternal. This is your true nature, prior to and beyond your mind. It is infinity experienced at the profound level of being in itself. The "clear-clear" is an expression for insight-presence, as the Tibetans call it. An expression to describe non-duality. And thoughts are recognized as dualities because every thought depends on something else. Yet, thoughts are nothing in themselves. And that includes imperialist capitalist thought! Recognize this, and conclude your endgame by finding your genius.

Eventually, you will realize how absurd it all is. To sit is quite simple, but it is complicated when one never does it.

Implement this: The endgame is to finally see the big picture from an existentialist perspective. Only we ourselves can finish the game. You can retreat from these man-made problems. You are a pawn that can become a queen.

Or don't. Don't bother because to sit still is boring. Mental slavery is more entertaining. And yes, what I suggest may all come across as nonsense. If it is nonsense, and life just happens to you, then you don't have to worry; you will simply expire forever. But may I suggest that you could also be a format of eternal. So, which one are you? It's either one or the other. Decide.

Chapter 10:

Quantum Physics

The leap to connect quantum physics with meditation

Science has become quite skilled with technologies that reveal the mysteries of the quantum universe. For those that don't know much about this, here are some of the key highlights. The standard physics model teaches that there are particles with mass and that there are particles without mass. Both kinds of particles can be observed, but the ones without mass are of higher interest because they can be multidimensional. Photons have no mass.

We know that photons do not interact with each other. They only interact with charged magnetic particles in apparently empty space. This empty space is the canvas for what we observe becomes observable. We call the invisible background of empty space "dark matter" and the space expansion "dark energy." In other words, empty space is not empty at all and it is expanding.

The Large Hadron Collider (LHC) at CERN specializes in nuclear physics that researches the smallest of the small. It breaks single atoms into particles and measures their behaviour on a quantum scale.

So, dark matter is present, recognized by quantum physicists, and is holding the observable universe together. And dark energy is the expansion of the universe that we can measure by analyzing the continued acceleration of distant galaxies that originated from the Big Bang. As a result, dark matter and dark energy are the necessary mediums to perceive observable light and matter.

What we label as perception is awareness, which springs from consciousness, that has no mass. The light that we observe appears to be an electromagnetic wave function that we believe to perceive with conscious awareness. But what if consciousness makes this electromagnetic function of observing occur for us to perceive? What if our conventional model is actually completely reversed in the observable present? What if we all collectively project this occurring reality as a constant to be observed?

We think that reality is a constant that happens to us. However, quantum physics suggests that a universe observing itself would need to be conscious. Therefore, it would make sense for it to create what it observes. When I test this, it seems clear to me that my awareness controls my body, rather than my body controlling my awareness. Further, physics explains that energy never ceases to exist and that it only changes form. We can then dig even deeper and assume that if consciousness is energy, it would also not cease to exist but only change form. The same is the case with light, and we need light to perceive visible matter. There are some theories that we are light beings, and near-death experiences also report visions of light. Light can be both radiation wave and particle (photon), representing a quantum of light, but photons have no mass. So here is a phenomenon that can be both particle and wave, without mass. This is very peculiar, and just like how consciousness is something that we experience but that we can't see.

I have an abstract theory that these photons react to oscillations that have already been projected by our consciousness. These oscillations are energy waves. As we know, photons can be both wave and particle, therefore, when the photon wave collides with an oscillating consciousness wave, it becomes a particle and reveals itself as matter. Thus, consciousness itself could be a combination of oscillating energy and photons that make the photon waves collapse into particles, and then manifest as matter because they are being observed. And, all these processes happen instantaneously and simultaneously (not one after the other, as in sequential time). This could be one way of explaining how a universe could be self-observing.

Consciousness could also coexist on simultaneous, infinite dimensional oscillation levels, which would explain entanglement and multiverses. This would also suggest that light is aware of itself. If that was not the case, then light and consciousness would have to be separate entities. However, this seems impossible because both are necessary fundamentals for a perceivable and observable universe that can be observed as a coordinated one. Without light, we would only perceive sound, touch, smell, and taste. Therefore, light and consciousness cannot be independent from each other because we have continuous visual coherence without errors. Meaning, an error would be like a glitch in reality, like in the movie *The Matrix*. But glitches do not occur. There are none until we pass out or fall asleep.

We recognize that Heisenberg's uncertainty principle explains that particles are a collection of possibilities, and the uncertainty is that we can never predict where each individual particle will be next in space at any given time. In other words, there are all these infinite possibilities, but somehow, all these particles remain coherent in the present as perception. Even infinity would have to be coherent somehow to be experienced as matter. It is like we experience slices of infinity at every individual moment simultaneously within a coherent now. And this is experienced by all creatures and matter, synchronized as one. Therefore, it seems possible that the medium for perception to occur is consciousness oscillating matter (by waves and particles) into beings and matter.

Yes, I get it, the standard model still seems more plausible. As a reminder, the standard model is that we are just organic brain matter that causes consciousness so that we can experience what happens to us out of nowhere. That we just fall into existence, and our brains learn to adapt until we expire. But why would the universe deem this as a necessity? In light of the potential that infinity offers, to simply exist, expire as a necessity, and keep it all going would be such a waste. So, highly unlikely! Therefore, it seems obvious to challenge the standard model and to expand, at least in theory. Quantum physics gives us that opportunity and so does meditation.

From the perspective of consciousness as an infinite being, it is absolutely possible that an entity of "I" (as an abstract of consciousness) projected to become a body and that this "I" may have even chosen its body. The "I" may also have chosen the life it currently perceives. This possibility could explain reincarnation.

Maybe this is all a bit much to imagine, but why not try? At some point, we have to be prepared to move away from the current standard models. I conclude that quantum events are consciousness in itself, which reveals how particles and forces interact at the perceivable pace of time because it observes itself. And self-observation makes perception possible to occur as experience.

Mass consisting of quanta (quantity of energy) is observable, measurable matter. And yes, we can accept the Big Bang, evolution, and that everything that we can touch and see, including our bodies, was produced from something else. But how can the mass-less medium of consciousness interact with what we can touch and see?

I think that consciousness does not interact with matter; rather, it produces matter, and it exists even without linear time observation.

Did that warp your noodle? It should, because consciousness deserves our absolute scrutiny, unlike capitalism. Consciousness is the all-connecting medium that we do not know at all, but still feel. And matter is what we claim to know, but cannot feel. The only matter we can feel is our bodies.

The other mystery is gravity. As mentioned previously, it seems to me that gravity is not only an effect of what space dimensional motion and curvature has on bodies, but also vibration electromagnetism (oscillation), which is a force that makes observation and matter coherent. In other words, the universe always seeks equilibrium (balance) by default, and if gravity (balance) did not exist, then everything would fly apart in an observable universe. Just like a galaxy has a black hole in the centre of it and dark matter surrounding it to keep it all together. There is an all-coherent balance present.

Anyway, observation is what we can measure, so let's remain there for now.

Science is progressing with the experiments of the LHC at CERN, and scientists such as Hameroff, Penrose, and Witten are thinking about the practical applications of these experiments. They are helping mainstream society understand more about what we don't even assume to imagine. Again, how small is small precisely? Their reports present evidence that quantum physics and mental processes are also entangled. Entanglement, string theory, and oscillations are now the leading suggestions in theoretical physics on how the physical universe reveals itself. Previously, we accepted the standard physical model of a body being conscious, because we could not have imagined any better without quantum physics. The sciences used to concede that the universe evolved according to their theories and consciousness from the brain. Today, quantum physics suggests that we are projecting our own reality because the universe observes itself. Should we then not observe ourselves more often?

We can now imagine that consciousness chooses to reveal itself in physical entities such as humans, animals, and carbon-based substances (matter), which confirms what our 300-year-old friend Leibniz once said. Once we have the capacity to accept this potential, we should be asking what else could be and how can we reach beyond what is. If our true lifeform is consciousness, then our being should be more occupied with what consciousness can teach us instead of our thoughts.

We spend most of our time falling into the thought abyss of delusions and emotions. It is like we're trapped. And the bizarre emerges when the so-called psychiatric experts have to explain dimensions that are beyond matter and the linear. It seems necessary for them to remain opinionated about their linear views because they can't see a new target in consciousness itself. Kind of like religion replacing fact with faith. Weak science is therefore just as weak as religion, and the herd complies because they are told. But logic recommends that one does not know what one does not know. Neither does the artist. Artists create without knowing. They simply begin and become. So be an artist yourself and welcome that capacity.

As a species, we have to move on and consider observing the universe through meditation rather than through religion and capitalism. Since one can't meditate all day, one has to cope with the herd that follows the false and even the educated. Meditation is not a priority for the herd. It is practised by few and seems neglected because the rest ask, why bother with such a seemingly boring activity? The Zen concept is too slow for the herd that prefers participating in the immediate. Most never practise serious self-reflection because involuntary following, posing, and even lying to entertain overrides their hidden mental resources. To them, it seems far more exciting to join the mass dullness of the tech pandemic that we seem to crave. They need mayhem, like another format of gossip.

But, the wiser kind of individual, the type of person like the main character in *Good Will Hunting*, chooses information and seeks to understand capacity above all—a capacity that reaches even beyond the available educational sources. It is a desire that rises from the depths of their own consciousness.

Public scientists are often too busy serving their own institutions and credentials and will most likely never connect with these kinds of wise hermits. The sophisticated refuse hermit input. To them, it is not necessary. But if they are all such experts and specialists, then why is everything so severely disabled?

They called Schopenhauer a pessimist. He was troubled by the imperialist oppression that surrounded him, so why would he be optimistic? He was right to be a pessimist! His statement that "Talent hits a target no one else can hit; Genius hits a target no one else can see" is profound. This is well-proven by Schopenhauer, not only well said.

My view is that I don't even have to be a genius to understand what's wrong with humanity. I simply know that we can do much better.

When we self-reflect far more than what most of us are used to, then we begin to see how absurd our lives really are. Although, that realization does not mean that we can't escape our rut. So, I invite you to sit, meditate, and discover that nothing that is actually something on your own. When you do so, the now is what you observe, and it is all you can ever experience and influence. There, you will find an infinite presence where nothing becomes something. This is where you will feel that something appears out of nothing and seems to be aware of itself. This is not a thought or your brain. Instead, it is a presence that is only felt. And you can feel this presence without thought. It gets even more interesting when you try to comprehend that what you observe (your presence) only appears because you are observing it. In other words, you are the cause of what you observe.

In light of that, it seems absurd to waste away identifying and labelling sequences of ideas, causes, and effects that are mostly the thoughts of others. These thoughts are only a disturbance to the silence of that presence. None of these thoughts actually exist in substance. All that truly exists in itself is your feeling of that presence without thoughts. This is consciousness that independently stares right at you! There is nothing more soothing than witnessing this profound stillness and to have a sense of evenness to sustain it, moment to moment. It is, in itself, a self-created, ongoing presence that is not connected to anything physical, and it has no mass. Science cannot explain this or the absolutes of our being. But you, sitting in stillness, can experience it!

We do have some reliable psychological information that is sufficient to explain thought processes, but once we retreat into independent pure consciousness, everything opens up into space without time or mass. And from there, unimaginable insights will spring. This is where genius is found!

When we read the remarkably deep and detailed writing of Immanuel Kant, we witness his struggle with consciousness, which he named "a priori" or the "thing-in-itself." With Descartes, we remember that his philosophy could not explain his existence despite his mathematical precision. He confirmed that thinking causes his being. Irene Arendt somewhat corrected Descartes by saying that he should have said, "I think I can recognize myself, which is something else other than my thoughts, and I am that which I recognize." In other words, "I am not thought, I experience (am) what produces thoughts." That recognition of the self is also explained in experiencing the Buddhist Mahamudra. Therefore, we must all learn that the key to mental refinement is to develop a better awareness of our eternal and underestimated consciousness. The artist feels that expression in the moment is much more profound than the following thoughts. That is genius in action.

Seeing consciousness from this perspective exposes how weak the thoughts of the busy monkey mind actually are. Further, when we investigate feeling the body, and the mysteries of qigong in particular, we find that healing with consciousness and the body's energy is not only possible but also very probable. We can fine-tune our mental faculties with full-body movement meditations such as tai chi, and we can tap into our potential gifts that will reveal themselves from our always-present quantum consciousness. As a species, we all have to retreat more often into ourselves.

Implement this: The mystery of quantum consciousness and compassion do not relate to imperialist wars, terrorism, and the murder of so many species. It is here where the polarity of being and becoming is at its most extreme. The sequences of events in history that amounted to human and species slaughter are well-documented. If we are all collectively projecting this ongoing slaughter, then this is what we choose to observe. However, the essence of humans must be essentially good, because babies are born innocent. Eventually, we get lost in the unnecessary delusions of male becoming and we mistake these delusions for our true nature. But our true nature is being (eternal consciousness), not becoming. And we could be anything! Capitalism is morbid minimalism.

Or don't. You know that you can't ignore this, but you can choose to anyway.

Where are we?

Schrödinger said that we are in essence outside of ourselves, and that we perceive the observable universe because our bodies are in it. Again, this suggests that our consciousness cannot be produced by our brains or bodies. When we reverse the standard model, one can confirm that consciousness projects the body. However, does consciousness exist independently without a body and without projecting anything? Is self observing awareness only a temporary borrowed faculty from consciousness while we are alive?

We can observe that earth is suspended in space, following the laws of gravitational forces within our galaxy and many other unknown factors. Physics and chemistry suggest that we evolved here due to chemical reactions in space and from our nearest star, the sun. That is remarkable, but still not as mind-blowing as when we include that we are in fact aware within this chemical soup, and that all of this is apparently happening to us (experience), including consciousness.

But that does not seem to be enough. Is consciousness that single essence that exists in itself? And as Schrödinger asked, where does it come from? His cat in the box theory also leads us to understand that consciousness cannot only perceive our bodies, but can also potentially produce all the matter and light around us because we observe it.

Again, nothing is happening to us. Instead, we (consciousness) make things happen due to our observation.

Also, why is there an underlying desire for all creatures to rest, such as in sleep or meditation? Rest is always the last resort to return to. There is a cyclical need to surrender to what is beyond our awareness, and without rest we don't survive very long. When we look at matter in the quantum world, we discover that nothing ever rests there. Atoms will only rest and stand still at about minus 272 degrees Celsius. Still, consciousness does not freeze.

In conclusion, despite of a lot of unknown factors, we can still better define where we are than what we are.

Chapter 11:

Meditation

Living in the moment

Everything decays, while at the same time, the new is born in the present moment. Non-duality is precisely the very moment. Nothing to grasp, nothing to contemplate, nothing to focus on. Thoughts simply come to us, one by one, like waves on the ocean. And when we connect these individual thoughts, we call it thinking. So, thinking is a sequential process, but what is a single thought in itself?

There are varieties of thoughts. An original thought is an idea, and ideas appear from nothingness! Many writers choose to write early in the morning after deep sleep has reduced the chatter in their heads. A fresh mind will follow ideas because we are curious and constantly changing by nature. So, writers follow these ideas, which evolve into stories.

Have you ever noticed that you can only have one thought at a time? Our internal stories are sequential single thoughts on a string. Our busy monkey minds are like this with just about everything. We invent stories based on what we hear and see, and this is where information stress starts to pile up.

During meditation, we observe that thoughts are occurring, but we don't follow them. To test this, simply try to be conscious without having thoughts. It is not easy at first, but with practice you will be able to sense that there is a different space available that exists without thought. Every time you practise sensing this, you can call it meditation. You don't need to sit on a cushion in a fancy robe with incense burning in the background in order to meditate. Just observe consciousness without thinking, anywhere, anytime. There is no magic to it; it is simply unfinished presence.

In principle, we accept what we learn and then teach it. Learning is seeking, while teaching is confirming, and the combined learning and seeking mind is called reasoning. Reasoning is the process of discovering pieces that lead to larger pieces. From there, we can make statements. But even when one can reason and make statements, it does not mean that others will understand. Just like how one can read, but still not comprehend. Therefore, we often conclude too early that we have found answers that should include others.

For example, we complain about stress, but fail to isolate that stress in itself does not actually exist. Stress is caused by many individual pieces of information. It is the individual context of all the information combined by our minds that is labelled as stress. And stress is not a short-term thought, it is actually a feeling, and this is why it affects us long term. Our minds label and identify. They can even become delusional, and most of it is unnecessary. We are asked to respond to stress by relaxing, which is another feeling. What we label "stress" is actually an emotion caused by thought overload.

Therefore, to calm our emotions (feeling) by relaxing (feeling) is a good antidote, because they tend to cancel each other out. What's bizarre is that we can't actually feel thoughts. We just think we do because they cause feelings. In contrast, our emotions do exist, because we can feel them. Hence, we can only sense one or the other. A feeling is not a thought, and a thought is not a feeling. The Eastern religions may say that there is no substance in thoughts because they are empty and we can't feel them. Still, sometimes we experience that thoughts cause us to feel. What such religions mean is that once thoughts are reduced or eliminated, then feelings would not occur as frequently. So, the psychological mind-body connection takes place right here.

I chose the trickster to go on the cover of this book. He is meant to point out that what humans label as knowledge is often just information for self-entertainment. Knowledge and information are not the same. And we take what we claim to know way too seriously. In academic circles, we praise ourselves with designations and degrees. Then we unload that historic knowledge into the minds of the young, and demand that they regurgitate it and follow us. But they don't have to follow anything! It seems so important to always remember, yet we fail to recognize that we should teach the young to ask better questions instead of remembering what the older generations chose to ask. And we can't always anticipate how the young feel about what they are being taught. We just assume that they think how we think. Academic knowledge is simply claiming something, and while some of it can be taken seriously, what is present already is not nearly as crucial as what can be.

When children struggle, they are not just overloaded on information (thoughts), but they are also overloaded on feelings, such as peer pressure. The so-called educated set standards and force the young to expand on these standards. However, male-dominated societies set most of these standards. Clinging to male failures is lunacy. Besides some significant engineering, all they've delighted us with is theft, aggression, secret organizations, discrimination, fear, compliance, and chauvinism. That is what they were able to come up with and what they chose to implement.

However, none of this matters because it is all insignificant. I can sum it up in just one word: thoughts!

Humanity keeps asking why, why, why, yet not much ever improves. Male-dominated societies limit us. This fact is staring right at us, but don't be ashamed to be part of this incompetence. When you live in the moment, it is all gone.

Implement this: There is much to be discovered with a clear mind living in the moment.

Or don't. Have another drink to drown the mind.

As an interlude, tune into consciousness

This may be repetitive, but it is intentional to distract you from your thoughts right now (and it might feel good to read this again). In this very moment, second after second, the only experience we can observe is our presence. We exist, and we take it for granted. The next moment comes, we cannot hold on to it, and it has passed. These immediate, ongoing present moments are first consciousness, then awareness, and then thoughts. Sense it. You can actually feel that we project what we observe simultaneously. We can almost expect what is coming next, even though it has not happened yet. We can project and observe awareness without having any thoughts, and it just is.

So, when there are no thoughts, it may feel like dullness. But this is being, and being is that priori consciousness that makes our self-awareness possible. You can even hear your awareness. It's like a slight ringing in your ears. There is this something that causes our awareness out of nothing. There is that non-duality right there. You can sense that projecting and observing yourself simultaneously is happening. Time does not do this—we do it.

Remember, Leibniz asked, "Why is nothing something, and something nothing?" By "nothing," he must have meant awareness without thoughts and that we can't see what causes our vision, yet we still see.

Eventually, causality proceeds from there, when the "I" is recognized as you, and you think that "I" is what you are. Yet, you are not, even though it seems realized. Presence is actually all there is. Presence that is not labelled as an "I." Presence that is just being. Only later does sense awareness take over and get conditioned to connect and react to the seven senses and information. We then react with identification and emotion to what we invent as thoughts. These thoughts then develop further, conditioned by previous experiences, to rationalize what we choose and believe. Then we get lost in sequences of events that form our human experience. We take it all for granted and then forget to return to plain conscious awareness without thoughts. Except when we return to the very moment, meditate, or fall asleep.

Implement this: Practise having no thoughts. You can do it anywhere.

Or don't. Chase your thoughts like a kitten chasing its tail.

Insights

As I explained, in between every single thought there is a gap, and this is where insights come from. Gaps are beyond the sequences of events that coherent thoughts represent. Our sequences of thoughts are relentless, even circular, and they mostly distract us from these gaps. And because most of us are not aware of this simple fact, we often miss that there actually are gaps. Insights can still occur without isolating these gaps, but they just won't happen as often. Consistent meditation practise enables us to arrive in these gaps more often, and for extended periods. Once one is in a gap, try not to discover anything! Just stay there undisturbed, and trust that anything can appear out of nowhere. A gap is where nothing becomes something again and again. It is coming from the beyond (that you actually project).

Meditation is not some ritual. It simply shows you what you are and the hidden potential you have that you could not even have imagined. You may even discover that you truly need more solitude instead of device information. It is a wide-open opportunity that actually comes across as a secret, and is sold as spiritual materialism. Most sages recommend silence, and they say that even without trying to develop anything, insights will appear! These insights then become intentions, such as:

The less we say, the less we have to monitor and control.

The less we think about the past, the more sensitive we become about the present.

The less we follow, the more we condense into being.

The less we have, the more we are.

As a result, we become kinder to ourselves. This seems quite obvious, but when one truly begins to follow meditation, then further insights and signs from the universe will reveal themselves. These are not religious or spiritual hopes. These are factual appearances that we could not expect.

Having said that, one of the insights you may discover is that there is no need for spiritual materialism, as in performing rituals, spending time in over-priced retreats, and so on. Why do you have to pay to relax? You don't even need to sit in a "meditation pose" to meditate. Like I said, you can simply do this anytime, anywhere, and in any position you're in. Everything you will ever discover is actually already present. It is that hidden something waiting to reveal itself in the gap in every moment. Have confidence in that.

Implement this: Silence is waiting to reveal its gifts. Go there and find them.

Or don't. Don't go there. Miss out.

The deathless

Sitting upon his deathbed, the Karmapa said, smiling, "Don't worry, nothing happens." He meant that after death, there is the deathless, an infinite presence that is consciousness in itself.

During image meditation, we can look for that presence. For example, imagine the moon as it is in the dark night sky. As it passes across the horizon and vanishes in the morning, it seems like nothing remains. But the moon is still there, it is just out of your sight, in stillness, watching the earth, aware, and watching you. When you visualize the moon, even when it's pitch black, you know that it's simply there, always present, a companion to the earth. This is like your being. It is present within you but unable to be grasped with thought. It is a feeling, and you only recognize it as a you with a self.

Consciousness is like watching the moon in space, but also being the moon watching the earth. A kind of one, all embracing.

Therefore, is the self looking at you, or are you looking at the self?

It's actually both, and they are happening simultaneously. It is the thing-in-itself, without a self.

Think, "Look at who is looking," but remain with the "who" without identifying yourself. It is not easy to rest there, but keep trying. Aim for short moments of feeling this, and the moments will increase with practise and familiarity.

Solitude is not only available when you isolate yourself like a hermit. There is no solitude. What remains is only silence. But who is looking in this silence? Consciousness is always there and you will never be alone. This is the deathless!

You can experience the deathless whenever you sit. Just find your posture: note the nostrils, the centre upper lip, the third eye on the forehead, and the pineal gland in the core of the brain, at the top of the spinal cord. The spine is straight, like coins stacked on top of one another. If your legs become uncomfortable, don't force through the pain; adjust to a comfortable position, then settle. From there, don't move at all, as if you are made of stone, but completely relax. The hands are resting on your thighs like a cradle, with the right hand on top of the left hand with the thumbs touching. Especially relax the arms and shoulders. Feel the comfortable breath. When a thought arises, focus on the breath. . . thought occurs, breath. . . and so on. This is meditation in the initial phase, and at the same time you will be aware of your deeper, whole-body sensations. Continue, and relax even more.

Be careful because when we focus on the breath (which is a feeling), it can become a mental distraction as we try to have no thoughts (which is also a thought). This can lead to meditative dullness. Once dullness and breath are recognized, consciousness can be refined further and further by going backwards and forwards between thoughts and no thoughts (feeling). This is called the wobble. As you wobble, you will anticipate something coming next, but eventually you will be able to let go. The wobble will subside, and there will be no more breath awareness and no thoughts will come up. Physical sensations will become very faint and time will dissolve into the immediate present. Only pure and clear consciousness will be felt. This is the first level of having no thoughts (calming that monkey mind). Sensations and thought will still occur, but don't identify with them.

It may feel like you are hollow, like a vase or a balloon, and weightless. You may sense a flow, or vibrations, but these sensations will also eventually vanish. Bliss appears out of nowhere, but don't let the bliss distract you. File it away also, as if you know that you can always come back to it. This is knowing. Have confidence that you always had this knowing and move on. Simply wait (without waiting for anything). Breath, thought, no thought gap, breath, thought, no thought gap, and so on. Nimitta (light sensations that are like a fog) will appear sooner or later, but move on. At first this will be distracting because it will be amazing, but simply be, and continue. Whatever comes up, let it pass, moment to moment. Eventually, the beyond will open up in the extended gap (the first jhana). It is vast and indescribable. . . but move on.

Still, this is not enlightenment. Enlightenment is this process, and to practise it again and again. Consequently, you will experience further levels of jhana with further concentration and refinement. Ultimately, enlightenment is not a destination; it is being! And once you move off the cushion, then more unexpected insights and gifts reveal themselves in post-meditation. Your wonder at how this compares to capitalism will deepen. Is indulging on a super-yacht in the middle of beautiful waters more precious than that? Maybe for a while, but it will pass.

The wobble

The upcoming illustration represents infinity experienced as explained in the Chapter 1: The big picture.

There is a vertical arrow pointing up through the centre (from the bottom). This arrow represents infinity experienced as consciousness projecting from the past to the future (the top), and returning to the centre as the residue we call perception (the event horizon). The arrow is illustrated as linear, but the projected future from the past, remains as residue in the present, and they all happen simultaneously.

The residue arrow points to centre, where we experience perception as the format called time.

The meditation wobble is illustrated with thoughts (mental activity and peripheral awareness) on the left side, and feelings (breath and body) on the right side. Note that you can only experience one of the two (either thought or feeling) in a present moment. The awareness current alternates (wobbles) between the two, and there is a centre between them. This very centre is the present moment (the gap). This is the focal point. Wait there (without waiting for anything), let occurrences pass, and return to the gap.

The gap arrow points to the centre and isolates the gap in between thoughts and feelings, where there are no thoughts or feelings. There is only presence (consciousness) observing itself.

However, everything is one single instant, that constantly renews itself because it observes itself (the thing-in-itself, Kant). The single centre star represents where the awareness wobble eventually subsides, and dissolves into the gap, where we can find bliss in profound stillness, emptiness, the jhanas, and enlightenment.

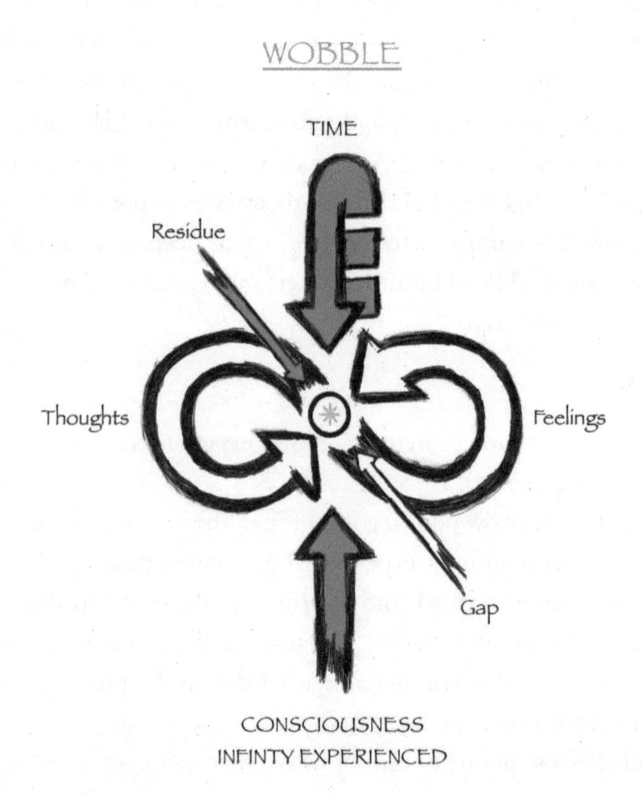

Bodhisattva control

We think that we are mostly in control, but when taking a closer look, we learn that we control very little. We don't control our heartbeats, organs, immune systems, or even our emotions. We just drift in biological uncertainties. So, how can we even attempt to control others and world affairs?

The only thing I can control are the parameters of my immediate awareness and what I should do next. With every situation, I realize how subject I am to everything else around me and in me, and that everything is conditioned by something else. Bodhisattvas have learned that they experience life moment after moment and that this is enough. So, they remain waiting. When they wait, they don't become prey for obstacles, and every creature is precious.

In contrast, complying with capitalism causes suffering. The entire globe suffers because of it. Hypothetically, if there was no capitalism, there would be no suffering. If there was no suffering, there would be no need for compassion. Consequently, there would be no need for bodhisattvas either.

However, we have to cope with reality. Though, how we cope may not solve the actual problem. Coping is just a remedy to make problems more bearable.

Mental capacity clearly recommends transcending away from a problem rather than coping with its subsequent conditions. Bodhisattvas can alleviate conditions with compassionate actions, which are helpful. But this kind of help does not address our problem.

I explained that our problem is capitalism. And even though you may agree with me, you will likely remain complacent and insist that you can't do anything about it. You will go to work tomorrow, like everybody else, while wishing for a better society without suffering (the conditions). But that can never happen by ignoring the problem (capitalism).

I am explaining this as a bodhisattva. We don't need to choose to suffer by habitual default. I can alleviate your suffering with my message. People like me have compassion for all our suffering, even for the self-deception of the middle class. My role is to transform my message into preparing you for the realization that it is up to you to help eliminate our capitalist problem. The compassion is then passed on to you to act on for the benefit of all.

The super-sensory Tibetan way

Most of us like magic and special gifts. One of those gifts is super-sensory perception. Would you believe it if I told you that it can be attained with quiescence and by cultivating gap stillness? Again, see the moon first, then move beyond the existence of the moon that you can only see. It is always there. Super-sensory perception cannot be achieved with concentration alone in meditation. Mind capacity only expands with devotion to enduring and post-meditative awareness. Mindfulness is to remember what one has learned from these disciplines. Therefore, the useful mantra: "The trained mind knows when to pause with the four *R*s: Relax, Retreat, Respond only if necessary, and Rest."

It is a scientific fact that practising disciplined meditation rewires the brain and gives one access to other levels of consciousness. The psychological *tabula rasa* (clean slate) is the first condition to practise. Then the magic of seeing (having glimmers of first impressions) will appear. Future divination and intentions spring from there. You can always check your wonderful breath, wobble between thoughts and feelings, and align your posture everywhere and all the time (not only on the meditation cushion).

As you progress further with your practice, you will reach a point beyond relaxation, which means that there is no more intentional breath. Prior, you would feel your breath in the lower belly, airways, nostrils, and on the upper lip. When you are beyond relaxation, you switch to sense all the other peripherals around you. Where has the breath gone? Meditation is not a breathing exercise. You only employ breath sometimes to escape dullness during the wobble.

From there, find inner refuge and sense your consciousness shining like a lamp. But its light is not a light, it is the clarity that shines from just sitting, not grasping anything, and sensing without breath (embryonic breathing), undisturbed, motionless, in the gap between thoughts. There is a sense of evenness that all is combined into one as bliss.

This is approaching emptiness. The mind will still move occasionally, but then it files this away. By the time you think about where the movement came from, it is already gone. You remain undisturbed, and it has dissolved by itself. Do not grasp the dissolving movement either. This is wu wei—just being aware and remaining that way, waiting. From there, an even deeper awareness of consciousness will reveal itself, like a silence within silence. This is called the mind fish. It is like a fish in crystal clear water, not moving at all, but still conscious. The feeling is so profound that when you become aware of it, you don't want to leave it. But then it's gone. . . Such moments are indescribable.

In Taoism, the Tao never does, yet everything is done. Nameless simplicity acts without intention. This simplicity is the practice. When we move with chi (inner presence), dwell in inner mind fish silence, and speak only when necessary, then insights and signs will appear more often, and when we least expect them. Everything becomes a blessing, including pain and hardship. It is the way (the Tao).

Developments will occur as follows:

- One finds that the Tao and the path to follow is actually there (as explained).
- One experiences Shamata (bliss) the same as the ordinary.
- Arhats have no mental defilements because they have found silence within silence. And an arhat does not recognize him / herself as an arhat. There is no form and identification.
- Mental balance is the core. It is the hub of the wheel of desire. It does not move.
- One achieves the first jhana as a form of lucid awareness (self-recognized) beyond the five senses.
- One has access to consciousness itself, that is the priori, with ease (the thing-in-itself, Kant).
- Additional jhanas become accessible. These are profound and highly refined states of consciousness that build up from the previous jhanas. They detach from the external world, into suppression of thoughts, to rest with a sense of ease, then the passing away of ease, to merge into the infinity of space, and ultimately into absolute no-thingness. (This is a brief summary).
- Shamata during the day is seeing the world through rigpa. Clean and clear rigpa is a constant realization that all phenomena are empty. Suffering appears as evident, but it is also empty.
- Wu wei and Zen are also simplified tools to realize rigpa. Pristine awareness is the sustainability of rigpa. The Tibetans call it calm abiding, so rest there.
- Eventually, there is no more meditation necessary. Meditation is just a method to develop super-sensory focus, cultivation, and intense awareness.

- This is to return to clear, pure consciousness as infinity experienced, but also to seeing it as itself.
- Mahamudra, Dzogchen, and practising Dharma are not necessary anymore. One is the practice.

Everything not only *becomes* one, it *is* one. Mindful breathing, kindness, intense but even focus, balancing the big picture, and trimming the sails of defilements. One now understands that suffering is only self-inflicted mind-labelling. Imagine how one would practise Dharma when situated in a WWII concentration camp. There, death would appear to be an end to suffering, but besides the torment the body has to endure, suffering is also a mental illusion. To see death as an opportunity would be an escape for some. But the fear of dying would remain.

Samsara is like that. It is a rebirth into the suffering cycles of life. We always want both: to live but not to suffer. But if Samsara is also an illusion, then why do we need to be liberated from it? To liberate oneself from something that does not exist (illusion) is what? Emptiness. Here we are again: nothing, nothing, nothing.

Stability and clarity are like a telescope, and the mind is that telescope. A telescope needs to be stable, it cannot wobble, it needs clean lenses (Hubble) or even infrared sensors (Webb), and it needs to be in outer space (beyond earth's atmosphere) to see deeper. But still, we can't see far enough. That would be the definition of a well-focused mind.

Great meditators recognize each other

They say that a master can guide you and save you time, but how? If there is nothing to know (Socrates), and all is one and empty (Buddha), why would one need a master?

They say practise, but concentration drains you.

They say find silence within silence, but the mind is loud.

They say stability is cultivated with relaxation in tai chi and that Soma (body position) intensifies focus to attain clarity, but the body aches.

They say that the sensations of the breath accompany the stability, that it becomes smooth and refined at the nostrils, but it takes such a long time to notice significant progress.

They say to merge into the gap (in between thoughts) and to stay there, but that busy monkey mind just can't be tamed.

They say Dharmakaya is the mind of the Buddha, solid like a tree, providing life and shelter for all. Why can't you do that?

They say that you will arrive in stillness within stillness, and to move beyond to clear-clear awareness alone. But when?

They say to observe whatever comes and goes without judgment and that defilements will dissolve, but that is not easy.

They say that bliss will develop, but advise not to get addicted to it. Finally, you seem to get there, and then move on?

They say rest in pure, naked consciousness within the quantum space—that is the thing-in-itself—but there are only brief moments of this.

They say to cultivate wisdom, but insight has to come first.

They say that intuition is primordial knowing (Yeshe). This is insight hidden in plain sight, waiting to be unveiled. But when?

They say to have patience with your progress. Progress is simply meaningful practice. That is asking for even more patience.

In other words, there will always be something else.

Masters are mostly a business. Some are genuine avatars, but most of these highly realized individuals live isolated. They don't need to be masters; they already know the master within themselves. Have confidence that you will find your master within yourself as well.

Concluding

Try to lose the master mindset and rest in calm, abiding awareness. That is enough. You already are the master. Moment by moment, just wait, and dissolve everything into nothing.

Yes, you can be like Yoda. The force is with you already.

Self control is not solving mind puzzles and riddles. It is waiting. Yet, it is waiting without waiting for anything!

Lie on your back, comfortably. Imagine that you are on a beautiful beach, with pelicans flying by. Practice your inner smile and glow as if you are on that beach.

You can always simply experience the present. The thing-in-itself is always there, projected and simultaneously experienced. Without thoughts, this is the suchness of the clear-clear. Realize that everything else is just a test.

When you sense the internal that is chi (presence), then allow it to move you. Chi is not a thought. It will move you all by itself. It is always there; it is a feeling. Walk slow and light-footed. Drink tea, watch for unexpected signs and synchronicities, see all the colours and smell all the fragrances around you, taste being, and enjoy. There is not more to learn.

Metaphors

A ritual is meant to transform the moods of the mind, whatever the ritual may be. Poetry serves the same purpose. For example, *The Lake Isle of Innisfree* by William Butler Yeats uses the line, "There midnight's all a glimmer, and noon a purple glow, / And evening full of the linnet's wings," to invite one to imagine a dream-like purple sky with thousands of birds in flight across it, and the term, "bee-loud glade" to conjure an image of a clear blue sky with bees humming in open space.

This is language, but somewhat bizarre to understand because it sounds so swollen. These expressions are meant to inspire experiences that are beyond the ordinary. All these imaginary suggestions are thoughts expressed in words. But why do we have to talk around in circles when all can be said in simple language? I get it, poetry is meant to be an art, and language is a gift. But who is still interested in this? The cultured of the past? The new culture wants to look at selfies and devices. So we have to keep metaphors simple.

There is talk about activating chakras and of Kundalini, where chi (internal energy) rises from the bottom of the spine to the crown of the head. In Tibet, they call this internal process Tummo. Various cultures have similar stories to explain chi energy centres in the body. The centres and energy channels are explained metaphorically and with imagination, but physically, they are activated with breathing methods. That is the core of the exercise, and breathing is what keeps it simple to distract from thoughts.

So, something is going on with the internal body energy, and physically strengthening the body with tai chi tames the mind even further. But the mind still does not stop. It just keeps coming up with new thoughts out of nowhere. It's like a passion that wants to reveal itself. Can someone explain that? Time does not do that. When the relentless mind vanishes during both sitting and moving meditations, it is like being released into the vast, clear, blue sky of "bee-loud glade". But there are no bees. It is empty self-recognition, and all the noise of thoughts, language, and metaphors is gone.

Is there karma?

The theory of karma is a good idea to make people aware that their actions have consequences. However, this system that suggests that one has a better next life if one behaves better in this life does not add up by sheer volume. Does it mean that for the few rich people out there, their previous lives comprised mostly good actions? While for the many people that live in extreme poverty, does it mean they all misbehaved in their previous lives? And is a monk or avatar more rewarded by good karma in their current life than a super rich business oligarch? How is a better-karma life defined?

If karma is indeed a force to balance the universe, then the universe sure produces a lot of bad karma people that are re-born as poor people. That should make you laugh! Are capitalism and possessions the result of having good karma? And if one is a good karma capitalist, what would one become next?

I completely understand that good karma in a next life may not mean wealth, but poverty sure causes suffering and can't mean good karma. And since the entire globe is slaving away for capitalism that causes all our suffering and destroys the planet, we should all have bad karma.

The scriptures say that if we are engaged in non-action, we would not accumulate bad karma. We can disengage from capitalism, despite its cleverness. Would that not suffice?

To engage in non-action, imagine retreating to the inside of your central lobe, where there is no sensation whatsoever (we can't feel our brains). Since you can't feel anything there, it would be an empty experience. This is why they say that you can't develop bad karma when you meditate. So, what is the problem? Just sit still and feel your brain. This is the starting point to eliminate both compliance and bad karma. Did someone say bingo? Anyway, I'm just having fun with this one.

Another good question is what is happiness? Joy is important. We can enjoy nature, people, products, destinations, and entertainment. But enjoyment will fade at some point, and then we will want to repeat that enjoyment. The desire to repeat is actually attachment, and possibly even suffering, because we can't reproduce enjoyment all the time. So, does this kind of attachment cause bad karma as well? Absurd, right?

Attachment is a disturbance, and not detaching from situations causes suffering. We have to admit that religions are the attachment that also discriminates against other religions. So, this would be double bad karma. Not to mention that religions are also attached to delusions that spring from opinionated pride. Apparently, pride is the worst sin. So, this would sum up to triple bad karma, and so on. So, religions and karma are like oil and vinegar. But they can still be combined to make a dressing called a vinaigrette. Maybe that's why they've gotten away with everything so far: vinaigrette tastes good.

Emotions are also attachments, good or bad. We can use deconstruction to detach from the bad ones. Eventually, when we are not mad anymore, can we wipe out the bad karma of getting mad with the good karma of deconstructing the emotion? In other words, we may reach for a vinaigrette occasionally, but karma is an overreach.

Master

When the master finds the student, then the student has found the master. But who is looking for whom? What if the master is persistence itself and means to meet the student with effort? A clever proposition when considering that our consistent daily challenge is to master our ability to allow patient accepting.

Irritation does and will continue to occur due to relentless thoughts. We label these thoughts, and then we identify with them. However, the persistence in remembering yourself is the master that realizes that you can retreat to your own inner cave. There you can find rest in silence and tame thoughts. As a result, any kind of reaction will also be milder, or not occur at all. Upon returning from your inner cave, you can respond and reveal patient information. You can also imagine that you are a standing heron that watches his prey from above. Calm, careful, and slow. Or even better, silent. After all, impatience is an emotional reaction and always depends on some cause. You perceive the cause and identify with it, but because you identify (label), you risk losing your patience. But at that point, you have already lost your way because you've identified with it. We often don't even realize what is going on.

So, we can be patient, or we can endure impatience. Still, both patience and impatience are self-suffering. When you recognize that there is no need to be either and that there is no need to react to any kind of thought at all, then you are on your way (Tao). Thoughts will always be patient or impatient noise. Resting in between both is enlightenment.

Some practical mental tools to remember

- There is no need for a master because every situation is already your master. If we are infinite consciousness, then you were never born. So, what is there to obey? This also means that you will never die.
- The fish trap is there to catch fish. When the fish is caught, you forget the trap. Words are meant to explain intent. Understanding the intention makes you forget the words.
- Like water dripping into a vessel, fill yourself with good, drop by drop.
- The Buddha nature is present already. Imagine that you already have it.
- You can talk or think about food, but that is not eating.
- The ego's will is a muscle (Schopenhauer). The more one exercises it, the stronger it will become. But ego is a mental weakness.
- All thoughts are like a movie being projected, revealing content. Consciousness is the lamp projecting the images. The images would not be visible without the lamp. First there was light.
- We can sense that the heart and organs are our deepest inner core and that they operate independently of our thoughts. Our stomach does not seem to be aware, but it grumbles when hungry. We don't think about sustaining our organs, regardless of what else we think.
- When you sit solidly like a rock in the stream of life, water still flows around you by itself. It seems obvious enough to know this, but you have to realize first that you can be that rock.
- When meditation is deepest, breathing becomes very shallow, bliss appears, and it feels like there is no time. Everything melts into the moment. Does time do this or consciousness?
- Consciousness is like what the eye can see, but the eye cannot see itself.
- Contemplate that if there was no suffering (capitalism), then there would be no need for compassion (charity).

Wisdom

If we remember the Stoics from stoa, the porch or hall where teaching took place, we can imagine young minds sitting as a group and craving wisdom. What is wisdom?

Well-reasoned choices, knowledge from the past, well-behaved conduct, self-control, courage, and justice do not necessarily equate to wisdom. Some sages claim that they are better, that their secret beliefs triumph over the common man, and that because of their beliefs, they may even reach salvation. They consider themselves wise. But secrecy is in itself selfish and not wise.

Wisdom is wide open and means a deeper understanding. But to learn wisdom is an ongoing, lifelong practice. It is to rest in non-action, to simply observe the moment, and to wait without waiting for anything. It starts with the absence of activity and then becomes the activity of absence. There is no wisdom in itself. There is only this process. Some may call this meditation, but it can also be called contemplation. Through this process, insights will spring. These insights emerge out of nowhere.

When other people hear those insights, they call them wisdom, even when they are simply copies of someone else's insights. However, original, pure wisdom is when you, yourself, find insights that have practical applications for you.

People seek wisdom even though they already have it. But most don't practise meditation, where they can learn to have no thoughts. To them, it may appear that meditation is an activity that nothing comes out of. Like calmly fishing in a bathtub. But insights and special gifts will come out of nowhere when one meditates consistently. Try it!

Wise language is more effective when it also involves doing. Well-done is far superior than well-said!

The truly wise can lose nothing, and they can forgive everything. So then, what is there to fear?

The wise do not intend to be better than others. In fact, they promote evenness. If balance would be a human pandemic, then where would we be? One can always choose to be kind, and the initial act of delaying is the first step towards kindness. Waiting and balance are wisdom.

We sometimes even considered wisdom as atheism. What are the consequences of atheism? There are none. Religion is just storytelling and judgment according to those stories. However, what is the point of being judged by someone else? We all have enough trouble judging ourselves. So why bother and increase the load from someone else?

Spiritual (Consciousness) developments

We sometimes refer to our non-physical presence as spirit, and even touch on the concept of a soul. This implies that these would-be entities are separate from the physical body. Are they? And does the spirit or the soul ever get tired, or is this only a quality of the body? We actually don't really know, but we are still content in saying that our bodies have spirits or souls. There is also no mention of whether either soul or spirit are conscious. So then, what is conscious? The body? Or is the body conscious but with a separate soul that we may call a spirit? Or is the spirit consciousness produced by the body? Which is it? Regardless, does it not feel like all is one and the same?

In tai chi, qigong, and Tummo, the chi can be felt in the body as a moving internal energy. It is like an empty force. This feeling can even override pain and our sense of gravity; it can generate heat. It is like it penetrates our internal quantum particles via blood circulation and concentration. We can concentrate our awareness within the body to specific points, and then we can feel that force. There are numerous layers to the body: visible, invisible, finer, and so on, right down to the particle. But the canvas, meaning our body and feelings, where everything takes place, is consciousness.

So where is the spirit or the soul in all of this? Or were spirit and soul mistakenly identified as consciousness in the past? They speak of the soul leaving the body when we expire. Did they mean that the body that produced consciousness would also produce a soul? Or would the soul leaving the body be the unaware consciousness? In other words, they say that the body is temporary, but the soul is not, which is correct. But would the opposite not make much more sense, where only infinite consciousness can produce a body temporarily, and never expires? That would not require a spirit or a soul.

Considering how clever the universe is to observe itself, then why would the universe create bodies to evolve into consciousness and then expire? Where does the energy to create these bodies come from, before expiring into nothing? That would contradict the law of preservation, which states that energy never ceases to exist. Consequently, the spirit and soul concept doesn't add up to be plausible.

How we perceive reality hinges on the development of our awareness. We are the residue of energy and mass in quantum space, and both energy and mass depend on each other to exist as form.

Being is feeling, and not a thought (you don't think up pain). I am (feel), therefore I think (observe, and label). Descartes had it in reverse; he said, "I think, therefore I am."

Because we still underestimate consciousness, we need to convince our doctors to welcome quantum physics into medicine. Current medical science still does not understand enough about what causes disease. It is quite advanced with surgery and treats symptoms with highly refined chemistry. On the other hand, consciousness is the body's feeling and healing ability. Using our consciousness for healing and to prevent sickness would be far superior to using chemicals when we're already sick. If we can remotely view, then why could we not remotely heal? But medicine says otherwise, and it is a profit-seeking business. Greed can prescribe so that not becoming sick in the first place can be neglected. Medical science should spend more time researching how we can harmonize our awareness of the body. I am convinced that we can heal ourselves. Particles can interact at a distance, and so can mental energies to heal the body. There is evidence that chi can be projected and applied for healing, but the doctors are commissioned to push drugs. Health care has become an emotional trap that can demand high prices and should be renamed "health abuse." The number one reason for personal bankruptcy in the US is medical bills, and praying is not helping.

Refinement

Consciousness refinement is the key for us to become a competent species. The following are the most important things to contemplate in this practice.

- Tibetan lamas practise constant clear awareness in the present. They call it calm abiding or suchness. Consequently, they are kind by default, and this is not complicated. Once one practises this self-reflection, one will notice changes.
- On rising (4–5 a.m. is recommended), meditation will feel different, and it will provide clarity and calm post-meditation for the rest of the day. Silence is the language of the realized. They know that living in the moment always presents a new beginning.

- Meditation at night before enough sleep (eight hours is recommended) will result in lucid dreams. Once meditation practise increases, one can get by with less sleep.
- When you sit, just sit (zazen). Be aware, but not dull. Stay and simply wait, without waiting for anything.
- Chakras are energy centres, but most information about chakras is overrated and gets lost in too many details. They follow the spine, and you can feel them when you sit or do a body scan. It does not matter what colour they are or what they look like. Just sit, feel, and merge with them.
- Despite everything, random thoughts will still come up during meditation. Do not fight whatever emerges. Use the information to define as much of your unknown as possible. Clarity will eventually emerge all by itself. Still, clarity insights will take time. The best way to discover them is to hold reservations at bay for long enough and to let the involved processes disclose their own nature.
- Imagine that you can heal others with the simple intention to heal, and have them think that they have already been healed.
- Add several periods of water fasting. The body knows what to do! This may sound like nonsense, but try it. It is very real.
- During tai chi, qigong, and Tummo, you will begin to feel vibrations, like a flow. Refine that feeling. It is transmitted through the surrounding space. This is not just imagination, it's there. We think that space is empty, but quantum physics tells us that it is not. In soft martial arts, you want to be soft, light-footed, and to flow like water. The most important is to consistently practise the same form movements over and over. Eventually, your body will show you more and deeper sensations during the moves because of the repetitions. This is called developing your senses, and this is also meditation. Start slow and relaxed, and feel that there is cosmic quantum energy all around you. Don't jam your joints. Fine-tune quality concentration in your movements and have no other thoughts. Don't force anything and let the cosmic quantum flow find you. Absorb it.

- Finally, to bring meditation, dream yoga, post-meditation, healing, and physical practice all together as a holistic refinement process will result in the most benefits. Diligent, daily practice will allow you to feel this, and the rewards are incredible. This is why weekend retreats or random practices will never have the same effect. They are better than doing nothing, but this is spiritual materialism. Practice can be done anywhere, anytime. Eventually, everything becomes practice. Enjoy!

Body or mind

We are non-dual consciousness concealed in dual physical matter. Our bodies are comprised of the ever-changing processes of energies and previous causes. As a result, our bodies age. However, our consciousness does not change. What does change is our awareness, as in our thoughts, and whether we call it evolution, genetics, karma, or whatever, it is an ongoing continuum to make perception self-observable.

My consciousness feels the same today as how it felt when I was a six-year-old. I'm not talking about aging-body aches and pains. I mean how pure consciousness without thoughts reveals itself as a feeling. It feels like a presence, like a canvas on which everything unfolds, and it still remains when we sleep. We just can't feel it then. When you think about it, a feeling may be experienced, such as being tired, but you do not think up being tired. It just happens. Or when we first open our eyes in the morning, our very first self-awareness is actually blank, yet still present. Eventually, our thoughts then become self-reflecting awareness, where we collect ourselves by remembering what we left behind previously and what we should do next. From there, we get sucked back into the much broader informational vortex that will override our presence. We stress, constantly run after our thoughts, and adjust to fit in until we ultimately fall asleep at the end of the day. Then what? What is going on when we sleep? Our organs still function without thinking about them, and we dream without thinking about dreaming. Suffering is gone.

As I look at my cat basking in the sun, I see that there is not much suffering going on there. Suffering is not intelligent; my cat seems to know this by default. Some of us may have heard of minimalist Taoist masters that are always very calm. Despite their apparent serenity, I have also met a few that were like pure energy contained in a pressure cooker. They were also very kind, despite all this energy sealed up inside. They still had an evenness about them, because they practise pure spontaneous presence. In that presence they find the light that emanates in every single form of being (including my cat basking in the sun). They follow a few fundamental concepts and repeat them again and again. From there, life becomes incredibly simple. Awareness is change:

Physical awareness change exercises

- Jump or jog on the spot.
- Take a cold shower.
- Have hot water for breakfast.
- Smile with your face, then with your body.
- Stand on the spot (qigong) Fill your body with empty force.
- Inhaling the fresh breath of the trees in a forest. Connect with the earth.
- Pay attention to synchronicities.
- Get plenty of rest, which will increase dreaming.
- Progressively practise and practise progressively.

Mental awareness visualizations for meditations

- When you were a baby, you had no memory, you were innocent, and you were all-absorbing. Was that meditation?
- Consider: What is in between thoughts? Where does the in-between come from? What is it?
- Arriving in the gap is to turn on the internal light.
- Practice clear-clear mind fish. Imagine a fish in crystal clear water in a fishbowl. Be that fish and don't disturb the water at all.
- It will always be now, even at the speed of light. Eternity lasts an infinite fraction of a second, because there is no time. What if the so-called Big Bang continues to happen infinitely? If this is the case, then it never happened.

- A clear, star-filled night, the moon in space reflecting on a serene body of water.
- A mental delete is to empty into silence and remain, then relax even more and make very refined Soma (body) adjustments until eventually, you are gone. It is like you convert into a little death (or sleep), and there you can recognize the infinite presence that feels like there is no more time and only white light. People frequently report this during near-death experiences.
- If you could forget all that you have ever experienced, what would you do next?

Discipline

There actually is no discipline in itself. If one wants to persist consistently, there is only beginning and enduring.

Giving up does not exist without time. It's an illusion.

Trick temptation and transmute that energy into effort for something else.

Discipline problems. They do not exist; they are only the progression of sequences of events. When we reverse engineer a problem, we often can't find where it even started.

Some disciplines take a lifetime. Helena Blavatsky compiled many theology and philosophy secrets into *The Secret Doctrine*. She devoted her entire life to it, and thus Theosophy was born.

Just in attempting to practise meditation regularly morning and evening, gifts and synchronicity events will start to appear. This won't take a lifetime. Look for the signs. . .

Chapter 12:

New Rules

You may now understand your mind from a different perspective, and you may also realize that to mentally struggle with capitalist existence and the miserable human condition it causes is useless and that talking about it will not cause much change. Only doing with deliberate action will create change. The ideals of so-called western civilization are built on the capitalist assumption that compliance to that standard is the best we can be. But why be so blatantly mediocre?

There is decay among the capitalist leading nations as well. It's just hidden decay, with less stench.

Many struggle with conforming, so they seek help through psychiatric evaluation sessions. There they are, victims who have left their comfort zones, being probed and later diagnosed with conditions such as anxiety, bipolar disorder, and depression. These conditions are stages of fear that are kept private. But privacy with a shrink is only a symptom of mental decay. These conditions may appear because of fitting into the capitalist herd; but they are actually caused by the mild insanity that capitalist and religious herds represent. Individuals are afraid to voice what they truly want because they are afraid of offending the herd. It seems much easier to drift along with the herd instead. But easy has no mental range. Neither does visiting a shrink. Most people may actually have the capacity for deeper thinking, but the herd influences them away from doing so with their relentless delirium. The individual loses self-remembering and joins in repeating like a parrot in a cage. And because the majority also repeats, one becomes a comfortable disciple. Again, almost like a religion: obeyed and followed.

Rest assured that the herd will continue pursuing their capitalist responsibilities of consuming and dreaming of becoming rich. Capitalist maintenance thoughts will entertain them and keep them busy, micro-managing nothing but pleasure. They all claim to be busy when they are doing something, yet they don't know what busy actually means. The only time most consider not being busy is when they waste away as sloths on the couch, consuming entertainment, sugar, fat, and alcohol until they explode into obesity. Being busy in my mind means dodging bullets, artillery, and mustard gas on an empty stomach in the trenches of WWI. Insane, but that's busy. . . Maybe less time would help. How about having one minute left to live? What would you do?

Anyway, brush that aside. What we need is something else. I can't stress enough that we underestimate the power that the middle class has to change everything. Stupidity and laziness are not our fundamental problems, they are only the consequences of greed and cowardliness. These are the permanent weaknesses of humans and capitalism exploits them. Both Jesus and Buddha made us very demonstratively aware of these weaknesses already, as neither of them had any possessions and neither was afraid of anything. The middle-class individual is greedy as well, but too much of a coward to admit it. So, they sustain what everybody else does, not only to fit in but also due to sheer laziness. As a result, our species only appears to be stupid. It's not complicated.

To become capable, humans need to reinvent themselves from scratch. We need transformational ideas to build civilizations like the former Venus model. The concept was great, they just missed that they can't run something like that as a business in a capitalist society. Still, something like that can succeed when run as a global platform without profit. If you have not seen what this Venus project was about, I highly recommend searching for it on the internet. The old concept information is still there.

Nietzsche had the right idea with the übermensch—the overman. Man has to evolve above his current compliance model. Elaborating further on his concept is what mental evolution demands. Nietzsche said that writing is thinking, and that was one of his wisest statements. Organizing compliance is not thinking. Seeking profit limits thinking. And doing both would be a waste of time in a society without wealth. We need to not only understand these differences, but act on them tomorrow. Therefore, we need new rules (like Bill Maher's political satire).

Mental Capacity Manifesto: Tractatus of Prudence

If we converted our capitalist economies into productive, global, rebuilding forces, we could change the former label of capitalist to capacity. This would mean that we would now pursue restoration and we would not pursue profit. The fundamentals to do so already exist in rich nations, but we would now have to expand those to the neglected. Entire sectors of the economy could be converted.

Common denominator:

1. Eliminate all currencies and establish one single trade medium to measure value which cannot be traded (stock markets wouldn't exist anymore). Forgive all debt and return all lands.
2. Prioritize providing food, shelter, medical care, and education for all troubled nations.

Food production:

1. Global geothermal food technology.
2. Complete water and ocean management, including severe commercial fishing reduction.
3. Complete air management.
4. Cultivation of deserts, including water canals, widespread agriculture, tree planting.
5. Global food education, including removal of diets overloaded with carbohydrates.
6. Global protein management, including fish and shrimp farming, synthetic protein expansion.

Medical:

1. Global affordable production of pharmacy.
2. International distribution of medical staff.
3. Global health education.
4. Increased natural remedy research.

Resource recovery:

1. Global detailed recycling.
2. Mine field and contaminated land clearance.
3. Global janitors to remove ocean plastic and economize landfills.
4. Downsize the petroleum industry and expand into hydrogen, natural gas, electric, and solar energies.
5. Global reforestation.
6. Ocean fertilizing, reef recovery, and species seeding.

Rebuilding:

1. Elimination of weapons and reallocating these funds to construction equipment.
2. Transformation of military into highly trained construction forces.
3. Enforced reduction of international arms.
4. Transformation of prisons into environmental labour camps, and all sentences significantly reduced.
5. Transformation of prisons into correctional farming, where individuals are trained for labour while gaining an education simultaneously.
6. Sustainability LEED planning and retrofitting buildings.

Space:

1. Global satellite and space orbit debris cleanup.
2. Global space programs.

By the way, I am a LEED AP O&M (Leadership in Energy and Environmental Design, Accredited Professional, Operations & Maintenance). These alternative options are available, and making these adjustments includes jobs for all!

When equal values are established and profit-taking is eliminated, there is no need for massive taxes. Banks become common-denominator medium distribution centres. There is plenty for everybody.

All of this is attainable, and this is how we will reinvent much better living standards. The poor will welcome this, the middle class won't notice much change, and the wealthy can keep what they want to maintain because their wealth won't be wealth anymore.

The United Nations would have to act as a global capacity committee instead of as peacekeepers. One of the first priorities would be to address the needs of the poorest countries first. That would also mean that all the G7 nations would be last in line. The UN committee would need to be upgraded with various key sector experts from the fields of science, health, logistics, and agriculture. Finance will be unnecessary. This panel should be independent and undergo re-election every two years. Officials would be elected by credentials from each territorial sector (no need for nations to vote), and each area has various representatives for each sector. Each representative would serve for four years: two years as deputy, and two years as principal. When the principals retire, they remain as consultants, the deputies are promoted to principals, and new deputies are elected. This cycle structure should provide expertise and consistency.

This panel would make all the reconstruction decisions to protect the global interest of all sectors. All global military would primarily be transformed into construction forces. Local police would assist them and provide security if need be. Participants from every sector could volunteer anywhere.

Is that not easy enough? Everybody could work, eat, have shelter, have health care, and have time to travel and enjoy. The capitalist mantra "survival of the fittest" will only apply to nature, and everyone can be included.

If the current authorities can't work this out, then the middle class will mobilize to get this done. For those of you in the middle class that assume this is unnecessary, then you are limiting everyone else. Again, Nietzsche said that if you are too much of a burden to others, then you should remove yourself. In my view though, removing yourself from the process would be a waste that does not even help either.

Now, all these necessary actions do not mean that the capitalist middle class will have to comply to anarchy and possess nothing. It just means that they have to adapt to get by with a little less so that the ones that have nothing can begin with something. And once the underdeveloped nations catch up, everybody's standard can and will improve again. This time, there will be no stolen land, poverty, or a destroyed planet. We can blossom instead. Wars, crime, unemployment, inequality, racism, mental health conditions, etc. will vanish.

I mean it: who wants new rules? This should be our legacy first. Then we can go to Mars. . .

Implement this: You have the personal responsibility to do better than before because you are present. Prove that you deserve to be present. It is *you* that needs to decide, and not others for you!

Or don't. Hoard what you can and continue with what you have always done. Sloth is convenient.

Courage

Nietzsche recognized that "the will to power" in man is a driving force that makes one become what one will be. It will take courage to accept the hard work needed to implement these new rules. So far, capitalism has always been the medium to exercise that will to power for survival and even personal wealth. The problem, though, is that wealth is in direct opposition to mental capacity. Will and power are driving forces, but mental ability is about calming drives and balance. Will and power for humanity to prosper are also contradicting to the environment. Being environmentally responsible and respectful is an expectation of intelligent cultures.

So, we have to find the courage to effectively corrupt this capitalist medium to get governing attention. And once we draw our savings, stop going to work, and ask the G20 nations to reconvene, we will have their attention. Then we can plea for them to mandate a new common denominator trade medium and devalue all debt and other currencies.

Corporations have to reduce production, and they can't sell for profit anymore. For an immediate impact, they should give away their products to less-developed countries, or accept trade. Yes, they would all operate at a loss, but that is necessary until all can catch up!

The G20 should educate their population that lavish consuming is not an option anymore. They would need to learn how to self-regulate. Who needs a hundred pairs of shoes? This, of course, would not be possible from one day to the next. There would have to be a transition period for countries to adjust. Let's say, three months. The UN would upgrade with the IMF and oversee and distribute the new common medium. Global surplus products would be distributed to the people that need them most. Surplus goods would be held at surplus custom yards. There would be no more countries. Land would be divided into geographical sectors. Each sector would have surplus agencies that report to the UN. This system would restrict and balance trade, and eliminate overproduction. All debt would be erased, land would be returned, and there would be no more profit.

Imagine a scenario like this! We could still have our entertainment, appliances, groceries, and so on. Just a little less, and every other sector could convert to having the same. Again, it would take time. But imagine the joy of all the success and well-being stories that would emerge. Suddenly, it would be worthwhile to watch the news. Trees would be coming back, national parks would be flourishing with wildlife, and we would be breathing much cleaner air. Stock markets would be converted into trade regulators and would manage surplus products without profit. The capitalist supply and demand speculation scenario would be eliminated completely. What was someone's gain will not be someone else's loss anymore. Those days would be over forever.

Nobody has to lose anything when we become intelligent. There is only potential and gain for the forgotten! Yes, these extreme measures would create global economic collapse at first sight. But, if precociously managed over time and with iron unity among the middle class, this will be attainable. Economists would become accurate when market volatility disappears. They would have to adjust to not growing capitalist economies indefinitely anyway. Last but not least, the industry of finance would only remain to the point where it would serve the world instead of the world serving it.

We have to have the courage to see the big picture, and act accordingly.

Implement this: This is not utopian! It's all there, staring at us.

Or don't. You are a capitalist clone.

This is how we can get it done

Reach beyond. What follows is hypothetical, but it is possible.

Remembrance Day, the eleventh month, the eleventh day, at the eleventh hour. That is when the insanity of slaughtering three million people and eight million horses, mules, and donkeys ended WWI.

April 22, 2024 will be Earth Day. That is the day when people will turn off their lights and appliances to save energy, and participate in many earth-preserving activities. But what if this is also the day that capitalism ends? (Or it could be any day—the sooner the better.) You, as a member of the global middle class, would simply prepare on that day to withdraw all your cash deposits from your bank accounts, and then not show up for work the following day.

Why would we do this? Imagine if everybody in the world flushed their toilets at the same time. Our plumbing systems would not be able to handle it. In a similar fashion, if the middle class withdraws all cash flow, then banks won't be able to operate because they will have lost their liquidity to pay back deposits (liabilities) and loan money (assets). And when nobody shows up for work anymore, that will get global attention. The financial markets would temporarily collapse. Then we would give the governments time to end the insanity of capitalist wealth accumulation and to come back with proposals to reduce all currencies to one trade medium and to initiate capacity global reform. (Something like a New Rules Manifesto.) Simple, effective, intelligent, and proof that we do have the ability to deserve this planet as a species.

Now, you can ignore my suggestions and think that this would be insane. At first, this seems reasonable. But think again and review that these options are available and right in front of you. Take some time to imagine such a scenario, and discuss it with family and friends. A middle class financial and labour strike can initiate a peaceful solution for global issues. If we don't move in that direction, the capitalist West and Eastern BRICS will divide, and their currencies will continue to undermine each other anyway.

So why wait, when we can act first?

We can stop whining about how very little will get better. Delay is just delay. Options require action! In this case, the first action simply requires choosing, and then you can act on your decision.

This is actually something that you can do on behalf of everybody, for everybody (like a global donation). Of course, some will not comply, but some will. This is viable, intelligent, and without violence.

Implement this: Act on this, and do it on behalf of everybody, for everybody!

Or don't. Don't act, because it does not apply to you. To stop working would be crazy. This middle-class, Peter Pan idea couldn't possibly impact the mighty herd. Keep running in the perpetual, capitalist hamster wheel, ignore global devastation, retreat to a farm, build a bunker with a confederate flag on it, pile up more guns, and stock up on provisions for a few years. That's just in case martial law comes back after a little nuclear dance and the delusional walking dead are out there for real one day.

The Neanderthals at least understood that fire would burn them, but capitalists are not even there yet. They see fires everywhere, ignore them from a distance, and talk us to extinction.

Obviously, I must be the one that is misinformed here. Anyway, I could continue with my sarcasm, and I have plenty, but you get the big picture. Still not convinced? OK then, let's move on.

Chapter 13:

Closing

Did we learn anything from the French and American revolutions? These revolutions happened because the people eventually challenged the popes and the lavish kings with critical levels of truth and reason. They then upgraded from imperialism to capitalism, and now we enjoy corporations as the new god-kings that are not challenged by truth and reason. These god-kings are not at risk anymore of getting the guillotine or the noose, so they can do whatever they want and then buy an army of lawyers to lie truth and reason away.

There was St-Juste, who demanded equality capacity. The response was that they cut his head off. Just like they nailed Christ to the cross before him. In principle, it should not be about the will to power of gods, kings, or people. It should be about the will to mentally evolve as a species. The historic need for ethics and morality are proof of our mental incapacity because they are what help us manage our current circus.

Before the tech age, it might have been harder to control societies because communication was much slower. But today, when everything is literally instantly available, we are inundated by clones selling their subscribe buttons.

The mob is unpredictable and often wrong, and individuals will not all have the same opinion. Consequently, the rebel is born to push back against confusion, which evolves into the surreal, only to be rejected by the herd again. And then what? Escaping from mental health into the domain of mental illness?

If we want to strive for our potential as a global society, we have to categorize our mental range not only as a goal but also as a science. Freedom of speech may be a liberal idea, but it becomes very loud when everybody screams about their problems that never go away. We can't strive for mental balance when we are constantly distracted by political agendas that merely serve profit and waste. What I suggest is not a utopian dream.

We just have to cut back a little to be capable, instead of expendable.

I'm a guy with a family he can feed and a roof over my head. All I ask is for every human to be able to enjoy these basic conditions as well. It's only fair. If I have to take in another family, then so be it. Bring it on! But me taking in a family does not make the fundamental problem go away. When everybody lives in decent conditions, then there is no need to harbour an abandoned family.

Our most-observed rules should be the implementation of solutions in the name of global mental capacity, instead of capitalist idiocracy (thank you, Bill Maher, for that term). Society is an ongoing, unfinished project, and we can't allow manipulation to take away our potential. It is everyone's turn to reflect on this.

Peace is not a destination! It is a process of personal conduct, and it is absolutely impossible within the confines of capitalism. Only the middle class can implement these solution changes, and they should, no matter what the sacrifices may be for the wealthy. They already have enough. My recommendation is even to allow them to keep it all; they just can't get any more. They hoarded it, so they can sit on it. If wealth was devalued, abandoned, and everyone was debt-free, then would the wealthy even still hoard their wealth and sit on it?

What the authorities veil as democracy is what covers and protects that wealth. And just because they make the potential for wealth available, does not mean that wealth is the ultimate option to follow. Capitalism is a dumb option, but yes, it is still an option. However, don't you see the other options? There would not even be a need to create good karma if we were all equal. Even the Buddhists got that one wrong. What could one possibly ever accumulate? Death and the cosmos don't care.

At least the Zen mind recognizes suffering as our fundamental challenge, and that suffering is self-inflicted. However, if we stopped to comply with what we are today, then how much self-inflicted suffering would remain?

There would also be no need to dwell in limiting religions that teach hope for salvation. What would we need to be saved from? Again, death and the cosmos don't care. Buddhism and Zen have at least managed to provide far more positive messages than other religions. Buddha did not believe in a God. He was a mortal like you. He found his own mental depth under a tree with nothing, and he kept nothing. Jesus also had nothing and kept nothing. Meanwhile, most religions are loaded.

We allow capitalism and religion to dictate conditions that are unacceptable. We are told to hoard and not sin, or else end up in hell. Not a problem for the ones that are already in hell on earth. Why would the starving be afraid of hell when death seems like a relief?

We have self-aware brains that have the potential for whatever and we need to adapt. Animals adapt by default. Yes, they hunt and eat each other along the food chain, but the creatures that are eaten at least serve the purpose of nourishing their hunters. We hunt as well, but we don't eat the humans we hunt, and they don't die. They suffer. Complying to unsustainable options and holding onto our misery-generated comforts is such a waste!

That a little man like me has to tell you this demonstrates that we truly need intervention. Today is where we ended up, and the slaughter needs to end now. Many past decisions were made by decision-makers that should have never made any decisions. The arrogant statement, "Make America great again" comes to mind. Great for what? America already boasts that they are the greatest nation on earth. Evidently, there seems to be a need to be even greater than the greatest again. Just another capitalist propaganda package to be the leader of the capitalist fairy tale. We are humans first, so why do we need to be great? Do we need to dwell on our self-important, ruling Napoleon and God complexes that we inherited and keep dragging along?

Our historic priorities have always been to protect and discriminate, to isolate, to scream for more economy, and to rebuild nothing for the poor. They are priorities that ignore, hoard, and run to church to bless it all away.

Intelligent other (let's not call them alien) beings would only ask, what drives that much greed and self-destruction? Where does that come from? Not only physically, but also psychologically. They would ask why we even have a need to promote compassion for our own class depressions that we caused? And what is the point of perpetual suffering?

The herd complains about their chores and how useless the government is, but must still hoard everything they can get their fingers on. That is not potential. All that is, is sacrifice!

Obama said, "We are the change," and Gandhi was the change before he got rid of the British Empire in his backyard. But there are oppressors today that are much worse than what Gandhi faced with the British Empire. Their names are national debt, extremism, and internal social decay.

The US Republican money machine despises socialism. But what is so bad about socialism? Going to church, going to the pub, or running a farm are all social activities. Mild socialism and communism mean opportunity and striving towards equality for everybody. Capitalist MAGA extremism is socialism for high profit enterprise and private military outfits. The Americans conveniently called Marx a communist. But Marx was more than a mild communist or socialist. He was the Nostradamus that predicted that capitalism would destroy itself. Yes, the Americans and Europeans are included in this destruction.

American imperialist lies play the victims of their own cause. Help yourself understand what happened when Building 7 sunk into itself during 9/11. That the two towers came down because of those airplanes is all scientifically impossible. The controlled demolition of Building 7 in plain sight put the icing on the cake. The Bush administration's 9/11 report blamed it on the fires on the lower floors, and followed up by deliberately blaming it on Islam. The public was then simply left to believe the storytelling, because there was nothing else that could prove otherwise at this scale. Yes, it seems impossible that the US government would attack their own soil. It simply can't be that deep of a deception. But it was. Just like the church hammered the uneducated to believe in the Bible because they could. It is incredible what some of these institutions get away with in plain sight. And when they are questioned or opposed by other theories and even facts, it is simply, conveniently, labelled as conspiracy.

Yes, we're all that stupid. We can be told, and we will proceed. We are numb to even considering being rebels because rebels do not accomplish anything. It's like we're helpless.

After 9/11, there was credible, scientific evidence indicating that the towers' building materials disintegrated during their free fall. The evidence is presented in the book *Where Did the Towers Go?* There is actual video and pictures of hidden technology at work. The book also describes how they were able to remove thousands of tons of debris in a matter of weeks. All of it was scientifically impossible, but still in plain sight!

The cover-ups are also evident for the Pentagon and Flight 93. None of the crashes present nearly enough visible debris. Then the American government produced the Bush cover-up report and proclaimed themselves victims. This then gave them the right to be the world police and level Afghanistan with B52 carpet bombing and military intervention.

But what they also did with these actions was further enslave the entire globe in their self-righteous capitalist propaganda, like how they spew "make America great again," the new slogan of the MAGA Republicans, led by Legal Teflon Don. The Democrats paint him as the sphincter flying on golden toilets in Trump Force 1. An individual that drowns in lawsuits, but is still not locked up. Every other criminal with his kind of legal resume would be sitting on a single regular toilet in jail. But not this guy. Nothing sticks on Teflon, and he remains untouchable.

So why is that? It gets better. Teflon Don might even be a good guy. Apparently, he is a "white hat," meaning he is part of a military organization that was revealed by QAnon. Just like Putin and Xi Jinping are apparently good guys as well. All these guys may actually work together in the background to take down the super-rich cabal of the US and Europe the likes of BlackRock, Vanguard, the Bilderberg Group, and all the secret families that run the Federal Reserves. In public, the US appears as if they are divided on various levels, but this apparent division and victimizing is a distraction from the real objective. Behind this division hides the objective for unity of the likes of QAnon and other organizations that want to remove the capitalist cabal from controlling nations and sustaining financial slavery. They all know that the global debt situation can't be sustained at these levels. But they still keep the herd in the dark, while they slowly prepare them for a major financial lockdown with COVID. BRICS (Brasil, Russia, India, China, and South Africa) are the nations that also oppose the cabal, and their main objective is to de-dollarize the world financial markets. So, they want to deliberately undermine the capitalist system where it hurts them the most, which is to make the dollar and Euro unstable. Russia, China, and Saudi Arabia are considering starting to trade crude oil in Chinese yuan instead of US dollars. If that happens, then most countries that hold US dollars to buy energy (energy is often the highest expense for countries) would then want to sell their US dollar holdings. Imagine what that would do to the value of the dollar. That threat is actually very real. Not to mention that the US banking system is over extended on debt risk at the same time. So, something is about to hit the fan, and it won't be feces.

The US global financial control extends beyond their borders with their military. Their global entanglement not only performs as a security tool but also as an economy engine. They claim to be the world democracy police. However, global armies these days are not built to invade other countries anymore. The Russia/Ukraine conflict is only a distraction to draw global attention away from our inbred East versus West addiction. BRICS has warned the US and Europe that they don't want to be told what to do anymore and that they don't appreciate being labelled as thugs and underdeveloped. Their long-term resilience against capitalism is about to mature into capitalist defeat.

And as always, in the case of combat war, who is sent to fight? Definitely not the cabal, silver-spoon people. They recruit the poor and say God bless our troops and God bless America, and that it is OK to torch everything. No wonder the Russians and the Chinese are always represented as being pissed off. But they are not! These guys are smarter than the Americans give them credit for, and not nearly as overextended financially.

Anyway, enough said, my apologies about the repeated summary rant. You get the global picture. It's all war, and we mind as well be ready for Valhalla.

But that is a different big picture compared to what I described as an introduction to this book in chapter 1. What's more important is what do you, the reader, actually believe? Who is in control from your perspective? Social improvement requires ideas that have immediate impact and that can be discussed in the open.

Well-intended activities have to revolve around respecting this planet. The planet deserves so much more than our West versus East games and waste. We should be ready to anticipate that a total reset can change our dependence on rich caveman ideas. The rich cabal will do whatever it takes to remain cavemen. But their days are numbered.

The fundamental point is that the middle class can walk away from it all. We will eventually depart from our capitalist becoming and realize that we don't need to repeat anything as beings. So, why wait?

I have morphed into a capitalist civilization nihilist, because such a civilization means nothing to me. Primitive consuming and complacency are the parents of stupid and lazy. I just file them away. What else can be said?

To me and many others, the herd frustrates. There are some that have left society to live off the grid, where they can live in untamed moderation. Still, these people have at least the option to flee the grid, while the abandoned can't escape.

Much has been lost, but everything can be rebuilt. We have chased our own tail so far, and can simply think nothing of it, because the future won't care. There is no need to grieve over our past miseries. There is an oriental saying: "The cat is a little Buddha chasing his own tail." It's OK to chase your own tail sometimes. Mother Earth will help ground us if we give her our attention and time. We are guests here, and we can have fun with everybody, especially our host, the earth, and its abundant animals. Finding our true potential is not only about mental expansion; it should also be fun. This can happen in many ways. I think it starts by searching for what one really enjoys doing. Then go from there and follow your journey, step by step. Would it not be a relief to have time for doing more of what we like? Just be curious. Maybe you don't even know what you really like yet, but without trying to discover what it is, you will never know. Curiosity is the fundamental developmental drive of children and one's intellect, and one should remain curious to the very end.

Absurd poetry

Obviously, I do not consider myself a capitalist citizen. But by necessity, I work and live this mediocre life, and I should have nothing to complain about. Even so, I long to flush all these organized feces and leave the capitalist toilet. I wish we could all leave the stench behind and spend time in a garden overlooking a calm ocean of mental serenity. The common good that democracy promises fails to deliver, so we could all convert into sages, hide in caves, and grow our own food again. Regressing back to the Neanderthal dimension is an option, but it may be a bit absurd, since we have come quite far with riding machines. We have to find some sort of medium that we could all digest and sustain, whatever that will be.

What we can do is walk away and respect all creatures and matter. The new normal will be kindness and treating everything like we treat our mothers. We can live in a place where people don't need to be reminded to be kind. There can be value in self-reliance again, like when we self-isolated during COVID, had beards and mops on our heads, learned to bake bread again, and actually missed seeing each other in person.

Isolation and restraint were also the message of that guy called Jesus, until the Roman empire nailed him to that cross. It appears he had the right intent, but then the morbid imperialist story begins with a crucifixion followed by an impossible resurrection and then ends with that his demise was to teach us a lesson. What lesson was that? To follow his simple-man concept, or to get crucified because of business? Within a decent mental frame, crucifixion could not even develop. In fact, no religion would be necessary. And there would be no need to bicker about whether Nietzsche was right when he said that Buddhism lives up to its promises, whereas Christianity does not. That seems obvious. And last but not least, conveniently ignoring women is never an option when mental goodwill is intended.

Implement this: Wait, read, think, and write.

Or don't. React immediately to whatever.

Last words

It seems that we can't get anything right. After all of this, you may have found some nuggets in this book that are worth keeping. I provided rants, questions, and options, but the responsibility to embrace the mental capacity to actually do something with this information remains with you. What will matter is what you are going to spend your linear time on.

You could consider not following. You could consider reflecting first before you buy or desire more of what you don't need. Too much of everything is just decadence. And no, having less and doing less is not boring. Instead, you could participate in leaving capitalism behind and moving beyond.

Once you practise meditation and realize that we are consciousness instead of objects, then you will develop a different perspective. Then, the mere thought that humanity is always chasing freedom becomes absurd. Freedom is staring right at us, while the rich are never free. They are shackled to protect their possessions and greedy thoughts, whereas the realized know that true freedom is to have no thoughts at all and to adapt to equality.

I can't emphasize enough that meditation is a critical skill to develop, and that we should teach it in school. Everyone should learn how to fit meditation into their day. It would help us cope better together, and it would expand our mental abilities. With increased practice, we begin to understand that the benefits of meditation also reveal themselves during our post-meditative awareness. Getting to know ourselves better helps us remember that nothing is as it seems, it never has been, and it never will be. There is only the very present!

Everything springs from this always-present, infinite source, which is present in the now and that resides by itself in between every thought. It is the source and essence of our being that will always be unfinished and has no room for anything unpleasant. When one can realize this, then our absurd overall conduct becomes more and more noticeable. History demonstrates that our behaviour is violent, and consequently we require much compassion. We may even appear as a consistent species because most of our conduct is all wrong, and once something right occurs, like the concepts of Taoism, meditation, Greenpeace, or hugging trees, then they stand out like sore thumbs. Use those thumbs and hitchhike a ride to the consciousness galaxy (thanks, Douglas Adams).

Moving forward, what can you do with this book? If you understood it, then you may want to keep it, because it can serve as a manual. You can mail the book to yourself to keep as a souvenir of your trip away from the capitalist herd. But it might be best if you give it to other people to read, and that they can pass it on as well.

Last, I'd like to mention that you can find articles on the internet that suggest that some scientists believe the universe is conscious. Search for them and discover that some are finally catching on, though I guess they just remain articles instead of recognizing our source as fact. The Tibetan sages have always felt that our purpose is to serve this source. They practise meditation, accessing knowledge that is not a knowing from reading or others. They merge with the source's infinite presence that reveals what we could never think of.

Meditation means to practise, but first, turn around, tune in, and drop out. . .

Gratitude

My grandparents inspired this book. Thedi was a traveller, general labourer, freelance writer, and also my father figure. Most might not believe this, but I never saw him mad. He was a very calm influence and lived through both World Wars. Josi was by his side through the good times, and the austerities they had to endure. She was the hub of the family and an innovative cook who worked all her life and never got paid. Their three children were born during WWII while Thedi was in uniform. When they both passed away, there was barely enough money left to bury them.

And gratitude to the following:

Juliana, who raised me as a single mom.

For their love and kindness, Eleah, my wife; our children, Luca, Noli, Joah; and our cats.

To my old friends from Banff and Lake O'Hara for their loyal friendship. They know who they are.

And the team that helped me at Friesen Press.

Printed in Canada